Quentin Meillassoux

Speculative Realism

Series Editor: Graham Harman

Since its first appearance at a London colloquium in 2007, the Speculative Realism movement has taken continental philosophy by storm. Opposing the formerly ubiquitous modern dogma that philosophy can speak only of the human-world relation rather than the world itself, Speculative Realism defends the autonomy of the world from human access, but in a spirit of imaginative audacity.

Books available

Onto-Cartography: An Ontology of Machines and Media by Levi R. Bryant

Form and Object: A Treatise on Things by Tristan Garcia, translated by Mark Allan Ohm and Jon Cogburn

Adventures in Transcendental Materialism: Dialogues with Contemporary Thinkers by Adrian Johnston

The End of Phenomenology: Metaphysics and the New Realism by Tom Sparrow

Fields of Sense: A New Realist Ontology by Markus Gabriel

Quentin Meillassoux: Philosophy in the Making Second Edition by Graham Harman

Forthcoming titles

Romantic Realities: Speculative Realism and British Romanticism by Evan Gottlieb

After Quietism: Analytic Philosophies of Immanence and the New Metaphysics by Jon Cogburn

Infrastructure by Graham Harman

Visit the Speculative Realism website at
www.euppublishing.com/series/specr

Quentin Meillassoux

Philosophy in the Making

Second edition

Graham Harman

EDINBURGH
University Press

© Graham Harman, 2011, 2015

Edinburgh University Press Ltd
The Tun – Holyrood Road
12(2f) Jackson's Entry
Edinburgh EH8 8PJ
www.euppublishing.com

First edition published by Edinburgh University Press in 2011

Typeset in 11/13 Adobe Sabon by
Servis Filmsetting, Ltd, Stockport, Cheshire,
and printed and bound in Great Britain by
CPI Group (UK) Ltd, Croydon CR0 4YY

A CIP record for this book is available from the British Library

ISBN 978 0 7486 9995 7 (hardback)
ISBN 978 0 7486 9346 7 (webready PDF)
ISBN 978 0 7486 9345 0 (paperback)
ISBN 978 0 7486 9347 4 (epub)

The right of Graham Harman
to be identified as author of this work
has been asserted in accordance with
the Copyright, Designs and Patents Act 1988,
and the Copyright and Related Rights
Regulations 2003 (SI No. 2498).

Contents

Remark on Citations

Page references to works by Quentin Meillassoux appear in parentheses in the text itself, in the form of an abbreviation followed by a page number. For example, (AF 92) means page 92 of *After Finitude*. A key to the abbreviations of Meillassoux's works appears below, and full bibliographical information on these writings can be found in the list of Works Cited at the end of this book. References to works by all other authors appear as endnotes following each chapter.

Citations from Ray Brassier's translation of *After Finitude* appear courtesy of Continuum Publishing. Translated excerpts from the unpublished French manuscript of *L'Inexistence divine* (*The Divine Inexistence*) and the whole of the 'Interview with Quentin Meillassoux' appear courtesy of Meillassoux himself; both are published in the present work alone.

AF = *After Finitude*
BL = Berlin Lecture ('Iteration, Reiteration, Repetition')
BM = 'Badiou and Mallarmé'
CL = 'The Contingency of the Laws of Nature'
DI = *The Divine Inexistence*
DU = 'Decision and Undecidability of the Event in *Being and Event I* and *II*'
HE = 'History and Event in Alain Badiou'
IW = 'The Immanence of the World Beyond'
MS = 'Metaphysics, Speculation, Correlation'
NS = *The Number and the Siren*
PV = 'Potentiality and Virtuality'
QM = 'Interview with Quentin Meillassoux'
SC = 'Subtraction and Contraction'
SD = 'Spectral Dilemma'
SR = 'Speculative Realism'

Series Editor's Preface

With this book, Edinburgh University Press launches a new series in Speculative Realism. The Speculative Realism movement began with a now famous April 2007 workshop at Goldsmiths College, University of London (see pp. 77–80 below). In the brief ensuing period it has taken on a life of its own, especially among younger participants in the blogosphere. Books in this series may be either admiring or critical, but all will explore the ramifications of speculative realism for philosophy and the numerous disciplines in which this young movement has already had an impact: anthropology, archaeology, architecture, English literature, feminism, the fine arts, Medieval studies, musicology, rhetoric and composition, science studies, and others.

Speculative realism is best understood as a loose umbrella term for a series of vastly different philosophical enterprises. What all have in common is their rejection of what Quentin Meillassoux first termed 'correlationism'. Whereas realists assert the existence of a world independent of human thought and idealists deny such an autonomous world, correlationism adopts an apparently sophisticated intermediate position, in which human and world come only as a pair and cannot be addressed outside their mutual correlation. Accordingly, the dispute between realism and idealism is dismissed as a 'pseudo-problem'. Inspired ultimately by Immanuel Kant, correlationists are devoted to the human-world correlate as the sole topic of philosophy, and this has become the unspoken central dogma of all continental and much analytic philosophy. Speculative realist thinkers oppose this credo (though not always for the same reasons) and defend a realist stance toward the world. But instead of endorsing a commonsensical, middle-aged realism of boring hands and billiard balls existing outside the mind, speculative realist philosophies are perplexed by the *strangeness* of the real: a strangeness undetectable by the instruments of common sense.

Given that Meillassoux coined the central polemical term of speculative realism ('correlationism'), and given that his writings in English have been among the most popular works in this idiom so far, it is fitting that the first book in the series should be a study of his philosophy. Meillassoux was born in Paris in 1967, making him still a rather young philosopher. His debut book *After Finitude* (2006) had immediate and far-reaching impact, and his unpublished major work *L'Inexistence divine* (*The Divine Inexistence*) has been eagerly awaited for several years. I am pleased to report that the present book includes a 65-page appendix featuring translated excerpts from this unpublished but somewhat legendary work, which was written in 1997 and extensively revised in 2003.

Perhaps it is also fitting that I should be the author of this series-triggering book on Meillassoux's philosophy. He and I have worked in proximity for five years as original members of the speculative realist movement; moreover, we also have two of the most contrasting philosophies in the group. For Meillassoux, the familiar correlationist point that we cannot think a tree-in-itself without turning it into a tree-for-us is a powerful argument that must be overcome with delicate logical finesse; for me, it is a terrible argument from the start. For Meillassoux, the principle of sufficient reason must be abolished; for me, it is the basis of all ontology. For Meillassoux, only a commitment to immanence will save philosophy from superstition and irrationalism; for me, philosophies of immanence are a catastrophe. For Meillassoux, the human being remains a unique site of dignity and philosophical questioning, and marks a quantum leap from the pre-human realm; for me, humans differ only by degree from raindrops, dolphins, citrus fruit, and iron ore. My hope is that such contrasts have generated productive tensions in the book now before you. By reflecting on these tensions, the reader will be led into the midst of some of the most important internal debates of speculative realism. But there are other such debates, and as Series Editor I welcome proposals for books on all aspects of this new approach to philosophy.

Graham Harman
Cairo
February 2011

Preface to the Second Edition

Since the publication of the first edition of this book, interest in Meillassoux's philosophy has continued to grow, as has the amount of his work available in English. In the autumn of 2011 he published his second book, a sparkling study of the canonical French poet Stéphane Mallarmé, which is covered in Chapter 3 below. Meillassoux also made a significant career move in 2012, leaving his alma mater the École normale supérieure after many years of service for a new position as *Maître de conférences* at the Université Paris 1–Panthéon Sorbonne. This suggests that long-delayed recognition in his home country is finally beginning to arrive. There was even significant recognition in the art world, as in 2013 Meillassoux and his original Speculative Realist colleagues (Brassier, Grant, Harman) were ranked collectively by *ArtReview* as the eighty-first most powerful influence in the art world, the highest-rated philosophers on the list. In the meantime, Meillassoux's debut book *After Finitude* was either already translated or being translated into roughly a dozen languages. For this second edition I have made only minor stylistic changes to the text of the first edition. But I have also added a good deal of new material. An expanded Chapter 2 contains sections on various lectures and articles by Meillassoux not available at the time of the first edition. This is followed by a new Chapter 3, devoted exclusively to *The Number and the Siren*. The later chapters of the book have been renumbered accordingly.

Ankara
August 2014

Introduction

This is the first book-length treatment of the philosophy of Quentin Meillassoux (pronounced 'may-yuh-sue'), an emerging French thinker of the greatest interest. Meillassoux was born in Paris in 1967, the son of the anthropologist Claude Meillassoux (1925–2005), a household name among Africanists.[1] The younger Meillassoux studied at the famed École Normale Supérieure on the rue d'Ulm, and taught at that institution for more than a decade until accepting a position at the Sorbonne in 2012. His debut book, *Après la finitude* (*After Finitude*), was officially published in early 2006,[2] though copies were sighted in Paris bookstores late the preceding year. Little time was needed for Meillassoux's book to catch fire in Anglophone continental philosophy circles. In the words of Peter Hallward, a noted authority on recent French thought:

> Not since [Jacques] Derrida's 'Structure, Sign and Play' (1966) has a new French philosopher made such an immediate impact in sections of the Anglophone world . . . It's easy to see why Meillassoux's *After Finitude* has so quickly acquired something close to cult status among readers who share his lack of reverence for 'the way things are.[3]

Prominent among Meillassoux's teachers was the philosopher Alain Badiou, whose preface to *After Finitude* displays breathtaking confidence in the book: 'It would be no exaggeration to say that Quentin Meillassoux has opened up a new path in the history of philosophy . . . a path that circumvents Kant's canonical distinction between "dogmatism", "scepticism" and "critique"'.[4] Hinting at Meillassoux's larger unpublished work, Badiou adds that *After Finitude* is merely 'a fragment from a particularly important . . . philosophical enterprise'.[5] Slavoj Žižek tells us that

I

'the philosopher who addressed [the status of materialism today] in the most appropriate way is Quentin Meillassoux in his *After Finitude*.'[6] It is true that Badiou and Žižek share a number of points in common with Meillassoux's position, and thus their neutrality might be questioned. But when Meillassoux was invited to discuss his book at a salon hosted by Bruno Latour, he impressed even those of a different philosophical stripe: 'Meillassoux was great, three hours non-stop, I had to stop him! ... He is a force of nature and yet very quiet and amiable ... Everyone was greatly pleased and totally unconvinced!'[7]

Such ringing endorsements from some of the most celebrated thinkers of our time speak well of Meillassoux's first book. Yet his greatest impact has undoubtedly been among the young. If one book has been treated as the central monument of the newest trends in Anglophone continental thought, by allies and critics alike, it is surely this recent import from Paris. Within a year of its French publication, *After Finitude* had catalyzed the formation of the Speculative Realism movement in philosophy, and given birth to an extensive corpus of blog posts devoted to the book. Despite his clarity as a writer and friendliness as a colleague, Meillassoux quickly became something of a mysterious intellectual figure, largely due to rumors concerning the massive unpublished philosophical system to which Badiou alluded: *L'Inexistence divine*, or *The Divine Inexistence*. But there is no mystery at all surrounding his key polemical term, which has already entered the philosophical lexicon in what feels like permanent fashion. I speak of 'correlationism', Meillassoux's name for the dominant ontological background of the continental philosophy of the past century. Authors working in the continental tradition have generally claimed to stand beyond the traditional dispute between realism ('reality exists outside our mind') and idealism ('reality exists only in the mind'). The correlationist alternative, so dominant that it is often left unstated by its adherents, is to assume that we can think neither of human without world nor of world without human, but only of a primordial correlation or rapport between the two. Despite its inability to think anything outside the correlate of human and world, correlationism denies being an idealist position. After all, one can always claim that extra-human reality is not being rejected in idealist fashion since humans are always already immersed in a world, or something in a similar vein.

The roots of correlationism are easiest to locate in the Critical Philosophy of Immanuel Kant (though Meillassoux now speaks of David Hume as the first corelationist), released to the public in the distant 1780s and 1790s, but still forming the horizon for most philosophy in 2010. Kant's position has two simple but major implications. The first is the basic finitude of human knowledge, which Meillassoux's title *After Finitude* openly abandons. According to Kant, we are unable to have knowledge of things-in-themselves, but are limited to reflecting on the transcendental conditions of our access to the world: space, time, and the twelve categories of the understanding. By contrast, Meillassoux tries to show that absolute knowledge is possible despite the claims of Kant and his correlationist heirs, Husserl and Heidegger prominent among them.

But there is a second implication of Kant's position that Meillassoux fully accepts. Like most post-Kantian thinkers, Meillassoux greatly appreciates Kant's critique of 'dogmatic' metaphysics, which attempts to make proclamations about the world as it is without a prior critique of our ability to know the world. The typical form of the correlationist argument in our time, which goes significantly further than Kant himself, says roughly this: 'If I try to think something beyond thought, this is a contradiction, for I have thereby turned it into a thought.' Meillassoux is alone among the original Speculative Realists in finding this argument to be so powerful as to be initially unassailable. In his view the correlational circle of human and world is not a trivial error or word game, but rather the starting point for all rigorous philosophy. We cannot make a pre-Kantian leap into some dogmatically described exterior of thought; instead, the correlate of thought and world must be radicalized from within. In other words, the next step in philosophy must be an 'inside job', and our human relation with the world always retains philosophical priority over the relation between inanimate objects, despite Meillassoux's attempted proof that there must be things independent of thought. The knowing human subject is something special in the world, and it makes no sense to speak only of a 'difference of degree' between human and non-human experience, in the manner of figures such as G. W. Leibniz, Alfred North Whitehead, and Gilles Deleuze. None the less, Meillassoux does not follow the Hegelian path of turning the human–world correlate into something absolute in its own right. Instead, he tries to drive a wedge midway between Kant's position and Hegel's. Claiming that a position called 'strong corre-lationism' is possible, and describing how it differs from absolute idealism, Meillassoux then tries to radicalize strong correlationism into his own novel position: speculative materialism.

To summarize in reverse order, Kant holds as follows:

a. The human–world relation stands at the center of philosophy, since we cannot think something without thinking it.
b. All knowledge is finite, unable to grasp reality in its own right.

Meillassoux rejects (b) while affirming (a). But readers of my own books know that my reaction to Kant is the exact opposite, reject-ing (a) while affirming (b), since in my philosophy the human–world relation does not stand at the center. Even inanimate objects fail to grasp each other as they are in themselves; finitude is not just a local specter haunting the human subject, but a structural feature of relations in general including non-human ones. Yet the present book is meant largely as an exposition of Meillassoux's philosophy, and most of the critical counterplay between his posi-tion and my own is concentrated in Chapter 4. Otherwise I will adopt the voice of an advocate for this remarkable new thinker, who has already galvanized an entire generation of admiring supporters and detractors.

It should now be clear who Quentin Meillassoux is, and why many readers see him as one of the most original philosophers working today. But a word is also in order about this book's subti-tle: *Philosophy in the Making*. No one can predict what additional books by Meillassoux might have appeared fifty or even ten years from now. This makes it impossible to write about him in the same way that one writes of the deceased classic thinkers of yesteryear, or even of established living thinkers of advanced age. Instead of a completed philosophy, Meillassoux's is literally a philosophy in the making, a concept I borrow from the writings of Latour.[8] In *Science and Action*[9] Latour makes a distinction between 'ready-made science' and 'science in the making'. The former consists of established scientific facts, praised for their rationality in compari-son with the night of ignorance that came before. Such established facts become 'black boxes' taken for granted and never opened, thereby concealing an intricate history and internal organization. As Latour puts it, 'the impossible task of opening the black box is made feasible (if not easy) by moving in time and space until one finds the controversial topic on which scientists and engineers are busy at work.'[10] In the present case, the timing of this book ensures that the Meillassoux black box is already open, since it has never yet been closed: there is currently no such thing as the completed philosophical *œuvre* of the forty-six-year-old Quentin Meillassoux. At the time of this writing (June 2014) we stand somewhere between the published *After Finitude* and the unpublished *The Divine Inexistence*, with other works undoubtedly still to come. Part of the excitement of the current study is that I am aware of no other in-depth account of a young philosopher in the midst of emergence. There is even the possibility, both intriguing and alarming, that the present book might have some effect on the ultimate shape of Meillassoux's work. It is no longer possible to encourage Nietzsche in his loneliest hour or give feedback on the weaker arguments of St Thomas Aquinas; nor can they respond to their present-day critics from beyond the grave. By contrast, Meillassoux will be able to read and contest this book just like anyone else.

Notes

1. An enlightening obituary of the elder Meillassoux by Mahir Şaul, 'Claude Meillassoux (1925–2005)', can be found in the *American Anthropologist*, vol. 107, no. 4, December 2005, pp. 753–7.
2. Quentin Meillassoux, *Après la finitude*. Translated into English by Ray Brassier as *After Finitude*.
3. Peter Hallward, unpublished manuscript. Quoted with Hallward's permission.
4. Alain Badiou, 'Preface', in Meillassoux, *After Finitude*, p. vii.
5. Ibid.
6. Slavoj Žižek, 'An Answer to Two Questions', in Adrian Johnston, *Badiou, Žižek, and Political Transformations: The Subject of Change*, p. 214.
7. Bruno Latour, personal communication, 21 February 2007.
8. Latour himself had borrowed the phrase from Alfred North Whitehead's title, *Religion in the Making*, though in the present book I mean it in a thoroughly Latourian sense.
9. Bruno Latour, *Science in Action*.
10. Ibid., p. 4.

After Finitude

This chapter presents the main ideas of *After Finitude* (2006), the lucid and economical work that gave Quentin Meillassoux an immediate degree of fame in the Anglophone world. Here as elsewhere in the book, my summaries will inevitably be shaded by my own philosophical concerns. While Meillassoux and I have worked together in the context of the Speculative Realism movement, it is widely known that our intellectual differences are pronounced. I am none the less a passionate admirer of his philosophical imagination and argumentative audacity, and until Chapter 4 will try to keep my own views largely in the background. No one, however, can give a purely neutral survey of a philosopher, and my decisions about which aspects of Meillassoux's work are most important and most debatable will not be the same as anyone else's. Very different books about Meillassoux from this one are possible, and I hope competing accounts will soon appear. But from where I stand, there seem to be six ideas that function as pillars of *After Finitude* and of Meillassoux's philosophy as a whole. They are listed here in an order different from the author's own:

A. The enemy is correlationism. But it must be overcome from within, not by simply dismissing it in a naïve realist manner.
B. There is a position called strong correlationism that does not slip into the excesses of absolute idealism, and that can be radicalized into a new philosophy called speculative materialism.
C. When strong correlationism is radicalized, it yields the truth that only one thing is necessary: contingency itself.
D. The existence of a world *prior or posterior in time* to all human consciousness poses a greater intellectual challenge than the existence of things *spatially remote* from all

human consciousness. This is the theme of 'diachronicity', the expanded version of what Meillassoux initially calls 'ancestrality'.

E. The fact that natural laws are contingent does not require that they be unstable. This is where the transfinite mathematics of Georg Cantor enters Meillassoux's philosophy, in a slightly different manner from how it enters that of Badiou.

F. The distinction between primary and secondary qualities must be revived, and the primary qualities of a thing are those that can be mathematized.

Not only would Meillassoux present these themes in a different order, but he would also probably not even choose precisely these as the pillars of his book. In particular, Point D is one he would surely regard as somewhat trivial; it is not even addressed in the original French version of his book. But taken together, these six points are the basis for one of the most striking philosophies to have appeared in the young twenty-first century. They are also enough to place Meillassoux in a somewhat isolated position, since even his fellow Speculative Realists would agree with only the first half of Point 1 and either reject or ignore the others. His commitment to following his ideas wherever they lead brings him to the surprising doctrine of a hyper-chaotic world devoid of all necessity, in which the laws of nature can change at any moment for no reason whatever, and in which both ethics and politics hinge on a virtual God who has never existed but might exist in the future. This dazzling vision has brought Meillassoux countless admirers, but few if any literal disciples. For all the friendly clarity of his communication with readers, he is a thinker of rare solitude.

Correlationism

With his term 'correlationism', Meillassoux has already made a permanent contribution to the philosophical lexicon. The rapid adoption of this word, to the point that an intellectual movement has already assembled to combat the menace it describes, suggests that 'correlationism' describes a pre-existent reality that was badly in need of a name. Whenever disputes arise in philosophy concerning realism and idealism, we immediately note the appearance of a third personage who dismisses both of these alternatives as solutions to a pseudo-problem. This third figure is the correlationist, who holds that we can never think of the world without humans nor of humans without the world, but only of a primal correlation or rapport between the two. As Meillassoux puts it, 'the central notion of philosophy since Kant seems to be that of *correlation*. By "correlation" we mean the idea according to which we only ever have access to the correlation between thinking and being, and never to either term considered apart from the other' (AF 5). And given that few people in our time wish to defend a full-blown idealism of the Berkeleyan variety, only one option remains: 'every philosophy which disavows naïve realism has become a variant of correlationism' (AF 5).

To a large extent, Meillassoux views this trend unfavorably. At the end of his book, he openly declares his goal of 'waking us from our correlational slumber, by enjoining us to reconcile thought and absolute' (AF 128). This critique of correlationism launches the strange adventure of Meillassoux's philosophy. As simple as the concept may seem, it has already met with numerous misunderstandings, and hence should be discussed in some detail. The first point to be made is that correlationism is not a 'straw man', as numerous critics in mainstream continental philosophy have lazily asserted. The reason this concept has had such explosive force in continental circles since 2006, among both admirers and detractors, is precisely because the supremacy of the human–world correlate has long been the unspoken central dogma of these circles. Among analytic philosophers there has always been a respected and vigorous realist tradition, but in continental thought it was only in the early 1990s (by Maurizio Ferraris in Turin) that realist positions were openly defended, though even now they remain in the minority. Among continentals the debate between realism and idealism is still viewed, in the manner established by Husserl and Heidegger, as a pointless pseudo-problem. What one defends instead is the primordial interplay of human and world: whether that of thought and object (Husserl) or *Dasein* and *Sein* (Heidegger). But this is precisely what Meillassoux means by correlationism. While Husserl and Heidegger bequeathed numerous treasures to present-day philosophy, they shed little light on the autonomous reality of beings outside human thought.

But the second point to notice is that Meillassoux's use of 'correlationism' is not solely polemical. More specifically, he *does not* attack the human–world correlate in the name of a return to old-fashioned realism, despite the frequent and understandable misreading of his remarks on 'ancestrality' in that manner. Unlike Alfred North Whitehead, who openly declares that 'in the main [my philosophy] is a recurrence to pre-Kantian modes of thought,'[1] Meillassoux has no wish to be pre-Kantian. Indeed, he is highly sympathetic to Kant's critique of pre-1780s metaphysics as 'dogmatic'. When the objection is made to realism that we cannot think the unthought without turning it into a thought, for Meillassoux this is a crushing objection that needs to be craftily addressed by argument, not just an annoying word trick, as many classical realists hold.

And this is the third point that should be noted at the outset: Meillassoux wants to show that correlationism can be radicalized from within so as to yield absolute knowledge of things independent from us, while also avoiding the absolutization of thought found in German Idealism. For Meillassoux, there is always something outside human thought, and this something is purely contingent. Through precision labors that resemble the work of a gem cutter (to use Levi Bryant's description), he builds a new philosophy of the absolute by starting from the apparently devastating limits of correlationism.

But a fourth and final point must also be noted: the correlate has at least two distinct features, and Meillassoux rejects only one of them. In one sense the correlate entails a limit on human knowledge; in another, it grants a special philosophical privilege to the human–world relation over the relation between any other things. As the very title *After Finitude* indicates, what bothers Meillassoux about correlationism is its claim that we have no access to the absolute. By contrast, the other aspect of correlationism does not bother Meillassoux at all, though it lies at the very root of Whitehead's rejection of Kant: the special status of human knowledge of the world compared with how animal or inanimate entities interact among themselves and with other entities. To call Meillassoux a Hegelian would be a plausible oversimplification; to call him a Whiteheadian would simply be ridiculous.

None the less, for Meillassoux there are enough negative aspects to correlationism to keep his polemical side occupied for most of the book. While the traditional debate between philosophers revolved around the question of who has the best model of substance, since Kant this has shifted to a dispute over who has identified the true nature of the human–world correlate: 'is it the thinker of the subject–object correlation, the noetico–noematic correlation, or the language–referent correlation? The question is no longer "which is the proper substrate," but "which is the proper correlate?"' (AF 5). As Meillassoux observes, the quarrel between analytic and continental philosophy might easily be understood as a disagreement over whether language or consciousness is the best model of the correlate. Heidegger's replacement of consciousness and world by *Dasein* and *Sein* changes little, since being is still made the correlate of a human who is open to its mystery, to the point that it makes no sense for Heidegger to ask whether or not being could exist without humans. Meillassoux refers to this dominance of the correlational circle in a spirit of horror, calling it 'the Kantian catastrophe' (AF 124). He rightly adds that despite Kant's famous claim to have performed a 'Copernican Revolution' in philosophy, he is actually guilty of the opposite: a 'Ptolemaic Counter-Revolution' (AF 118). For whereas Copernicus removed humans from the center of the world by putting the earth in motion, Kant's insistence that reality revolves around the conditions of our knowing it makes a better match with Ptolemy's ancient geocentric astronomy. At the precise historical moment when science was leaping forward and seizing the absolute, Kant enslaved philosophy to a model of finitude that still dominates philosophy today. Yet despite this considerable downside of Kant's legacy, 'we cannot go back to being metaphysicians, just as we cannot go back to being dogmatists. On this point, we cannot but be the heirs of Kantianism' (AF 29). As he had already put it a few pages earlier: 'We must bear in mind the apparently unanswerable force of the correlationist circle (contrary to the naïve realist)' (AF 27). The absolute that Meillassoux so passionately wants to restore cannot be attained by leaping beyond finitude and dogmatically grasping an external reality conceived in naïve fashion, but only through the inside job of radicalizing the correlational circle from within, forcing it to yield secrets of the absolute that we never imagined were there.

Meillassoux's ambivalent feelings toward correlationism must be kept in mind as we consider his famous theme of 'ancestrality'. The topic arises early in the book through a brief time line that evokes the fleeting lifespan of humans in the history of the cosmos. The origin of the universe was 13.5 billion years ago; the formation of the earth, 4.56 billion years; the origin of life on earth was just 3.5 billion years before the present time; and *Homo habilis*, our johnny-come-lately cousin from Tanzania, is a mere

2 million years old (AF 9). Since the 1930s, scientific techniques have enabled us to determine the age of both fossils and starlight, thereby placing many entities at a date far older than all possible sentient observers. On this basis, Meillassoux points to a difficulty confronting the correlationist, who wants to view reality as a human–world correlate, but is now faced with scientific discourse about a reality that *precedes* any possibility of such a correlate. And here he introduces his two key terms for referring to such a reality: 'ancestrality' and the 'arche-fossil'. In his own words:

> I will call 'ancestral' any reality anterior to the emergence of the human species – or even anterior to every recognized form of life on earth . . . I will call 'arche-fossil' . . . materials indicating the existence of an ancestral reality or event; one that is anterior to terrestrial life. (AF 10)

Admittedly, this reference to ancestrality and the arche-fossil is not an unanswerable blow to the correlationist position. The correlationist can still counterattack as follows: the statement that 'the earth was formed 4.56 billion years ago' can be rewritten as saying that 'the earth was formed 4.56 billion years ago *for us.*' Although Meillassoux finds such objections wrong, he hardly finds them laughable. His appeal to the ancestral in *After Finitude* is not a 'proof' of realism in the naïve or dogmatic fashion, but is meant more in the spirit of an *aporia*. The problem for correlationism is that it cannot give a *literal* interpretation of scientific statements. For 'no variety of correlationism, no matter how vehemently it insists that it should not be confused with subjective idealism *à la Berkeley*, can admit that this statement's literal meaning is also its deepest meaning' (AF 122). And as Meillassoux puts it, if we 'suppose for a moment that the realist . . . interpretation harboured the key to the ultimate meaning of the ancestral statement [we] would then be obliged to maintain what can only appear to the post-critical philosopher as a tissue of absurdities' (AF 14). Among these supposed absurdities are the following 'naïve' ideas: being is not co-extensive with its appearance to us; what exists is temporally prior to its appearance to us; human sentience and cognition arose at a certain point in the history of the universe that might even be accurately dated.

All these notions are basic pillars of common sense and of natural science alike. Yet they make a dramatic contrast with the correlationist vision, whose defenders can easily heap scorn on common sense, but must respond to the natural sciences with a mixture of prudence and tenacity. Among correlationists, 'a philosopher will generally begin with an assurance to the effect that his theories in no way interfere with the work of the scientist.' However, 'he will immediately add (or say to himself): [scientific research is] legitimate, *as far as it goes*' (AF 13). The literal claim that the earth dates to 4.56 billion years ago must give way to a second, more sophisticated interpretation of this statement. We have seen that, instead of saying the earth is 4.56 billion years older than humans, the correlationist says that the earth is 4.56 billion years older than humans – *for humans*. No matter how skilled the sciences become at dating pre-human entities, the correlationist always has the trump card of turning all ancestral dates into dates *for us*. Despite Meillassoux's considerable sympathy for the correlationist argument, he dismisses these procedures with acid tones. We know of fundamentalist Christians who insist on the Biblical verdict that the world is only 6,000 years old, and who interpret scientific evidence to the contrary as God's way of testing our faith in the Bible. 'Similarly,' Meillassoux mocks, 'might not the meaning of the arche-fossil be to test the philosopher's faith in correlation, even when confronted with data which seem to point to an abyssal divide between what exists and what appears?' (AF 18). Correlationists do indeed *claim* that they are not merely trapped in a human interior, when they 'readily [insist] upon the fact that consciousness, like language, enjoys an originary connection to a radical exteriority (exemplified by phenomenological consciousness . . . transcending toward the world)' (AF 7). But Meillassoux rightly calls this supposed exteriority 'a transparent cage', and notes that in this way 'contemporary philosophers have lost the *great outdoors*, the *absolute* outside of pre-critical thinkers . . . that outside which was not relative to us . . . existing in itself regardless of whether we are thinking of it or not' (AF 7).

Later in the book, the theme of ancestrality expands into that of 'diachronicity', which no longer includes only events preceding human life, but those following the possible extinction of intelligent species as well. After all, 'the problem of the arche-fossil is not confined to ancestral statements . . . [but rather] concerns every discourse whose meaning includes a *temporal discrepancy* between thinking and being' (AF 112). Eventually we need to ask why a temporal discrepancy is more important for Meillassoux than the spatial discrepancy between human observers and unwitnessed events in distant galaxies and abandoned houses. But clearly, the post-human universe raises the same problems as the pre-human cosmos: just as we ask about the formation of the earth a billion or more years before the rise of terrestrial life, we can also ask about 'the climatic and geological consequences of a meteor impact extinguishing all life on earth' (AF 112). It should be noted that for Meillassoux diachronicity is not a matter of fact, but of possibility. After all, it *could* happen that human life will endure forever along with the universe as a whole. And it even *could* be the case that human life was present from the time of the Big Bang. 'Science could in principle have discovered a synchronicity between humanity and world, since there is nothing to rule out *a priori* ... the hypothesis of a human species as old as the cosmos' (AF 113). But even if this were the case, we could still raise the problem of diachronicity as a hypothetical scenario. We would still be able to speculate: *what if* our human ancestors were not as old as the universe itself? Would the human–world correlate then be threatened? Even in a world without genuine arche-fossils, they would live on as a valuable thought experiment in the same way as the 'possible worlds' scenarios of analytic philosophers like David Lewis.

We now have a sense of what Meillassoux intends with his valuable term 'correlationism'. Dogmatic realists claim that a world exists outside our thinking of it, and the much smaller group of absolute idealists denies any such world outside the mind. By contrast, the correlationist philosophies prevailing since Kant view 'realism vs. idealism' as a basically worthless dispute, and claim to occupy a more sophisticated middle ground: we can neither think the world apart from humans, nor humans apart from the world, but only these two poles in co-existence. While Meillassoux attacks correlationism, he does so only in part. His goal is not to replace the human–world correlate either with traditional realism or full-blown idealism: far from it, since he views Kant and correlationism as a rigorous forward step in the history of philosophy. If Meillassoux views Kant as a 'catastrophe', this is not out of nostalgia for the olden times of dogmatic metaphysics, which he explicitly and repeatedly denounces. Instead, the nature of the Kantian disaster is confined to a single word found in the title of his book: *finitude*. What Meillassoux seeks is a non-dogmatic version of the absolute, one that arises internally from the ashes of the correlational circle. If we arrange philosophies along a primitive three-term spectrum of *realist – correlationist – idealist*, the second of these is where Meillassoux sets up camp. But once he has done so, he immediately proclaims a new philosophy.

Speculative Materialism

Instead of remaining with the aforementioned threefold schema of realism, correlationism, and idealism, Meillassoux offers a subtler range of positions. The following list is important enough for the argument of *After Finitude* that it needs to be given a name for future reference. Let us call it 'Meillassoux's Spectrum', a list arranged from most to least classically realist in spirit:

- Dogmatic/Naïve Realism
- Weak Correlationism
- Strong Correlationism
- Very Strong Correlationism
- Absolute Idealism.

Most of these positions already existed well before 2006, though often under different names. Meillassoux's own Speculative Materialist philosophy is not yet included, but will emerge from a specific point in the list. Above all, his appeal to ancestrality and the arche-fossil should not be mistaken for Position 1: dogmatic/ naïve realism. Meillassoux is fully appreciative of the Kantian revolution in philosophy, despite the dark note of Kant's hymn to finitude. The best description of Meillassoux's strategy is that he initially places himself in Position 4: Very Strong Correlationism, working carefully to show that such a position can be maintained without collapsing into Position 5: Absolute Idealism. But rather than simply adopt Position 4, he turns it upside-down into a standpoint never known before, and which he calls Speculative Materialism.

In this section I will sketch the main features of these five positions, and show how Meillassoux hopes to escape the schema altogether. But first, we should dispense with some possible objections to it. One objection would claim that the Spectrum misses any number of possible intermediate positions; from experience, it seems that anywhere from three to seven new options are demanded by those who wish to one-up the Spectrum. The proper response to this objection is simply to note that seventy or even three hundred subtle new variants might also be added if one wished, without thereby proving that the added nuance is of relevance to Meillassoux's argument. In short, Meillassoux does not claim that these are the only possible human attitudes towards the realism/idealism question, but only that they are the most important variants for clarifying his own Speculative Materialism by way of contrast. He is not trying to write an encyclopedia of all possible philosophies, only trying to develop a specific philosophical standpoint and distinguish it from its neighbors.

Another possible objection would lament the 'linear' character of the Spectrum, with the implication that philosophies are much too complicated to be laid out along a one-dimensional number line. This objection is well founded, but in the present context it is quite irrelevant. True enough, there is no way to arrange such diverse modern thinkers as Deleuze, Fichte, Gadamer, Levinas, and Merleau-Ponty along a single linear co-ordinate system, given the vast range of subjects all of them address. But notice that it would be quite easy to arrange these thinkers in linear fashion if we did so according to available data on height, cholesterol count, or age at death. The point is that the linear ranking of *anything* becomes possible as soon as we focus on just one criterion. And thus it is in no way difficult to arrange philosophers in linear fashion according to how closely they approximate the classically realist version of the human–world relationship. This is precisely what Meillassoux's Spectrum does, for a limited but highly valuable purpose.

As we have seen, Meillassoux generally views correlationism as a *bad* thing. He introduces the term in a polemical spirit, and recommends that the correlationist model of philosophy be rejected. Yet the alternative he proposes is not a return to naïve realism of the pre-Kantian type. For in one sense it is true that ancestrality makes it 'incumbent upon us to break with the ontological requisite of the moderns, according to which *to be is to be a correlate*', since 'our task consists in trying to understand how thought is able to access the uncorrelated, which is to say, a world capable of subsisting without being given' (AF 28). Rather than following Kant's gesture of asking how synthetic judgments *a priori* are possible, Meillassoux asks as follows: 'what is the condition that legitimates science's ancestral statements?' (AF 27). And this question 'demands of us that we remain as distant from naïve realism as from correlationist subtlety, which are *the two ways of refusing to see ancestrality as a problem*' (AF 27). None the less, if forced to choose between naïve realism and correlationism, Meillassoux would embrace 'the apparently unanswerable force of the correlationist circle (contrary to the naïve realist)' (AF 27). We thus leave naïve realism behind for much the same reason as did Kant himself.

But like the German Idealists before him, Meillassoux is inclined to see a problem with thinking the things-in-themselves. This becomes clear from his next distinction, between 'a "weak" model [of correlationism], which is that of Kant, and a "strong" model, which seems to be dominant today, even if it is never thematized as such' (AF 30). The difference between the two forms should be clear enough. It is well known that while Kant's philosophy is based on our inability to know the things-in-themselves, he at least allows us to *think* them. By contrast, Meillassoux says, 'the strong model of correlationism maintains not only that it is illegitimate to *know* the in-itself, but *also* that it is illegitimate to claim that we can at least *think* it' (AF 35). Kant holds that we are able to make a few definite claims about the in-itself, such as that contradiction is impossible. But 'by what miraculous operation is Kantian thought able to get outside of itself in order to verify that what is unthinkable for us is impossible in itself?' (AF 35). For Meillassoux at this stage of the argument, non-contradiction 'can only be the norm for what is thinkable by us, rather than for what is possible in an absolute sense' (AF 40–1). And thus strong correlationism (which Meillassoux finds more formidable than the weak version) holds that irrational discourses about the absolute cannot be discounted (AF 41). In other words, for strong correlationism '*it is unthinkable that the unthinkable be impossible*' (AF 41). We simply cannot say anything at all about what lies outside thought. And here 'the strong model . . . seems to us to be represented as much by Wittgenstein as by Heidegger, which is to say, by the two emblematic representatives of the two principal currents of twentieth-century philosophy: analytic philosophy and phenomenology' (AF 41). For the Wittgenstein of the *Tractatus*, the structure of the world can only be 'shown' in a way 'that cannot be bound by the categories of science or logic' (AF 41). And for Heidegger, 'the very fact that there are beings, and that there is a givenness of beings' (AF 42) lies beyond all rational access.

Meillassoux has much to say about this strong correlationist position, and most of it is bad. Strong correlationism is linked with numerous distasteful trends in the contemporary world: fideism, skepticism, fanaticism, and the return of the religious in general. In so far as strong correlationism thinks no rational statement about the in-itself is possible, it leads directly to fideism: 'fideism is merely the *other name* for strong correlationism' (AF 48), as seen in the mystical leanings of Wittgenstein and the theological tendencies of Heidegger. All possibility of rational discourse about the in-itself has ended: 'What philosopher nowadays would claim to have refuted the possibility of the Christian Trinity on the grounds that he had detected a contradiction in it?' (AF 43). Though it might seem that recent criticisms of metaphysics would also entail a critique of religion, the opposite has happened. For while it is true that specific metaphysical systems have been toppled to the ground by recent philosophy, this procedure has merely opened up a vast space of the unknowable in-itself, untouchable by reason. The results are predictable:

> by destroying metaphysics, one has effectively rendered it impossible for a particular religion to use a pseudo-rational argumentation against every other religion. But in doing so – and this is the decisive point – one has inadvertently justified belief's claim to be the *only* means of access to the absolute. (AF 45–6)

As a result, 'even atheism . . . is reduced to a mere belief, and hence to a religion, albeit of the nihilist kind' (AF 46).

For Meillassoux, fideism goes hand in hand with skepticism. Against the frequent tendency to interpret religious fideism as a devious mask that conceals skeptical irreligiosity, Meillassoux holds that 'scepticism [is] an authentic fideism, which is dominant today, but in a form . . . *that has shrugged off every particular obedience to a determinate belief system*' (AF 46). Historically speaking, fideism 'was initiated by the Counter-Reformation, and Montaigne was its founding father' (AF 46). Indeed, Montaigne is a towering figure in Meillassoux's version of the history of philosophy, in some respects more important than Descartes as a founder of modern thought.[2] More generally, Meillassoux laments that while Greek philosophy once rationalized religion, religion is now used to derationalize philosophy (AF 47). Philosophy is subordinated to piety, and has become the voluntary handmaid of religion. Though it might seem that philosophy has been liberated from all religious pressures, 'it now considers itself to be the liberal servant of any theology whatsoever, including an atheology' (AF 47). Religious notions are no longer condemned for their *falsity*, since the question of truth has shifted entirely to the realm of belief. Instead, we have entered a moralized space in which 'the condemnation of fanaticism is carried out solely in the name of its practical (ethico-political) consequences, never in the name of the ultimate falsity of its contents' (AF 47). But rather than viewing fanaticism as the crude, primitive remnant of a pre-rational era, Meillassoux sees it as the very *product* of Western critical reason: 'It is thanks to the critical power of correlationism that dogmatism was effectively vanquished in philosophy, and it is because of correlationism that philosophy finds itself incapable of fundamentally distinguishing itself from fanaticism.' In short, 'the victorious critique of ideologies has been transformed into a renewed argument for blind faith' (AF 49). Western thought is now obliged to pursue the same balancing act found in Meillassoux's own philosophy: the need to avoid the extremes of (a) dogmatic contact with a metaphysical in-itself and (b) the fanatical skepticism of belief, as embodied by 'the pretensions of those who would present themselves as its privileged trustees, solely by virtue of some revelation' (AF 49).

We now return to Meillassoux's Spectrum, a term never used by the author himself, but still a good name for the gradation of positions he describes. Already we have mentioned naïve/dogmatic realism, weak correlationism, and strong correlationism. With each step in the series so far, Meillassoux becomes increasingly sympathetic to the position described, while remaining somewhat dissatisfied. We should also note a further distinction between two separate forms of strong correlationism described by Meillassoux. Since he does not name them, I will take the liberty of calling them Strong Correlationism and Very Strong Correlationism. The difference between the two is as follows. The Very Strong Correlationist takes it for granted that the de-absolutization of thought also results in de-universalization, so that each person becomes a sort of private fideist with a personal worldview impenetrable to reason. By contrast, the simple Strong Correlationists 'situate themselves as heirs of Kant's critical legacy'. Hence they will 'attempt ... to uncover the universal conditions for our relation to the world, whether these be construed as conditions for empirical science, conditions for linguistic communication between individuals, conditions for the perception of the entity, etc.' (AF 42).

The Very Strong Correlationists are found among postmodern philosophers. They 'dismiss every variety of universal as a mystificatory relic of the old metaphysics [and] will claim that it is necessary to think the facticity of our relation to the world in terms of a *situation that is itself finite*'. And thus the correlation in which we find ourselves has no universal features, but is 'anchored in a determinate era of the history of being, or in a form of life harbouring its own language-games, or in a determinate cultural and interpretive community, etc.' (AF 43). Although many different authors could be cited as examples of the Strong and Very Strong positions, it is most helpful to cite the shift from Husserl to Heidegger as an example of the turn from Strong to Very Strong. For Very Strong Correlationism, the correlate is marked by its *facticity*. And though Meillassoux will soon reject this notion in the name of the related and startling idea of 'factiality', Very Strong Correlationism turns out to be his preferred starting point on the Spectrum: the point at which he attempts to radicalize the correlate from within. But first, there remains a further shift along the list of options, and it is one that Meillassoux would not quite endorse: Absolute Idealism. We will approach this topic slowly, through a reflection on how the correlationist deals with science.

As a general rule, correlationism is careful not to denigrate the sciences openly: 'where science is concerned, philosophers have become modest – and even prudent' (AF 13). Philosophers assure us that their theories 'in no way interfere with the work of the scientist, and that the manner in which the latter understands her own research is perfectly legitimate' (AF 13). None the less, we have seen that they always want to one-up the sciences by treating their literal statements about the ancestral world as circumscribed by a deeper philosophical sense – a sense in which events that occurred billions of years ago only occurred billions of years ago *for us*. According to this attitude, 'although it is normal, and even natural, for the scientist to adopt a spontaneously realist attitude, which she shares with the "ordinary man", the philosopher possesses a specific type of knowledge which imposes a correction upon science's ancestral statements' (AF 13). Thus there seems to be a safe division of labor: science does the work of naïve realism and achieves amazing results; correlationist philosophy watches this work from an ironic distance with condescending praise and a gently raised eyebrow, never so gullible as to accept scientific realism in literal fashion.

But this leads us to the very paradox with which Meillassoux's book began. We ask the correlationist the following question: 'What is it that happened 4.56 billion years ago? Did the accretion of the earth happen, yes or no?' (AF 16, emphasis removed). The correlationist now tries to play a double game, conceding that in some way the statement is 'true', while also denying its *literal* sense. But this is meaningless for Meillassoux, who sees no point in a positivist or verificationist understanding of science. The literal sense of scientific statements is that they point to a real world outside its accessibility to us: 'Science does not experiment with a view to validating the universality of its experiments; it carries out repeatable experiments with a view to external referents which endow these experiments with meaning' (AF 17). In short, there can be no subtle middle ground between the claim that a world existed billions of years before the appearance of thought and the opposite claim that world and thought exist only as correlates of one another. Thus, 'the correlationist should stop being modest and dare to assert openly that he is in a position to provide the scientist with an *a priori* demonstration that the latter's claims are *illusory*' (AF 17).

This brings us to a colorful interlude that is actually somewhat perilous for Meillassoux's argument. For given that correlationism cannot be reconciled with literal ancestral statements, it follows that '[when] confronted with the arche-fossil, *every variety of idealism converges and becomes equally extraordinary* – every variety of correlationism is exposed as an extreme idealism' (AF 18). Or as he had put it earlier:

> it is as if the distinction between transcendental idealism – the idealism that is (so to speak) urbane, civilized, and reasonable – and speculative or even subjective idealism – the idealism that is wild, uncouth, and rather extravagant – it is as if this distinction . . . which separates Kant from Berkeley . . . became blurred and dissolved in light of the fossil-matter. (AF 17–18)

In other words, we now sense the real danger that correlationism is entirely indistinguishable from absolute idealism. And this would be a disaster for Meillassoux's book, for we will see that his own position makes sense only as a radicalization of the correlationist position, not as a variant of absolute idealism. Meillassoux's attempt to dismantle a flawed portion of the correlationist argument and turn it against itself presupposes that correlationism avoids melting into absolute idealism. We will return to this issue shortly, but for now let us note that Meillassoux is well aware of the danger:

> if strong correlationism can easily rebuff the realist . . . it is altogether more difficult for it to defeat the 'subjectivist' metaphysician . . . For how is one to legitimate the assertion that something subsists beyond our representations when one has already insisted that this beyond is radically inaccessible to thought? (AF 38)

Meillassoux proceeds roughly as follows. He asks us to make a distinction between two separate gestures; he then tries to drive a wedge between them by claiming that strong correlationism is able to make the first gesture while avoiding the second. The first gesture is this one: 'we cannot think a world without an entity . . . [that is] capable of "thinking" this world in the most general sense' (AF 37). This is merely the familiar point that we cannot think the unthought without turning it into a thought. The second gesture pushes things further, reminding us that since the Kantian thing-in-itself is both unknowable and unthinkable, 'it seems that the wisest course is to *abolish* any such notion of the in-itself' (AF 37). What makes this second point more extreme is that it claims to have positive knowledge that the in-itself does not exist. In other words, even though absolute idealism holds that *the in-itself* is unthinkable, it still maintains that *the absolute* is thinkable (AF 38). This absolute is simply found in the very conditions of the subject–object relationship rather than somewhere beyond it.

Some readers might even conclude that this is Meillassoux's own strategy. After all, his philosophy does seek the absolute, and it does so precisely by radicalizing the correlate from within rather than leaping naively into a reality beyond it. However, Meillassoux openly tries to avoid a slide into absolute idealism. Correlationism is marked by *facticity*, that famous Heideggerian term for the specific situation of humans in a world at any moment. But rather than simply adopting the meaning that this concept has in Heidegger, Meillassoux relates it to the difference between Kant and Hegel: namely, 'Kant maintains that we can only *describe* the *a priori* forms of knowledge [space, time, and the twelve categories] . . . whereas Hegel insists that it is possible to *deduce* them' (AF 38). For Kant the precise structure of the world is simply an undeniable *fact*, impenetrable to further explanation. And yet, 'as far as we know, no one has ever come back from a voyage into the in-itself with a guarantee that meaning is absolute' (AF 36). Even though it seems 'meaningless' for the correlationist to speak hypothetically of an in-itself, since by speaking of it he converts it into something other than an in-itself, *the meaningless is not necessarily the impossible.* Our inability to speak of an in-itself from inside the correlate does not entail that only the correlate exists and that it must therefore be absolutized. This absolute idealism is rejected, and we are left with nothing but facticity, which is 'the mark of our essential *finitude*' (AF 40). Yet the very title of Meillassoux's book indicates that he will not stop here. Instead, he will attempt to convert facticity ('the world is governed by structural invariants that can only be described, not deduced') into contingency ('physical laws remain indifferent as to what happens, whether any entity emerges, subsists, or perishes') (AF 39).

Already we have encountered the first of several perilous arguments on which the whole of Meillassoux's system depends. Already he has accepted the basic strong correlationist argument against naïve realism: we cannot think an unthought object without thereby turning it into a thought. In this way, everything we consider in thought exists only as a correlate of our thinking rather than as something in itself. Meillassoux is even willing to go a step further, and concede that the very notion of an in-itself is *unthinkable*, since the notion of thinking something outside thought is meaningless. This is what makes him sympathize with strong correlationism rather than the weak brand of correlationism found in Kant. And this notion that the supposed noumena are really just a special case of the phenomena, that things-in-themselves are reabsorbed by the circle of thought in so far as we are the ones thinking them, is usually seen as a step all the way into Absolute Idealism. But Meillassoux refuses Absolute Idealism, subtly attempting to create a position midway between Kant and Hegel, though only with the aim of overturning it and creating an inverted position of his own: namely, for Meillassoux the unthinkability and 'meaningless' character of the things-in-themselves does not entail their non-existence. In other words, even when we conclude that thinking an unthought thing is a completely meaningless notion, this *does not mean that unthought things do not exist.* What is meaningful for humans need not exhaust the totality of what is real. For 'the strong model of correlationism can be summed up in the following thesis: *it is unthinkable that the unthinkable should be impossible*' (AF 41). We can restate all of this in terms of Meillassoux's Spectrum:

1. Dogmatic/Naïve Realism: 'The things-in-themselves exist, and they are knowable.'
2. Weak Correlationism: 'The things-in-themselves exist. They are not knowable, but at least they are thinkable.'
3/4. Strong/Very Strong Correlationism: 'The things-in-themselves are unknowable and also completely unthinkable. In short, they are meaningless. But that does not mean that they do not exist.'
5. Absolute Idealism: 'The things-in-themselves are unknowable and also completely unthinkable. In short, they are meaningless. And that means that their existence is impossible.'

Traditionally, Kantians have been at Position 2 and Hegelians at Position 5. Meillassoux places various twentieth-century figures at Positions 3/4, preferring 4 for himself as we have already seen. But this Position 4 will soon be transformed into one of the most surprising philosophical positions of our time: Speculative Materialism, which tries to avoid the two extremes of absolute idealism and correlationism. To escape the former it must abstain from hypostatizing the correlate of thought and world; to avoid the latter, it must move beyond finitude and think the absolute. Thus,

> every materialism that would be speculative, and hence for which absolute reality is an *entity without thought*, must assert *both* that thought is not necessary (something can be independently of thought), and that thought can think what there must be when there is no thought. (AF 36)

Contingency

Weak Correlationism is the familiar Kantian position that the things-in-themselves can be thought but not known. But for Absolute Idealism, to think the things-in-themselves outside thought is to turn them into objects of thought, and thus there is no way to point beyond the human–world correlate at all. Wedged between these two positions is Strong Correlationism. In one sense it agrees with Absolute Idealism that we cannot claim to think the unthought without falling into performative contradiction. But unlike Idealism, it holds that our inability to *think* the unthought does not prove the *nonexistence* of the unthought. This Strong Correlationism serves as the launching pad for Meillassoux's own position, Speculative Materialism. As we will see in the present section, his strategy is to transform our supposed ignorance of the things-in-themselves into an absolute *knowledge* that the things-in-themselves exist without reason, and that they can change at any time for no reason at all. In this way the cautious agnosticism of Kantian philosophies is avoided, but so is the collapse of reality into thought found in German Idealism. In their place, Meillassoux offers a wonderfully bizarre metaphysics of absolute contingency in which anything can happen without reason and without warning. It is precisely this vision that ranks him as one of the boldest speculative thinkers of our era.

Žižek reminds us of the Wagnerian theme that you can be 'healed only by the spear that smote you'.[3] Meillassoux proceeds in a similar spirit, comparing his own strategy against correlationism with the German Idealist transformation of Kant: 'we too must absolutize the very principle that allows correlationism to disqualify absolutizing thought. This is precisely what various subjectivist metaphysicians did – they turned the correlation itself ... into the model for a new type of absolute' (AF 51–2). Stated differently, 'we are going to put back into the thing itself what we mistakenly took to be an incapacity in thought' (AF 53, emphasis removed). Ultimately this will yield what Meillassoux calls the principle of unreason, 'whereby everything in the world *is* without reason, and is thereby capable of actually becoming otherwise without reason' (AF 53, emphasis modified). Or as he ominously puts it:

> Everything could actually collapse: from trees to stars, from stars to laws, from physical laws to logical laws; and this not by virtue of some superior law whereby everything is destined to perish, but by virtue of the *absence* of any superior law capable of preserving anything, no matter what, from perishing. (AF 53, emphasis added)

What turns out to be absolute is not the correlate itself (as for absolute idealism), but the *facticity* of the correlate (AF 52). It is time to see why Meillassoux thinks this is the case, since this step lies at the very center of his philosophy.

A dogmatic believer and a dogmatic atheist are arguing about the afterlife, and along comes a correlationist (AF 55). It sounds like the opening of a joke, or of a comic philosophy dialogue in the manner of Giordano Bruno. In many ways Meillassoux has the mind of a good dramatist, and often enough his most important passages take the form of imaginary debates between rival positions, or of fictional speeches by possible philosophers who have never walked the earth. In this case Meillassoux's first two characters are dogmatic simpletons, but each new persona arriving on stage is increasingly complex. The Believer claims that the existence of an afterlife can be proven, and the Atheist claims with equal vigor that the afterlife can be disproven with absolute certainty. Meillassoux, channeling the comic spirit of Molière, now brings a Correlationist on stage. In the eyes of this third character the two disputants are equally naïve, since one can only maintain a strict agnostic position on the afterlife. 'For just as I cannot know the in-itself without converting it into a for-me, I cannot know what will happen to me when I am no longer of this world, since knowledge presupposes that one is of the world' (AF 55). The Correlationist seems to have gained the upper hand, and a more primitive drama might end here with the trite lesson that absolute knowledge of anything is impossible. But Meillassoux develops the theme for another four pages, and the climax is a disturbing proposal that might well have been staged by Beckett or Artaud.

We are familiar with how the agnostic philosophy of Kant is often converted into full-blown idealism: the thought of things outside thought is still a thought; the noumena are just a special case of the phenomena. On a similar note, a fourth persona takes the stage in Meillassoux's dramatic conversation: the Subjective Idealist. This familiar stock figure tells us that the two Dogmatists and the Correlationist are equally wrong since 'all three believe that there could be an in itself radically different from our present state, whether it is a God who is inaccessible to natural reason, or a sheer nothingness' (AF 55). But this entails the obvious contradiction of trying to think something outside thinking. It follows that 'I cannot think of myself as no longer existing without, through that very thought, contradicting myself' (AF 55). Accordingly 'my mind, if not my body, is immortal' (AF 55). Idealism boldly claims to cancel anything lying outside the correlate, including death itself. The Dogmatic Atheist was simply wrong to have such faith in human extinction. The Dogmatic Believer was right that we can never die, but wrong to think that the afterlife could be anything radically different from the world we already know. And the Correlationist was wrong to believe in the possibility of something other than thought as well.

The spotlight now returns to the Correlationist, who is not so easily defeated by this idealist trick. It was easy to triumph over the two naïve Dogmatists, but admittedly harder to defeat the Idealist. The Correlationist can prevail against the other three positions simultaneously only by declaring that *all* are too absolutist in the their views. Even though the first two are Dogmatists, while the Subjective Idealist is the opposite of dogmatic by not going beyond the bounds of thought, all of them think they can give an absolute reason for their views on the status of death. By contrast, the Correlationist holds that 'my capacity-to-be-wholly-other in death (whether dazzled by God, or annihilated) is just as thinkable as my persisting in self-identity' (AF 56). This is due to the *facticity* of the thought–world correlate in the eyes of the Correlationist, which means that the conditions of the correlate can only be described, not explained. Whereas the Subjective Idealist finds it impossible for anything to exist outside thought, the Correlationist admits that an in-itself sounds meaningless but denies we can know that what is meaningful to us exhausts the realm of possibility. We simply know that the thought–world correlate exists, not that it *must* exist. The Idealist justifiably says that we *cannot think* the unthought, but it does not follow that the unthought *cannot exist*.

But now comes the fifth and final character of the drama: the Speculative Materialist, a dramatic projection of Meillassoux himself. And here we see the intimate and inverted link between Meillassoux's own position and what he calls Strong Correlationism. For whereas Strong Correlationism can be read as an epistemological claim about our finitude, ignorance, and need for skeptical agnosticism, Speculative Materialism reverses these claims into an *ontological* doctrine. In other words, the Strong Correlationist thinks we cannot know which possibility about the afterlife is true, but the Speculative Materialist thinks we *can* know that *any* of them could be true, and without reason. This apparently hair-splitting point is actually the key to Meillassoux's entire system, and is worthy of closer attention.

Consider again how the Correlationist is able to defeat the Subjective Idealist. The Idealist holds that the nonexistence of thought is unthinkable and therefore impossible, meaning that death simply cannot occur. The Correlationist had countered by saying that something might very well exist outside the thought–world correlate. But notice that the existence of this possible otherness *cannot itself be inscribed within thought*, or else the Correlationist would collapse into the position of the Idealist. In other words, the Idealist might say 'we cannot think a tree existing outside thought, and therefore no tree exists outside thought,' and the Correlationist might counter with 'we cannot think a tree existing outside thought, and yet such a tree might exist nonetheless.' But notice that this latter claim already pushes beyond the closed circle of thought. For it cannot mean that '*for me* we cannot think a tree existing outside thought, yet such a tree might exist none the less *for me*,' since this is a simple contradiction. Instead, it means that '*for me* we cannot think a tree existing outside thought, yet such a tree might exist nonetheless *in spite of my not being able to think it*.' To say otherwise would be a collapse into Idealism. The possibility of death means an actual possibility *of death*, not *of death for me* as something merely thought. In Meillassoux's words: 'I think myself as mortal only if I think that my death has no need of my thought of death in order to be actual' (AF 57). And as he wittily concludes: 'If my ceasing to be depended upon my continuing to be so that I could keep thinking myself as not being, then I would continue to agonize indefinitely, without ever actually passing away' (AF 57).

In short, facticity is only facticity if its limitedness is *absolutely* limited – only if the possibilities other than the thought–world correlate are possibilities that do in fact lie outside the correlate. If we say 'there might be trees outside thought *for thought*,' then nothing is gained, and Subjective Idealism is the only possible game in town. Correlationism is true only if Subjective Idealism *might be wrong*. But if it might be wrong, then it is *absolutely true* that it might be wrong, and Correlationism is no longer a merely agnostic position. Rather than remaining trapped in the circle of merely human finitude, it has finally discovered something genuine about reality. But for this very reason, it instantly turns into the Speculative Materialist position of Meillassoux himself. The only way for Correlationism to remain different from Idealism is to replace the absolute status of the thought–world correlate, not with finitude and ignorance about the otherness of the world, but with absolute knowledge that the world might be other than we think. As Meillassoux puts it: 'the correlationist's refutation of idealism proceeds by way of an absolutization (which is to say, a de-correlation) of the capacity-to-be-other presupposed in the thought of facticity' (AF 57).

But the Correlationist fought back against the Idealist, and will certainly fight back against the Speculative Materialist. For example, the Correlationist could claim that just as the Idealist might be wrong about thought being absolute, so too the Speculative Materialist might be wrong about the absoluteness of thought being impossible. Here as ever, the Correlationist has tried to seize the upper hand by showing that the alternative positions are too absolutist in spirit. But this time the strategy does not work. The Correlationist is essentially claiming that all of the characters are on the same footing: Dogmatic Atheist, Dogmatic Believer, Dogmatic Idealist, and Dogmatic Speculative Materialist. All think that they are right and the other positions are wrong. If we simplify and say that the Atheist holds that X is necessary, the Believer that Y is necessary, and the Speculative Materialist that both X and Y are real possibilities, the Correlationist thinks that 'what we are dealing with here is three possibilities of ignorance [the three different positions] and not with two real possibilities [as the Speculative Materialist holds]' (AF 58, emphasis modified).

Meillassoux's response to this last-ditch argument is simple: it contradicts itself. For here again, the only way the Correlationist can hold open the various different possibilities is with the tacit claim that the possibilities are *absolutely* possible. They cannot simply be possibilities for thought, or Subjective Idealism will win. Meillassoux now addresses the Correlationist, in his own voice, in a lengthy and intricate passage that can be drastically shortened as follows:

> Let me make myself clear, for this is the crux of the matter . . . The very idea of the difference between the in-itself and the for-us would never have arisen within you, had you not experienced what is perhaps human thought's most remarkable power– its capacity to access the possibility of its own non-being, and thus to *know* itself to be mortal . . . Consequently, you are perfectly well able to distinguish between the possibility of ignorance and the possibility of the absolute. But this possibility is always based upon the same argument – it is because one can think that it is absolutely possible for the in-itself to be other than the given, that what I believe to be really possible may not be really

possible. Once this has been conceded, you are caught in an infinite regress, for every time you claim that what I call a real possibility is merely a possibility of ignorance, you will do so by way of an argument that works . . . [against Idealism] only by thinking as an absolute the possibility you claim to be de-absolutising. (AF 59)

The entire drama can be summarized briefly as follows. The Atheist and the Believer are both derailed by the Kantian point that we cannot have access to reality outside our conditions of access to it. The Idealist is defeated by Meillassoux's point that the meaninglessness of thinking a world outside thought does not mean a world outside thought is impossible. And finally, the Correlationist is defeated by being transformed into a Speculative Materialist. For the Correlationist avoids being an Idealist only by insisting that there *might* be an in-itself different from the for-us, and this 'might' has to refer to a real in-itself, not just an 'in-itself-for-us'. The Correlationist claims to abstain from any form of the absolute, but can only be a Correlationist by holding that there are *absolutely* a number of different possibilities. Meillassoux concludes: 'We have now identified the faultline that lies at the heart of correlationism; the one through which we can breach its defences' (AF 59) – namely, there is no way to avoid making *either* facticity *or* the correlate absolute. If we say that everything is the correlate of an act of thought, then we have absolutized the correlate and become Subjective Idealists. Or, we can escape this position by de-absolutizing the correlate and saying that, after all, there might be something outside it. But this means *absolutizing facticity*, by saying that it is absolutely true that there might be something outside the correlate of thought and world. The Correlationist cannot have it both ways by saying: 'there absolutely might be something outside thought, yet maybe this is absolutely impossible.' In other words, once we escape the prison of Dogmatism, we can only be Idealists or Speculative Materialists. The standard agnostic version of Correlationism turns out not to be entirely agnostic, in spite of itself.

Another way of looking at it is that facticity itself cannot be factical. The point of facticity for Meillassoux, we recall, is that it means that the correlate of thought and world can only be described, not deduced. It is merely there, and we cannot know exactly why – in contrast with subjective idealism, which thinks it can deduce the necessity of the thought–world couplet. But we have just discussed how correlationism leads to the *absolute* possibility that reality could be other than the correlate, and this shows why facticity itself cannot be factical. In other words, if the specific features of our facticity can only be described and not deduced, the same is not true of facticity itself. And here Meillassoux coins a new French term, *factualité*, which Ray Brassier (with Meillassoux's explicit approval) has rendered in English as 'factiality'. As Meillassoux puts it: 'From now on, we will use the term "factiality" to describe the speculative essence of facticity, viz., that the facticity of every thing cannot be thought as a fact' (AF 79, emphasis removed). While facticity means that the structure of the correlate can only be described rather than deduced, factiality means that *facticity itself* is something that *can* be deduced. Such a deduction is precisely what Meillassoux tried to provide in the debate between the Speculative Materialist and the Correlationist. If facticity can be taken to mean that there is no necessary reason for any feature of experience, the hidden surprise here is that *facticity itself* is necessary. That is the meaning of factiality, to which Meillassoux attaches the expected adjective 'factial': 'We will call "factial" the type of speculation which seeks and identifies the conditions of factiality' (AF 79). The analysis of the conditions of factiality now becomes the explicit goal of Meillassoux's philosophical enterprise: the discovery of what he calls 'figures', or necessary features of factiality. To give a few examples, non-contradiction turns out to be one such figure or necessary feature (AF 69–70), as does the fact that there must be something rather than nothing (AF 80), and the fact that every mathematical statement can be absolutized (AF 126). As Meillassoux says on the final page of the book: 'the factial is defined as the very arena for a speculation that excludes all metaphysics' (AF 128, emphasis removed).

At first, it might seem that not much is gained when we move from the Correlationist to the Speculative Materialist: 'What the sceptic construed as ignorance – everything is possible – we now construe as knowledge, but knowledge whose content seems as indeterminate as the most complete ignorance' (AF 65). Or as Meillassoux puts it even more humorously, as if imagining a possible heckler: 'instead of saying that the in-itself could actually be anything whatsoever without anyone knowing what, we maintain that the in-itself could actually be anything whatsoever and that we know this' (AF 65). But we have already seen the significant difference between the two positions. Whereas the Correlationist merely says that we are ignorant of what may or may not lie outside the correlate, the Speculative Materialist does attain to a certain kind of absolute knowledge. After all, the Correlationist 'is incapable of disqualifying *any* hypothesis about the nature of the absolute' (AF 65). But '[the Speculative Materialist knows] two things that the sceptic did not: first, that contingency is necessary, and hence eternal; second, that contingency alone is necessary' (AF 65). It is from this apparently subtle difference between Meillassoux and Correlationism that an entirely new speculative philosophy will be constructed.

In one of his most effective war cries, Meillassoux proclaims that 'we are going to put back into the thing itself what we mistakenly took to be an incapacity of thought' (AF 53, emphasis removed). Whereas it might be thought that the lack of reason for anything is derived from the finitude and ignorance of human knowledge, Meillassoux actually claims the opposite: the doctrine of finitude is generally associated with a *hidden* reason, one that humans simply cannot grasp. With his turn toward absolute knowledge, Meillassoux strips the world of any place where shadowy hidden reasons could reside. The reason for things having no reason is not that the reason is hidden, but that no hidden reason exists. And 'this absence of reason *is*, and can *only* be the *ultimate* property of the entity' (AF 53). The entity holds no cryptic properties in reserve, as if in Heideggerian fashion; Meillassoux could never support a doctrine of truth as unveiling, since there is never any veil for him in the first place. The world is a surface without depth or potential, though there is still a *virtual* dimension to Meillassoux's system that we will soon discuss. 'There is nothing beneath or beyond the manifest gratuitousness of the given – nothing but the limitless and lawless power of its destruction, emergence, or persistence' (AF 63). But the important thing for now is that facticity, converted into factiality, is 'the real property whereby everything . . . is capable of actually becoming otherwise without reason' (AF 53, emphasis removed). The absence of an ultimate reason for anything is what Meillassoux also calls the 'principle of unreason', though he prefers 'factiality' to 'unreason' on the grounds that the latter might sound merely negative.

But there is one possible misunderstanding that must be avoided. In the popular mind necessity is often linked with stability and contingency with flux. It is easy to see why. If there is no reason for anything to be the way it is, there would seem to be no pillar of its reality, no hidden infrastructure supporting its being in a stable state. The usual view of contingency, in short, associates it with what Meillassoux calls 'precariousness'. For it 'designates a possibility that is bound to be realized sooner or later, so long as physical and organic laws remain as they have been up until now' (AF 62). To say that everything must eventually perish would amount to a metaphysical thesis about the nature of the cosmos. By contrast, Meillassoux '[does] not see by virtue of what there would be a reason necessitating the possibility of destruction as opposed to the possibility of persistence' (AF 63).

Another key Meillassouxian term for this absolutely contingent state of everything is *hyper-chaos*. Whereas an absolute is supposed to provide an unyielding foundation, hyper-chaos seems to be anything but an absolute, since for it 'nothing would seem to be impossible, not even the unthinkable' (AF 64). Those who fear that philosophies of the absolute lead to rigid crystallizations of reality should have the *opposite* worry about Meillassoux, who shows a nice poetic touch in admitting the chaotic world that results from his principles:

> If we look through the aperture which we have opened up onto the absolute, what we see there is a rather menacing power– something [senseless], and capable of destroying both things and worlds, of bringing forth monstrous absurdities, yet also of never doing anything, of realizing every dream, but also every nightmare, of engendering random and frenetic transformations, or conversely, of producing a universe that remains motionless down to its ultimate recesses, like a cloud bearing the fiercest storms, then the eeriest bright spells, if only for an interval of disquieting calm . . . It is a Time capable of destroying even becoming itself, by bringing forth, perhaps forever, fixity, stasis, and death. (AF 64)

This hyper-chaos is so contingent that even *flux* is contingent. An eternally frozen universe is just as likely as our present changing world, and so is a cosmos where all melts away into sugar. Meillassoux openly admits that the victory of contingency must seem like a Pyrrhic victory (AF 64).

It is well known that Leibniz based his philosophy on two major principles: non-contradiction and sufficient reason. The former can roughly be defined as the principle that nothing can be both A and not-A at the same time and in the same respect. God can flood the world or refrain from flooding the world, but cannot do both of these things simultaneously. (Some of the more radical occasionalist thinkers of early Islam allowed God to do this as well, and thereby abandoned the principle of non-contradiction, which Meillassoux never does.) The principle of sufficient reason contends that for everything that exists, there is a reason why it exists rather than not existing. The philosophy of Meillassoux is perhaps unique in accepting non-contradiction while *rejecting* sufficient reason. After briefly introducing the views of Leibniz on this question, Meillassoux positions himself rather clearly: 'Hegel saw that [his acceptance of] the absolutization of the principle of sufficient reason . . . required the devaluation of the principle of non-contradiction. Strong (Wittgensteinian-Heideggerian) correlationism insisted on deabsolutizing both the principle of reason and the principle of non-contradiction' (AF 71). While the reading of Heidegger here is debatable (his 1929 'On the Essence of Ground'[4] can only be read as a poignant tribute to sufficient reason), the real interest is Meillassoux's alternative: 'the principle of unreason [by contrast] teaches us that it is because the principle of reason is absolutely false that the principle of non-contradiction is absolutely true' (AF 71, emphasis removed). We should now look briefly at Meillassoux's treatment of each of these key principles, which shed much light on his own way of thinking.

As seen in the five-way dramatic dialogue, the principle of unreason can be proven using reason without being deducible from anything else. In other words, it is *anhypothetical*, in Aristotle's sense rather than Plato's (AF 60–1). And Meillassoux's unreason is obviously incompatible with Leibniz's sufficient reason: 'There is no reason for anything to be or to remain the way it is; everything must, without reason, be able not to be and/or be able to be other than it is' (AF 60). We saw already that the absence of any reason is linked for Meillassoux with the lack of anything hiding beneath 'the manifest gratuitousness of the given' (AF 63). When Meillassoux eventually argues in favor of an in-itself, it will not be a concealed in-itself of the Kantian or even Heideggerian variety, but something that is both independent of thought *and* something that can in principle be given to thought, rather than an inaccessible noumenon lying beyond the distortions of conscious access. Later Meillassoux even claims that Occam's Razor can be applied to the notion of real necessity, since reality can be explained without recourse to hidden causes (AF 107). Whereas Leibniz admired sufficient reason in a spirit of *gravitas*, Meillassoux views it as a scandal. 'So long as we continue to believe that there must be a reason why what is, is the way it is, we will continue to fuel superstition, which is to say, the belief that there is an ineffable reason underlying all things' (AF 82).

Meillassoux defines dogmatic metaphysics as the belief that at least one entity is necessary. Pushing things further, belief in the principle of sufficient reason is the ultra-metaphysical doctrine that *everything* is necessary, since everything has a reason for being the way it is. In addition to fueling superstition, this doctrine also serves as the virulent cradle of ideology, which Meillassoux defines as 'any form of pseudo-rationality whose aim is to establish that what exists as a matter of fact exists necessarily' (AF 33–4). The belief that things happen for a reason also has nefarious political consequences, since it lends an air of rational necessity to whatever the status quo may be. In this way, the critique of metaphysics and the critique of society go hand in hand as noble human endeavors:

> The critique of ideologies, which ultimately always consists in demonstrating that a social situation which is presented as inevitable is actually contingent, is essentially indissociable from the critique of metaphysics, the latter being understood as the illusory manufacturing of necessary entities. (AF 34)

Hume's destruction of the principle of sufficient reason awoke Kant from his dogmatic slumber, (AF 124) and Meillassoux hopes to awaken his readers in much the same way.

His rejection of the principle of sufficient reason is closely linked with his refusal of another of the classic pillars of metaphysics: belief in a necessary being. Traditionally this has been God, but Meillassoux is opposed to any sort of necessary being whatsoever. If we give a reason for anything, and then a reason for this reason, followed by yet another reason for this second reason, it is clear that we will soon have an infinite regress (Meillassoux assumes this is impermissible, without explaining why) unless we posit some sort of final necessary being.

> If thought is to avoid an infinite regress while submitting to the principle of reason, it is incumbent upon it to uncover a reason that would prove capable of accounting for everything, including itself – a reason not conditioned by any other reason. (AF 33)

The rejection of a necessary being is one of the crucial moments of Meillassoux's philosophy, but he handles it with a certain brevity. As he sees it, any belief in a necessary entity ultimately hinges on something like the famous ontological argument for the existence of God, which 'secures the existence of an X through the determination of this X alone, rather than through the determination of some entity other than X – X must be because it is perfect, and hence *causa sui*, or sole cause of itself' (AF 33). Meillassoux's rejection of the ontological argument (he refers to Descartes rather than Anselm) resembles that of Kant, which Meillassoux restates in especially lucid fashion. For Kant, he says, contradiction can exist only between an already existing entity and one of its predicates. If we assume that a triangle exists, then it can only have three sides, but no contradiction exists if we attribute four sides to a non-existent triangle. 'Thus, the subject of a proposition can never impose its existence upon thought solely by virtue of its concept, for being is never part of the subject, it is never its predicate' (AF 32). Or even more concisely, 'there is no "prodigious predicate" capable of conferring *a priori* existence upon its recipient . . . there is no contradiction involved in conceiving of a determinate entity as existing or not existing' (AF 32). The collapse of the principle of sufficient reason means that no metaphysical statement can ever be true (AF 65). Thus, what we most need is a kind of necessity that does not require a necessary entity (AF 33), and only one possible path remains (AF 51): the necessity of contingency itself.

We now move to Meillassoux's treatment of the principle of non-contradiction, which he accepts. Indeed he not only accepts it, but also tries to enforce it beyond what he sees as an excessively soft version of non-contradiction in the tradition. For instance, Aristotle is often seen as the absolute champion of non-contradiction, but in Meillassoux's eyes his reason is not good enough: 'what Aristotle demonstrates . . . is that no one can *think* contradiction, but he has not thereby demonstrated that contradiction is absolutely impossible' (AF 61). And this leaves him open to the familiar rejoinder of the Strong Correlationist, who would say that the fact that no one can *think* a contradiction without presupposing the law of non-contradiction does not prove that contradiction does not exist. But Meillassoux has larger ambitions, since he wishes to prove that contradiction is not just impossible for us, but impossible in its own right. To show this, he gives us a clever proof that is both simple and intriguing. Namely, Meillassoux holds that there cannot be a contradictory entity because if there were, it would have to be *necessary* (AF 67). And since necessary entities have already been shown to be impossible, contradictory entities cannot exist. Despite the massive chaos of Meillassoux's world, in which anything can arise at any moment with no reason at all, 'the only thing that could never arise and perish in such a chaos . . . would be a contradictory entity' (AF 69). For if a contradictory entity existed, it would include opposites, and hence there would be no alterity that would allow it to become something else. In other words:

> this entity would also prove incapable of undergoing any sort of actual becoming – it could never become other than it is, since it already *is* this other. As contradictory, this entity is always-already whatever it is not. Thus, the introduction of a contradictory entity into being would result in the implosion of the very idea of determination . . . Such an entity would be tantamount to a 'black hole of differences', into which all alterity would be irremediably swallowed up. (AF 70)

For closely related reasons, Meillassoux also thinks he is in a position to provide a proof that the thing-in-itself exists, by which he means not that there is something noumenal hidden behind all accessibility to us (he has already rejected this option) but simply that 'there is' something. While the tendency in our cynical era is to mock such questions as 'why is there something rather than nothing?' as touchingly gullible and naïve, Meillassoux thinks it is a real question for which he is able to offer an answer.

> It is a matter [he says] of demonstrating that it is absolutely necessary that the in-itself exists, and hence that the latter cannot dissolve into nothingness, whereas on the contrary, the realm of the 'for-us' is essentially perishable, since it remains correlative with the existence of thinking and/or living beings. (AF 71)

Meillassoux's proof that something must exist runs from pages 73 through 76 of the English version of *After Finitude*, and pays detailed attention to possible objections. None the less, we can summarize it briefly.

We have already seen that facticity itself cannot be just a fact; it must be necessary, or else correlationism would collapse into idealism. This led us to the principle of factiality: everything that exists is absolutely contingent. But Meillassoux observes that there might be both 'weak' and 'strong' versions of the principle of factiality. The weak version would simply say: *if* something exists then it must be contingent, but perhaps nothing exists. The strong version, by contrast, says that something *must* exist, and it must be contingent. In this way, the famous Leibniz/Heidegger question 'why is there something rather than nothing?' is transmuted into the following Meillassouxian question: 'can one, contrary to the preceding thesis which confines itself to the weak interpretation, justify a strong interpretation of the principle of unreason?' (AF 74). His answer is that one can, and there is an easy way to see why. If it were merely the case that *if* something exists then it must be contingent, then the facticity of that thing would merely be a fact, since we would already have supposed that its existence was not necessary. But while establishing the principle of factiality, we already saw that facticity cannot be a fact. Therefore, something must exist that is contingent in order for contingency to be necessary. And that something obviously must be something in-itself, since the kingdom of the for-us is entirely dependent on the existence of human or at least animal life, which is purely contingent. Hence there is something that exists in itself. Or as Meillassoux dazzlingly puts it: 'it is necessary that there be something rather than nothing because it is necessarily contingent that there is something rather than something else. The necessity of the contingency of the entity imposes the necessary existence of the contingent entity' (AF 76).

Just two paragraphs later, as if still reeling from the audacity of his own argument, Meillassoux grows reflective about the nature of our craft: 'Philosophy is the invention of strange forms of argumentation, necessarily bordering on sophistry, which remains its dark structural double' (AF 76). What makes Meillassoux so audacious is precisely his willingness to let everything hang from the threads of his proofs, and thus to invite charges of sophistry from anyone who happens to be unconvinced.

Diachronicity

We have already discussed Meillassoux's concept of ancestrality, which confronts the correlationist with the existence of realities pre-dating the existence of the thought–world correlate. But late in *After Finitude*, he proposes a useful and unsurprising expansion of this concept. Ancestrality is now redefined as 'diachronicity'. What this means is that we must also include events *following* the possible extermination of human thought along with those that occur before it exists:

> Closer inspection reveals that the problem of the arche-fossil is not confined to ancestral statements. For it concerns every discourse whose meaning includes a *temporal discrepancy* between thinking and being– thus, not only statements about events occurring prior to the emergence of humans, but also statements that are *ulterior* to the extinction of the human species. (AF 112)

The emphasis added here to the phrase 'temporal discrepancy' is Meillassoux's own, but if he had not done so I would have added it myself. For it is indeed the *temporal* discrepancy between human beings and a reality pre- or post-dating them that interests Meillassoux. He is unimpressed by contemporary entities that are *spatially* remote from all intelligent life: whether it be incidents in the Andromeda galaxy, the core of a black hole, or the interior of a watermelon before it is cut open to view. I lay special emphasis on this point, since Meillassoux's preference for time over space as the source of challenge exerts influence on at least two other portions of his philosophy.

First, when Meillassoux undercuts the principle of sufficient reason, what he seems to be attacking are the sorts of reasons that we find if we look backwards in time: namely, *efficient* causes. He openly holds that a chunk of gold might remain a chunk of gold or just as easily turn into silver, wax, or flesh, and any of these possibilities would occur for no reason at all. Yet there is another sense of 'reason' aside from that of efficient causes lying behind us in time. There are also the so-called material and formal causes, which are now studied by the branch of metaphysics called 'mereology', or the study of parts and wholes. In mereological terms, the reason that gold is gold is not just the history of its production by solar and geological forces. Instead, gold is gold because of its molecular and atomic structure. If Meillassoux wants to claim that gold exists without reason, then he should do so not just in the temporal sense that gold might arise *ex nihilo*, or that it might suddenly vanish, or change into dust, milkweed, cowbells, or a Zen monk posing riddles. Instead, he should also be willing to claim that the lack of sufficient reason applies even to the *present* instant, in such a way that the supposed laws of composition are violated. Not only would there be the possibility that gold will disappear or transmute in the next moment. Much worse than this, there would also be the possibility that gold in this very moment is composed not of protons arranged into gold atoms and then into gold molecules, but that gold might actually be made of silver, water, plastic, raw meat, fields of microscopic flowers, a troupe of minuscule acrobats, or even made of skyscrapers and mountain ranges much larger than the chunk of gold itself. Yet Meillassoux is silent on this question. As shocking as it might be that gold could appear or disappear suddenly for no reason, it is even harder to imagine existent gold made of something other than the known materials of gold. For this reason, the *synchronic* principle of sufficient reason is perhaps more threatening to Meillassoux's position than the diachronic sort. If someone were commissioned to write an article entitled 'Meillassoux's Mereology', it would be difficult for this person to find much to say. The composition of entities in the present moment does not seem to be an issue that concerns him: his focus is always on *temporal* discrepancies, *temporal* lack of reasons, or the *temporal* overturning of physical laws.

Second, the very question of physical law is another place where Meillassoux's preference for diachronic questions over synchronic ones leads him to an unexplained anomaly. He says, for instance, that 'although we maintain that the laws of nature could actually change for no reason, nevertheless, like everyone else, we do not expect them to change *incessantly*' (AF 84–5). But the real mystery is why Meillassoux sees any need for 'laws' in his system at all. Recall that he has already launched the most dazzling theory of contingency that the history of philosophy has ever known. The principle of sufficient reason has apparently been burnt to ashes. For Meillassoux even more than for Hume, there is no necessary connection between one thing and anything else. Unlike the occasionalists, those Humeans *avant la lettre*, he does not even have God as a last-ditch connection between disconnected things. Everything seems to exist in a perfectly independent state of contingency, which ultimately should mean: invulnerability to the influence of anything else. And yet, the very concept of a physical law assumes exactly the opposite. Where there is a law, one thing is able to influence another, whether it be a planet drawing apples towards its center, or a fire melting artworks, windows, and toys. A law means that one entity or field influences another in a specific way whenever these make the appropriate sort of contact. To say that 'the laws may change over time' is certainly radical, but it does not allow for complete contingency. For rather than being contingent, as Meillassoux promises, things are tied to necessary laws now as much as ever, but simply to laws whose character might change suddenly for no reason. Here once more, Meillassoux seems entirely focused on *diachronic* contingency, and does not seem bothered if the principle of sufficient reason continues to operate in a single instant.

In the French edition of *Après la finitude*, three asterisks appear at the bottom of page 36. It is there, between pages 36 and 37 of the French original, that Meillassoux inserted some new material for the English edition and requested that Ray Brassier add it to the book during the translation process. This new material runs from pages 18 to 26 of the English version of *After Finitude*, split off by a trio of asterisks on both ends. (It has since been incorporated into the French edition of the book, at Meillassoux's request.) From pages 18 to 22, Meillassoux considers the question as to why the spatial inaccessibility of contemporary entities is not as challenging to correlationism as the ancestral reality of things pre-dating us in time. He shows himself to be entirely unmoved by this question, for reasons we will now consider.

We imagine, then, that someone objects that ancestral events in distant primordial time are no more challenging to correlationism than are spatially concealed events in the current moment, whether they be those on a distant planet or occurrences in an abandoned house in the countryside. In both cases, something is happening that is not registered in any thought–world correlate. Meillassoux's response has a somewhat complicated structure. He imagines an *idealist* making the objection that space and time are two cases that should be treated in the same way, and that both can be shown to be equally harmless. In rebuttal, Meillassoux decides to concede the idealist's point that spatial distance is harmless, and that events *very distant* in time are also harmless. But he follows these concessions by insisting that ancestrality presents a much deeper problem than either of these examples, and thus cannot be disposed of by the idealist's claims. These claims can be summarized as follows. The objection based on ancestrality is merely banal. It relies on the privileging of space over time, even though (and here I agree with the idealist) 'an event occurring in an immensely distant galaxy, beyond the reach of every possible observation, would in effect provide the spatial analogue for the event occurring prior to terrestrial life' (AF 18). After all, in both cases there is no witness. But rather than using this point to say that spatial distance is also a challenge to correlationism, the idealist tries to show that both spatial and temporal distance are equally innocuous for the thought–world correlate. As the idealist sees it, the fact that something is unwitnessed is no objection at all: indeed it is 'unoriginal . . . [and] grossly inadequate' (AF 19). After all,

> the *lacunary* nature of the given has never been a problem for correlationism. One only has to think of Husserl's famous 'givenness-by-adumbrations': a cube is never perceived according to all its faces at once, it always retains something non-given at the heart of its givenness. (AF 19)

According to the idealist, this problem is easily solved simply by

> [introducing] a counter-factual such as the following: *had there been a witness*, then this occurrence would have been perceived in such and such a fashion. This counterfactual works just as well for the falling of a vase in a country house as for a cosmic or ancestral event, however far removed. (AF 19–20)

The idealist says that in the end this does not even conflict with science, which also tells us that 'had there been a witness' at the Big Bang, then that witness would have perceived such-and-such events occurring.

Meillassoux agrees with the idealist that the spatial argument is harmless and trivial, but also finds the idealist's use of it to be 'sophistical' (AF 22). For Meillassoux, the spatially distant is simply a variant of the temporally *ancient*, which he will try to show is by no means the same thing as the ancestral (AF 20). (It is again revealing that he never mentions any spatial analogue of the ancestral, such as an inaccessible parallel universe; time alone poses a paradox in his eyes.) While the 'argument from the unperceived is trivial and poses no threat to correlationism' (AF 20), the ancestral does not just mean an extremely old event that no one happened to perceive. Instead, 'it designates an event *anterior* to terrestrial life and *hence anterior to givenness itself*' (AF 20). In other words, 'the arche-fossil does not merely refer to an unwitnessed occurrence, but to a non-given occurrence' (AF 20). The vase falling in an empty country house does not strike Meillassoux as an interesting objection to correlationism, 'because this objection bears upon an event occurring when *there is already* givenness' (AF 20). The falling vase at 7:02:00 p.m. on 31 October 2010 and some remote human consciousness at that same instant must be considered as synchronic. And for Meillassoux, the synchronic absence of an unwitnessed event can always be recuperated through the old 'Had There Been a Witness . . .' Maneuver. However, 'the ancestral does not designate an absence *in* the given, and *for* givenness, but rather an absence *of* givenness as such. And . . . only a specific type of *temporal* reality is capable of capturing [this]' (AF 21). We are dealing here with something not merely lacunary, but rather 'prior to givenness in its entirety' (AF 21, emphasis removed). In short, the problem is 'how to conceive of a time in which the given as such passes from non-being into being?' (AF 21, emphasis removed).

Meillassoux even claims that the counterfactual trick of saying 'Had There Been a Witness . . .' does not work, 'since this would presuppose precisely what is being called into question: if a consciousness had observed the emergence of terrestrial life, the time of the emergence *of* the given would have been a time of emergence *in* the given' (AF 21), whereas we are trying to speak of a problematic time prior to givenness itself. Yet to insert one criticism into this otherwise expository chapter, it seems that perhaps Meillassoux is the one who is presupposing what is being called into question, when he assumes that a vase falling in a lonely country house can be no challenge to the thought–world correlate. After all, he has still never *demonstrated* why spatial remoteness from all givenness is less threatening than temporal anteriority to all givenness. We find no clear argument in *After Finitude* as to why spatial absence is a mere 'lacuna', while an event predating the correlate is some sort of unique undermining of the correlate. His proposed difference between an absence *in* the given and an absence *of* givenness as such is clearly asserted, but no evidence is presented as to why this is more than a verbal subtlety without a referent. While in practical terms it is easier to travel to the country house and see the shattered vase than it is to go back in time and observe the Big Bang, it has not been demonstrated that there is some sort of special ontological fissure between these two cases. The correlationist seems no better able to account for the falling vase than for the ancestral formation of the earth.

And furthermore, there is a sense in which this dispute between spatial and temporal distances is not even the heart of the matter. For quite apart from ancestral Big Bangs and lonely falling vases, we need to ask what happens in the case of a vase that is *currently* present to some consciousness. Let us imagine that we are in the country house ourselves, staring directly at the vase before, during, and after its fall to the floor. The vase holds water and flowers, even as we perceive it. But it is not our *perception* of the vase that holds these other items; only the vase itself does this. This is not simply because our current perception of the vase is not yet good enough. Even if we were to study it for half a century, pouring a lifetime's energy into understanding the vase – perhaps with the use of advanced supercomputers or direct epiphany through the assistance of angels – the situation would still not change. For no amount of knowledge about the vase can ever step into the world and replace that vase's labor in the cosmos. Only the vase itself can perform this labor. In short, Meillassoux should never have conceded the point about lacunary perception, because *even in the case of direct physical presence* an entity outstrips the thought–world correlate in a manner that is never merely lacunary. Just as all the steel in the world cannot build a song, all the perceptions in the world cannot build the very realities that they perceive. Yet Meillassoux is so committed to a model in which nothing is hidden behind the given, that whenever the given occurs in his writing, it immediately seems to be thoroughly saturated with human access. In other words, the present moment of time contains no mysteries for this philosophy, including those distant portions of the present moment that no one can see. For this reason, Meillassoux can only challenge the unfettered reign of human access by imagining a time when givenness did not exist at all: the ancestral. And here, he believes, there is no lacuna, since no perception yet exists to miss any of the facets of the world as it is perceived.

But the reason the 'Had There Been a Witness . . .' Maneuver fails is not, as Meillassoux holds, because we can conceive of a possible time in which witnesses are *ex hypothesi* unthinkable. Instead, it fails because even a witness cannot reduce the thing to a correlate of our awareness, even when that thing is pressed directly against our skin. More will be said on this point in Chapter 4 below, since it makes up the crucial difference between Speculative Materialism and Object-Oriented Philosophy.

Contingency Without Instability

We now come to one of the more remarkable claims in Meillassoux's book. The theory of absolute contingency at the heart of *After Finitude* invites us to imagine a wild cosmos of sudden shifts, transitions, and mutations without reason. This philosophy allows for the possibility of miraculous births and disappearances of the strangest possible entities, none of them foreshadowed either by the current state of the world or by any latent potentials hidden beneath what is given to consciousness, since Meillassoux allows for no such thing. Instead, his world might seem like a torment of constant upheavals, not the gradual, river-like fluxes of Heraclitus or Bergson. None the less, we do not seem to experience a world that is quite this outlandish. Even the worst atrocities of human history have occurred in stable geographic locales; the most punishing earthquakes and tsunamis are later analyzed calmly in accordance with known scientific laws; drug-induced visions at least offer a few consistent spirals and triangles that endure for up to a second, in colors already known to everyday visual experience; private nightmares in the dead of night at least present generally humanoid or fungoid adversaries whose names change only every five or ten seconds. What Meillassoux announces as basic ontological truth is something immeasurably worse than any of these bizarre scenarios: a landscape of totally unfettered chaos. And it might well be asked why we never seem to experience anything resembling such a hyper-chaos. If anything can change suddenly for no reason, then we might wish to know why this does not happen more often, or why the world *seems* to operate according to stable underlying laws.

Meillassoux's world is even more startling than that of David Hume. He admires Hume, however, and in a sense claims only to radicalize the deeper truths hidden in Hume's ideas. As everyone knows, Hume denies that we can have knowledge of any laws, any necessary connection between one event and another. It is only the *senses* that seem to indicate that the world is stable. Reason can give us no *a priori* truth other than the law of non-contradiction, and because of this fairly minimal restriction on possible events, 'reason informs us of the possibility that our billiard-balls might frolic about in a thousand different ways (and many more) on the billiard-table, without there being either a cause or a reason for this behaviour' (AF 90). Prior to Meillassoux, the three basic solutions to the problem of causation (and of sufficient reason more generally) were the dogmatic *metaphysical* claim to uncover hidden reasons for what happens, Hume's *skeptical* claim that we cannot know these reasons, and Kant's *transcendental* demonstration that while 'it is not absolutely necessary that causality governs all things, *if* consciousness exists, then this can only be because there is a causality that necessarily governs phenomena' (AF 89). According to Meillassoux, all three of these approaches share something in common: none of them questions causal necessity. This is obvious in the case of the metaphysical and transcendental approaches, but Meillassoux goes so far as to claim that 'Hume too never really doubts causal necessity – he merely doubts our capacity to ground the latter through reasoning' (AF 90). And thus, 'we should not be surprised at the ease with which scepticism turns into superstition, for to assert and believe that there is an unfathomable necessity to the way of the world is to be prepared to believe in a great deal of providence' (AF 91).

The only escape from such superstition, and indeed from any ideological prison, is to 'believe in reason, and thereby to purge reality of the hinter-world of causal necessity' (AF 91). This brings us back to one of the central problems faced by *After Finitude*: 'Once reformulated, Hume's question is in fact the one we raised earlier. If laws are contingent, and not necessary, then how is it that their contingency does not manifest itself in sudden and continual transformations?' (AF 92). The unification of contingency and stability now becomes Meillassoux's primary concern. And for those who find it preposterous that the universe might remain relatively stable even after being handed over to pure contingency, he offers a suggestive analogy. Early in the nineteenth century, the Russian geometer Nikolai Lobachevsky attempted to prove Euclid's parallel postulate via *reductio ad absurdum*. Euclid's postulate says that, given a line and a point not on the line, only one line can be drawn through the point that is parallel to the initial line. Lobachevsky's assumption was that if we were to begin by assuming that an *infinite* number of parallel lines could be drawn through that one point, then manifest absurdities would result, and Euclid's postulate would be proven. But things worked out differently for Lobachevsky. Instead of obtaining the desired *reductio* proof, 'he discovered a new geometry, which is just as consistent as that of Euclid, but differs from it' (AF 92). In the wake of this analogy, Meillassoux proposes a similar exercise for speculative philosophy. That is to say, we might also think we could prove the existence of causal necessity through a similar *reductio* proof, showing the absurdities that would result from the opposite state of affairs. But Meillassoux holds otherwise:

> our wager is that what happened to those geometers in the case of Euclid's postulate will also happen to us – little by little, we will discover that the acausal universe is just as consistent and just as capable of accounting for our actual experience as the causal universe. (AF 92)

Alluding to the close of *The Communist Manifesto*,[5] Meillassoux ends with an appeal to the philosophical workers of the world: 'we have nothing to lose by moving from a causal to an acausal universe – nothing except enigmas' (AF 92). In some ways, the future reception of Meillassoux's thinking hinges on whether the reading public can accept the Lobachevskian flavor of an acausal universe.

The first step in this enterprise can be found in one of Meillassoux's few extended references to a living philosopher. I speak of Jean-René Vernes, author of the still untranslated *Critique de la raison aléatoire*[6] (*Critique of Aleatory Reason*), as well as a champion bridge-player and the inventor of the board game Risk. The subtitle of Vernes's book, *Descartes Against Kant*, already shows his affinity with Meillassoux. What Vernes attempts in his lucid but little-known book is to '[expose] the reasoning upon which both Hume and Kant implicitly rely when they assume that the necessity of laws is obvious' (AF 95). And Meillassoux basically agrees with Vernes's account of the problem. The major difference is that Vernes remains a 'Euclidean' when it comes to the question of causal necessity; he really *believes* that causal laws are necessary. In other words, Vernes is not just summarizing the implicit argument of Hume and Kant, but is actually convinced by it. By contrast, Meillassoux finds the argument deeply flawed.

The strategy of Vernes is to apply the laws of probability to the events within the universe and then to the universe as a whole. Meillassoux's initial description of Vernes's position sounds much like a self-description: 'Contrary to Kant's identification of the *a priori* with necessity and of the empirical realm with contingency, for Vernes it is the *a priori* that presents us with contingency, while it is experience that presents us with necessity' (AF 95). While experience shows us one thing happening over and over again, reason presents us with a vast number of alternatives; a hundred different things (Hume) or even an infinite number (Vernes) might follow from the simplest collision of billiard balls. On this basis, it may be wondered why we believe in any necessity at all. Vernes's response, as Meillassoux puts it, 'is that our assumption in this case is exactly the same as that which would lead a gambler to suspect ... that a die that always lands the same face up is *very probably loaded*' (AF 96). We might already be suspicious of a die that landed on the same face many times in succession. But

> what if the dice we are playing with have been landing with the same face up not just for an hour, but throughout our entire lives, and even as far back as human memory stretches. And let us suppose that these dice are not just six-sided, but possess millions and millions of sides. (AF 96–7)

In this case it is obvious what we would infer: the dice must be loaded. There must be a hidden reason that explains the invariant result in which not all possibilities occur with equal frequency.

According to Vernes (and Meillassoux), the probabilistic argument for causal necessity is simply a matter of extending this same gambler's reasoning about hidden causal factors from events found within the universe to the universe as a whole. We can thus imagine our universe as one of many possible universes,

> each governed by different sets of physical laws; universes in which the impact of two billiard-balls does not conform to the laws that govern our own universe but results rather in both balls flying off into the air, or fusing together, or turning into two immaculate but rather grumpy mares, or into two maroon but rather affable lilies, etc. (AF 97)

In other words, we imagine a universe of all possible universes, as if each possible universe were positioned on the face of a many-sided die. It now happens that I find that the die 'always lands with the face representing "my" universe up ... Every time it is thrown, this dice-universe invariably results in the same physical universe' (AF 97). Given the vast number of possibilities, it seems completely impossible that such a recurring coincidence could be the result of chance. And thus, 'by an inference that is generally executed too quickly even to be noticed' (AF 98), we infer the existence of a necessary reason. For Vernes that hidden reason is called 'matter', but for Meillassoux this is really no better than calling it 'Providence'.

The point of Vernes's frequential argument is that stability would be incredibly lucky unless the dice were somehow loaded by a hidden structure of matter that guides the law of chance in a specific direction. But as Meillassoux sees it, we must distinguish between chance and contingency. Chance is in fact a parasite on physical necessity, since every game of chance requires an unfaltering necessary framework. For instance, a roll of the six-sided die assumes that there are only six possible outcomes of the throw.

> If from one throw to the next the dice imploded, or became flat or spherical, or if gravity ceased to operate and they flew off into the air, or on the contrary, were projected underground, etc., then there would be no aleatory sequence, and it would be impossible to establish a calculus of probabilities. (AF 99)

By contrast with chance, Meillassoux intends to develop a concept of contingency, which affects the very framework in which chance events occur. But rather than merely giving a negative account of contingency, he wants to give a positive account of the apparent stability of chaos, and he finds the tools to this end in the mathematical realm of the transfinite. Vernes's probabilistic argument requires a numerical totality of possible events, but the transfinite renders this impossible. Just like Badiou, Meillassoux now finds himself in the company of Georg Cantor.

When the number of possibilities in any situation is finite, no matter how large, then we can calculate the probability of each of them occurring. Nor is infinity even an obstacle to calculating probability, as Meillassoux describes clearly with the example of breaking a length of rope (AF 102). However, in order for the laws of probability to hold, there must be 'a totality of conceivable possibilities' (AF 102), whether finite or infinite. And here Meillassoux repeats his previous distinction between (a) cases occurring within the universe and (b) the universe a whole. For in the first sort of case we are always dealing with a given totality of finite or infinite size. But as for the universe itself,

> when I attempt to apply probabilistic reasoning to [it], I assume – without there being anything in experience that could validate this assumption – that it is legitimate to consider the conceivable as

another instance of a totality of cases. Thus, I subject the conceivable to a mathematical hypothesis: I turn it into a set, however large. (AF 103)

We now turn to Cantor, famously imported into continental philosophy by the works of Badiou. 'For we now know – indeed, we have known it at least since Cantor's revolutionary set-theory – that we have no grounds for maintaining that the conceivable is *necessarily* totalizable' (AF 103). Cantor detotalized number, showing that there is no greatest infinity: no Whole that would encompass all others.

> It is possible to construct an unlimited succession of infinite sets, each of which is of a quantity superior to that of the set whose parts it collects together. This succession is known as the series of alephs, or the series of transfinite cardinals. But this series itself *cannot be totalized*. (AF 104)

The quantity of all quantities does not just exceed the grasp of the feeble human mind; it does not exist at all. Meillassoux concedes that while this is true for the standard Zermelo-Fraenkel axiomatization of set theory (the same one preferred by Badiou), 'we cannot rule out *a priori* the possibility of selecting an axiomatic in which the realm of possible worlds would constitute an ultimate and determinate numerical totality' (AF 105). But at least we have one axiomatic that allows us to detotalize the possible, and this alone renders invalid an inference such as Vernes's, since he merely *assumes* that the possible can be totalized.

Thus, 'we have no way of knowing whether the possible can be totalized in the same way as the faces of a set of dice can be totalized' (AF 105). And this leads Meillassoux to another ontological split reminiscent of the one he makes between time and space: we *can* use probabilistic reasoning for events occurring *within* the universe, but simply not for the universe or the laws of nature as a whole. He speaks here of 'the illegitimacy of extending aleatory reasoning [such as Vernes's] beyond a totality that is already given in experience' (AF 105). Stated differently, 'we should restrict the claims of aleatory reasoning solely to objects of experience, rather than extending it . . . to the very laws that govern our universe' (AF 105). Just as spatial lacunae are not allowed to challenge the correlationist argument in this philosophy, intra-worldly events are not allowed to outstrip the probabilistic argument. Instead, laws of nature are allowed to exist for as long as we are speaking of intra-worldly events. The contingency of laws lies not in a fragile hold over the cases they govern (their hold is perfectly secure), but only in the fact that the laws themselves can change suddenly without notice.

One other point is worth mentioning here. When speaking of the intra-worldly possibilities that can be totalized, even if they are infinite, Meillassoux uses the term *possible*. But when speaking of the non-totalizable realm of possible cases, he uses instead the term *virtual*. The word 'virtual' appears rarely in *After Finitude*. (I count just two occurrences.) For instance, he seeks to '[establish] that the possibilities of which chaos – which is the only in-itself – is actually capable cannot be measured by any number, whether finite or infinite, and that it is precisely this super-immensity of the chaotic *virtual* that allows the impeccable stability of the visual world' (AF 111, emphasis added). But the word is rather common in Meillassoux's other writings, and turns out to be the central concept of *L'Inexistence divine*.

Primary Qualities

We close this summary of *After Finitude* by returning to the opening page of the book. The very first sentence of the French edition (expanded to two sentences in English) runs as follows: 'The theory of primary qualities seems to belong to an irremediably obsolete philosophical past. It is time it was rehabilitated' (AF 1). Just a few pages later Meillassoux shows his cards, declaring that his own theory of primary qualities is that 'all those aspects of the object that can be formulated in mathematical terms can be meaningfully conceived as properties of the object in itself' (AF 3, emphasis removed). He admits that this will seem naïve or dogmatic, since correlationism does not think any access to the in-itself is possible at all. And as a result, the correlationist will claim that 'the mathematical properties of the object cannot be exempted from the subjectivization that is the precondition for secondary properties' (AF 4). But we have already covered the latter portions of Meillassoux's book, and thus his response to this complaint is already known, even if his complete argument that primary qualities are mathematizable qualities has not yet been published. 'This is the enigma which we must confront:

mathematics' ability to discourse about the great outdoors; to discourse about a past where both humanity and life are absent' (AF 26, emphasis removed).

We now skip ahead to the final chapter of *After Finitude*, where Meillassoux returns to the theme of the mathematization of nature. It is here that Galileo emerges as an unexpected hero of the book. For unlike the Greek astronomers, 'Galileo . . . conceives of movement in mathematical terms, and particularly the movement which appears to be the most changeable of all: the falling of terrestrial bodies' (AF 115). In short, for Galileo 'the world becomes *exhaustively* mathematizable' (AF 115). And what this means is 'a world capable of autonomy – a world wherein bodies as well as their movements can be described independently of their sensible qualities' (AF 115). Galileo joins Descartes in employing a mathematized natural science to theorize a world existing apart from humans, while also joining Copernicus in removing humans from the center of the world (AF 116). In short, modern mathematical natural science gives us a cosmos in which thought is contingent, and in which 'thought has become able to think a world that can dispense with thought, a world that is essentially unaffected by whether or not anyone thinks it' (AF 116).

Galileo also destroys *a priori* knowledge about the world; we '[have] to be satisfied with reconstructing it as a fact' (AF 124). This leads to the interesting claim that Galileo sets the table for the philosophy of Hume. Indeed, 'the Hume-event constitutes the second philosophical ratification of the Galileo-event by demonstrating the fallaciousness of all metaphysical forms of rationality' (AF 125). Yet Meillassoux's related claim that the rejection of metaphysics entails a rejection of sufficient reason seems to work much better for Hume than for Galileo, whom one can hardly imagine upholding the contingency of natural events, even if he thinks they can only be described rather than deduced. In another bold but debatable moment, Meillassoux endorses Badiou's opinion that 'there is no fundamental episode in philosophy since Plato that has not proceeded via a re-interpretation of its originary alliance with mathematics' (AF 103). What seems indisputable, however, is Meillassoux's point that Kant's supposed Copernican Revolution is in many ways a Ptolemaic Counter-Revolution (a view he shares with Latour, an otherwise very different thinker). At the precise moment when modern science was trying to give us diachronic knowledge about 'the nature of a world without us' in which 'the truth or falsity of physical law is not established with regard to our own existence' (AF 114), the Ptolemaic Kant restored humans to the throne of knowledge.

Meillassoux is fond of saying that the mathematical is *the possible*: 'every mathematical statement is not necessarily true, but absolutely possible' (AF 126). The meaning of this is easy to explain. That at which mathematics points is not an ideal referent lying outside space and time that endures forever in Platonic eternity. Instead, mathematics refers to the structure of the given: 'all those aspects of the *given* that are mathematically describable can continue to exist regardless of whether or not we are there to convert the latter into something that is given-to or manifested-for' (AF 117). In other words, the mathematical is not *deeper* than the given; primary qualities are not somehow buried beneath human access. Instead, the difference between primary and secondary qualities is one that plays out entirely *within* the realm of the given. Some aspects of the given can be conceived as existing even if I were to vanish, while others cannot; the former are the mathematizable ones, and they count as the primary qualities. And this allows mathematizable realities to borrow the best of two worlds: 'this dia-chronic referent may be considered to be contingent while simultaneously being considered to be absolute' (AF 117, emphasis removed). That is to say, (a) primary qualities are contingent just like everything else, since they do not belong to some sort of special eternal realm outside the given, but (b) they are also *absolute*, since they can possibly exist outside human thought, even if in contingent rather than necessary form. For instance, 'the meaning of the dia-chronic statement about a radioactive decay older than all terrestrial life is only conceivable if it is construed as absolutely indifferent to the thought that envisages it' (AF 117). And more generally, 'what is mathematizable cannot be reduced to a correlate of thought' (AF 117). Mathematization answers the question of how thought can think what exists when there is no thought, which Meillassoux calls 'the most urgent question' (AF 121) posed by science to philosophy. The non-correlational manner of knowledge possessed by science is what allows us to call it *speculative* (AF 119). And since speculation opens up on the things-in-themselves that must exist outside thought, speculative philosophy must also be a speculative *materialism*.

It is often assumed that the end of metaphysics also means the end of the absolute. But for Meillassoux the end of metaphysics simply means the end of any belief in a necessary entity. In Meillassoux's view, modern Galilean science abandons *a priori* certainty in favor of a factical world that must simply be described rather than explained. But Meillassoux finds a new absolute in science: its ability to describe things that have reality outside human thought. He goes so far as to say that 'philosophy's task consists in re-absolutizing the scope of mathematics' (AF 126). Stated in terms reminiscent of Kant, the question philosophy must answer is not how *a priori* synthetic judgments are possible, but 'how is a mathematized science of nature possible?' (AF 126). While this phrase might have sounded painfully dull in isolation, it should now seem rich and suggestive following our survey of *After Finitude*.

Notes

1. Alfred North Whitehead, *Process and Reality*, p. xi.
2. This is made especially clear in Meillassoux's still unpublished November 2008 Toulouse lecture, 'Le Cogito contre le sujet – ou comment sortir de l'anthropologie par le doute'.
3. Slavoj Žižek, *Tarrying with the Negative*, Chapter 5.
4. Martin Heidegger, 'On the Essence of Ground', in *Pathmarks*.
5. Karl Marx and Friedrich Engels, *The Communist Manifesto*.
6. Jean-René Vernes, *Critique de la raison aléatoire, ou Descartes contre Kant*.

2

The English Articles

After Finitude was not published in English until 2008, but in the two years since its appearance in French, it had already built up a following in the Anglophone world. This was nowhere more true than in the United Kingdom, the cradle of the Speculative Realism movement catalyzed by Meillassoux's book, and to which he belonged as a founding member. The independent philosophy journal *Collapse*, based first in Oxford and then in Falmouth, also deserves credit for having published the first of Meillassoux's writings to appear in English. Three of the articles were translated from the French by journal editor Robin Mackay, while the fourth was a lecture delivered in English by Meillassoux himself. We have now seen additional articles by Meillassoux in English, and will consider them here along with his 2012 Berlin Lecture, technically still unpublished (though it has always been available as an online recording).

'Potentiality and Virtuality' was originally published in French in the journal *Failles* in the spring of 2006. *Collapse* printed an English version in its second issue, in March 2007. In this piece Meillassoux extends his reflections on transfinite numbers into a more detailed discussion of 'virtuality' than was found in *After Finitude*, thereby shedding light on one of the key topics of *L'Inexistence divine*. The English translation was reprinted in the anthology *The Speculative Turn*,[1] which appeared in early 2011.

The third issue of *Collapse* was published in November 2007, and contained two separate works by Meillassoux. The first was his remarkable 'Subtraction and Contraction', which appeared in French in the same year in the journal *Philosophie*. This breathtaking article employs an ingenious method, treating a single passage from Deleuze as though it were a lonely pre-Socratic fragment, then reconstructing Deleuze's philosophy by means of this 'fragment' and a detour through Bergson's *Matter and Memory*. While the article is often mistaken for an expression of Meillassoux's own views, it is really an exercise in philosophical fiction, with the author constructing a strange but plausible system rather different from his own. No comparable case comes to mind of a philosopher generating an alternative system to his own as an intellectual exercise.

Also contained in *Collapse* III is the text of Meillassoux's lecture at the first Speculative Realism workshop, held on 27 April 2007 at Goldsmiths College, University of London. It was the event that launched the now popular philosophical movement of the same name. The four participants spoke in alphabetical order: Ray Brassier (London), Iain Hamilton Grant (Bristol), Graham Harman (Cairo), and finally Meillassoux himself (Paris). His lecture was delivered directly in English, and defended the correlationist argument as a serious position that is hard to defeat. This formed a marked contrast with his colleagues Brassier, Grant, and Harman, none of whom finds the correlational circle especially formidable.

In May 2008 came the fourth issue of *Collapse*, containing 'Spectral Dilemma', which first appeared in French in the journal *Critique* in early 2006. Until the publication of the present book and its long Appendix featuring excerpts from *L'Inexistence divine*, 'Spectral Dilemma' was the most ample discussion in print of Meillassoux's concept of the virtual God, and the ethics entailed by the inexistence of this God.

In 2010, slightly too late to be treated in the original writing of the present book, Meillassoux's 'The Immanence of the World Beyond' was published in an anthology edited by Conor Cunningham and Peter Candler. 'History and Event' appeared in 2011 in the cutting-edge Australian open-access journal *parrhesia*. In the same year, 'Metaphysics, Correlation, and Speculation' was published in *Pli*, the highly regarded student-edited journal at Warwick University in England, while 2012 saw the appearance of 'The Contingency of the Laws of Nature' in *Environment and Planning D: Society and Space*, one of the blue-chip journals of geographers. Also in 2012, Meillassoux's Berlin lecture 'Iteration, Reiteration, Repetition' was widely disseminated as a leaked document. In 2013, Meillassoux returned to the pages of *parrhesia* with his essay 'Badiou and Mallarmé', staging a confrontation between his philosophical mentor and his favorite poet. And finally, 2014 saw the publication in English translation of another important article by Meillassoux on Badiou, entitled 'Decision and Undecidability of the Event in *Being and Event I* and *II*'. In what follows, all of these new articles will be grouped thematically rather than treated in chronological order.

Potentiality and Virtuality

We recall Heidegger's idea that every philosopher is guided by a unique thought:

> Every thinker thinks one only thought. Here, too, thinking differs essentially from science. The researcher needs constantly new discoveries and inspirations, else science will bog down and fall into error. The thinker needs one thought only. And for the thinker the difficulty is to hold fast to this one only thought as the one and only thing that he must think; to think this One as the Same; and to tell of this Same in the same fitting manner.[2]

Žižek has made a similar point more recently: 'we philosophers are madmen: we have a certain insight that we affirm again and again.'[3] And for yet another variation on this theme, we need look no further than Badiou's Preface to Meillassoux's *After Finitude*:

> It may be that, as Bergson maintained, a philosopher only ever develops one idea. In any case, there is no doubt that the philosopher is born of a single question, the question which arises at the intersection of thought and life at a given moment in the philosopher's youth; the question which one must at all costs find a way to answer. That is the category to which we must assign this book by Quentin Meillassoux. (AF vii)

Practitioners of most disciplines can be expected to cover new facts in each new work. But philosophers need to rethink the whole of their previous work each time they write something new, and this inevitably involves a bit of repetition. Imagine someone trying to travel across France using the technique of an Olympic long jumper. That is Quentin Meillassoux. Each time, he returns to the starting point, running again through the ground already covered in order to build up momentum, and then jumping a bit further than the last time. While some observers might laugh at this method of travel, it is really the only way for a philosopher to break fresh ground.

But while the philosopher must do this, there is not always a good reason for the commentator to do so. Most of Meillassoux's articles begin with some more or less condensed version of his general arguments about correlationism, contingency, the transfinite, and so forth. But since we have already covered this material in its most systematic form in connection with *After Finitude*, there is no reason to follow Meillassoux as he runs back through this material in each of the articles. We can focus on the *jump* of the long jumper instead of his running start. We can focus, that is, on what each of his articles *adds* to his previous position. In the case of 'Potentiality and Virtuality', most of what is new can be found in the concluding Section 5, 'Ontological Consequences of the Non-All', which runs for twelve pages. We need only begin with a few brief words on the earlier sections.

Meillassoux begins the article with a complaint: '"Hume's problem," that is to say, the problem of the grounding of causal connection, has known the fate of most ontological problems: a progressive abandonment, legitimated by the persistent failure that various attempts at solving it have met with' (PV 55). Here, the analytic philosopher Nelson Goodman is cited as a perfect example of this trend. After concluding that Hume's problem cannot be solved, Goodman simply changes the subject, asking instead: 'which rule, or set of rules, do we apply when we . . . make inductive inferences?' (PV 56). Against this pessimistic evacuation of all metaphysical problems, Meillassoux holds that Hume's problem *can* be solved. There follows a compressed dozen pages on some of the key ideas of *After Finitude*. We hear again about the truth of non-contradiction and the falsity of sufficient reason, since logical necessity must not be doubled with a purely fictitious causal necessity (PV 59–61). The frightening power of chaos makes another brief appearance (PV 61). The laws of nature could change at any time for any reason, but this does not entail that they must change *frequently*, and Meillassoux again cites Cantor and Vernes in making this case (PV 62–6). As he puts it, 'laws which are contingent, but stable beyond all probability, thereby become conceivable' (PV 67, emphasis removed). Since there is no Whole of possible worlds, we cannot call it either probable or improbable that the laws of nature would change suddenly for no reason. This leads him to the concluding twelve-page Section 5, 'Ontological

Consequences of the Non-All' (PV 69–81), which we will now consider in some detail. While this final section of 'Potentiality and Virtuality' is not especially surprising to those who have already read *After Finitude*, it does add a few new elements to the mix.

The goal of this section, following Cantor, is simply to assume the non-totalizability of cases and see what follows from it. There are perhaps three points of special interest in these pages, and we can proceed from easiest to most difficult. First, there is Meillassoux's critical discussion of the so-called anthropic principle. Second, we have his discussion of the origin of life. Third and finally, there is his crucial consideration of the difference between chance and contingency and the related difference between potentiality and virtuality.

The anthropic principle in science, when formulated as the so-called Weak Anthropic Principle, is simply the view that the present conditions of the universe must obviously be compatible with intelligent life, since we are intelligent life forms and we are here observing the universe. The variant known as the Strong Anthropic Principle takes a big step further, and holds that the appearance of humans requires such a bizarre coincidence of fine-tuned physical constants that there must be some hidden finality governing the process.[4] As Meillassoux puts it:

> one imagines oneself able to vary in an arbitrary fashion the initial givens of a universe in expansion, such as the numbers which specify the fundamental laws of contemporary physics ... One is then in a position to determine the evolution of these artificial universes, and one notes, in almost all cases, that these latter are incapable of evolving towards the production of the components indispensable for the emergence of life and, *a fortiori*, of intelligence. (PV 77)

From these considerations, the emergence of intelligent life seems highly improbable. Meillassoux states that 'this result, which emphasises the extreme rarity of universes capable of producing consciousness, is then presented as *deserving of astonishment*' (PV 77). In this way, 'anthropism ... reactivates a classical *topos* of finalist thought: the remarking of the existence of a highly-ordered reality ... whose cause cannot be reasonably imputed to chance alone' (PV 78).

As for the Weak Anthropic Principle, it does not view our existence as astonishing at all. The whole point of the principle is to eliminate our awed pondering of the highly unlikely conditions needed to generate our existence. 'Yes,' the Weak Anthropist says, 'it was statistically far more likely that a cold and lifeless universe would have been generated rather than our own, but then we would not be here to pose the question.' This attitude has become quite pronounced in recent reflections on the 'string theory landscape'.[5] Given the vast number of possible string theories, and the apparent impossibility of choosing between them on *a priori* grounds, some theorists play the anthropic card by saying that the one that is true must be the one that allowed us to be alive to construct a theory about it.

In this respect, the Weak Anthropic Principle shares with Meillassoux the feature of not being astonished that human life exists. Yet the reasons are completely different in the two cases. For the Weak Anthropist the problem is solved in *ad hoc* fashion: the emergence of intelligent life *really was* extremely improbable, and we just happen to be here as the beneficiaries of it. Meillassoux, by contrast, holds that the emergence of life cannot be called either probable or improbable. We feel astonished before extremely unlikely coincidences, and thus astonishment is based upon probabilistic reasoning (PV 78). But if the coincidence is neither likely nor unlikely, then a different mood is required. What is interesting is that Cantor's discovery of the many different infinities is usually presented as something astonishing and awe-inspiring, even by Cantor himself. But for Meillassoux, Cantor is the key to a *non-* astonished approach towards even the strangest advents in the cosmos. This is one of the hardest of Meillassoux's ideas to accept, yet it may be one of his most promising, and is certainly among his most original. The disappearance of the laws of probability (as concerns the structure of the world as a whole) pushes us away from merely considering the likely outcomes within our known universe, and invites us to consider the basic possible contours of that universe itself. This point will become extremely important in *L'Inexistence divine*, where we can no longer say that a World of justice is utterly implausible, and hence that World is no longer a ridiculously unrealistic political and ethical object.

Next, we turn to Meillassoux's related reflections on the origin of life, which will also play a major role in *L'Inexistence divine*. He begins by complaining about a stale, recurring approach to the problem of life visible 'from Diderot's hylozoism, to Hans Jonas' neo-finalism' (PV 79). The staleness results from our being limited to just two possible options, both of them bad in Meillassoux's eyes: namely,

> either one decides that matter already contained ... subjectivity in some manner, in too weak a degree for it to be detected, or that these affections of the living being did not pre-exist in any way within matter, thus finding oneself constrained to admit their irruption *ex nihilo* from that matter. (PV 79)

The problem with the latter option is not the phenomenon of *ex nihilo* emergence, which Meillassoux defends himself. Instead, the problem is with the traditional assumption that *ex nihilo* emergence requires 'a transcendence exceeding the rational comprehension of natural processes' (PV 80). This would entail 'the irrationalism that typically accompanies the affirmation of a novelty irreducible to the elements of the situation within which it occurs' (PV 80). In other words, we are first presented with a choice between a continuist model in which human life differs from stones only by degree, and a model that advocates a sudden leap from non-life to life. Such debates between the continuous and the discontinuous recur throughout all areas of human thought, and while in principle the debates are worth having, Meillassoux is right to imply that they easily turn into stale trench wars if no clever alternative solution is found.

Meillassoux's own approach is as follows. At first the continuist approach might seem like the rational one, while the model of sudden jumps might seem like the irrational one that requires the miraculous intervention of a transcendent God. But Meillassoux's new twist on the problem is to import sudden leaps *ex nihilo* into the rational, immanent sphere. In other words, his goal is 'to *reverse the signs*, making of every radical irruption the manifestation, not of a transcendent principle of becoming (a miracle, the sign of the Creator), but of a time that nothing subtends (an emergence, the sign of the non-All)' (PV 80). Even more colorfully, he tells us in a footnote that 'every "miracle" thus becomes the manifestation of the *inexistence* of God, insofar as every radical rupture of the present in relation to the past becomes the manifestation of the absence of any order capable of overseeing the chaotic power of becoming' (PV 74, note 7). This is all perfectly clear. What remains unclear is as follows: even if novelty must be 'irreducible to the elements of the situation in which it occurs'

(PV 80), why should this entail its disconnection with sufficient reason altogether? No one would argue that the Pyramids of Giza existed *in nuce* in the cliffs from which the stone was cut. And only an extreme occasionalist would argue that it was God who created the pyramids *ex nihilo*, rather than workers and slaves toiling to assemble the pyramids from blocks of stone. As Meillassoux puts it near the end of his article, 'in every radical novelty, time makes manifest that it does not actualize a germ of the past, but that it brings forth a virtuality which did not pre-exist in any way, in any totality inaccessible to time, its own advent' (PV 80). We should now turn at last to Meillassoux's concept of virtuality, which registered only the slightest trace in *After Finitude*.

One of the least pleasant features of continental philosophy since the mid-1990s has been the appearance of solemn Deleuzian tribunals, clad in hoods and sitting in shadow, accusing everyone with whom they disagree of 'confusing the possible with the virtual'. Often the meaning of this charge is left entirely unclear. For this reason, Meillassoux's remarkable clarity about his own potential/virtual distinction comes as a welcome relief. From his Cantor-inspired distinction between the infinite and the All,

> [there] results the possibility of clearly distinguishing between the notions of contingency and chance, and indeed between the notions of potentiality and virtuality. *Potentialities* are the non-actualised cases of an indexed set of possibilities under the condition of a given law ... *Chance* is every actualization of potentiality for which there is no univocal instance of determination on the basis of the initial given conditions. Therefore I will call *contingency* the property of an indexed set of cases (not of a case belonging to an indexed set) of not itself being a case of a set of sets of cases; and *virtuality* the property of every set of cases of emerging within a becoming which is not dominated by any pre-constituted set of possibles. (PV 71–2)

On one level this is clear and simple, and the point was encountered already in *After Finitude*. Events covered by a given law fall within a range of *potentialities*, and we can speak of *chance* when speaking of events occurring in this highly limited context. And in fact, the laws of probability are never questioned by Meillassoux at this level. Yet when considering the laws themselves, we must speak of *virtuality* rather than potentiality, and of *contingency* rather than potentiality, because time has 'the capacity to bring forth situations *which were not at all contained in precedent situations*' (PV 73), thereby implying that at the local level of analysis (that of cases indexed under a given law) situations *are* contained in the precedent situations.

In short, it might look at first as though, with his distinction between the pairs chance/potentiality and contingency/virtuality, Meillassoux were distinguishing between two different ways of *looking* at the world and arguing that the second is correct. It would be as if he were saying: 'Some people believe in chance and potentiality, but in fact these do not really exist, since there is really nothing but contingency and virtuality.' But this is not the case. Rather than endorsing one of these pairs and dropping the other into the rubbish bin of false ideas, Meillassoux preserves them both in a division of labor. On what I have called the local level, the level of cases governed by laws, he finds it perfectly acceptable to speak of potentiality and chance. It is only when ascending to the status of the laws themselves that he thinks virtuality and contingency must be brought into play. What he gives us is a two-world theory. Laws do exist, and for the most part they do function. But precisely through this admission that laws exist, Meillassoux concedes that the principle of sufficient reason is operative much of the time. After all, laws do involve a specific connection or relation between one entity or field and another. And this means that laws are binding, or necessary; the fact that a new necessity might some day arise without reason to replace the current one does not change the necessity of the relation here and now. Only when rising to the level of the laws themselves, which can always change for no reason, does the principle of sufficient reason collapse. Stated as an example, if the vase falls off a table in the aforementioned country house, it is certainly bound by the law of gravity. Meillassoux simply adds the proviso that the law of gravity exists for no reason and could change at any moment. If, instead of smashing on the floor, the vase flies into the sky or silently hovers, this is not because the vase breaks a law of nature, but because the law of nature changed suddenly and without warning.

Stated differently, Meillassoux is giving us a *taxonomy* of two different spheres of being: there is the realm of the potential and the realm of the virtual, or the realm of chance and the realm of contingency. It is true that even in the world ruled by laws, one might endorse an 'aleatory' vision in which one cannot 'deduce in univocal fashion the succession of events permitted by the law, but one can *index* these events in their totality' (PV 70). Yet this is only a '"caged freedom", that is to say the possibility of the advent without reason of one of those cases permitted by the initial universe; but not the freedom of extracting itself from such a universe to bring forth cases which do not belong to the set thus defined' (PV 70). And Meillassoux adds that 'the belief in chance is inevitably a metaphysical belief, since it incorporates the belief in the factual necessity of determinate probabilistic laws, which it is no longer possible to account for except via the necessity of supposed deterministic laws' (PV 70–1).

Someone might claim that Meillassoux's distinction is merely a matter of knowledge, rather than of two districts of reality. For as he puts it: 'To be more precise, we must say that the distinction potentiality/virtuality is gnoseological rather than ontological, in so far as it designates essentially a difference in our *cognitive* relation with temporality' (PV 74, note 7, emphasis added). This de-emphasizing of any ontological rift between potential and virtual, the apparent dominance of the virtual throughout all portions of reality, seems even more complete when Meillassoux goes on to say that 'the perpetuation of a universe of already-known cases (the constancy of laws) itself also *escapes all consideration in terms of potentiality* (one possible case in a set of others)' (PV 74, note 7, emphasis added). For example, imagine that you pull out a familiar pack of cards and draw one card at random. The Ten of Clubs is chosen, and there is nothing any more disturbing about this result than about any other. Now you draw a second card, and find the Joker in your hand. Neither of these events is especially disturbing, since both were foreseeable within the range of available possibilities. But now you draw a third card, and instead of one of the familiar types of cards you find an expressionist portrait of George Washington, backed by the familiar stars and stripes of the American flag. After a long moment of shock, you recall that there is indeed an ardent American patriot and bohemian dandy among your friends, and that it would have been just his style to smuggle such a card into your deck ahead of time; with this reflection, you are briefly calmed. But on the fourth draw, the card turns into a dove and takes flight through the window – and not even your decadent bohemian friend could have engineered such an event.

The question now before us is whether drawing the Ten of Clubs and drawing a card that turns into a dove are ontologically the same. And here there is some ambiguity in Meillassoux's views. For on the one hand, 'even if the case which comes to pass is already indexed [such as our Ten of Clubs – G.H.], it is only foreseen upon condition – an unforeseeable and improbabilisable condition – of the maintenance of the old set of possibles' (PV 74, note 7). But all this really means is that the law that has indexed a given set of possibles should not be assumed to remain in existence as if by inertia. If a law is to endure from one moment to the next, this requires a 'factual re-emergence', just as the God of al-Ash'ari or Descartes had to recreate the universe from scratch in every instant. But this does not mean that the Ten of Clubs and the magical dove are ontologically the same. The former simply requires the re-emergence of the same law, while the latter involves a new law altogether. As Meillassoux puts it, still in the same rich footnote:

> the virtualising power of time, its insubordination to any superior order, lets itself be known, or is phenomenalised, when there emerges a novelty that defeats all continuity between the past and the present. *Every 'miracle' thus becomes the manifestation of the inexistence of God*, in so far as every radical rupture of the present in relation to the past becomes the manifestation of the absence of any order capable of overseeing the chaotic power of becoming. (PV 74, note 7)

We should not be misled by the scare quotes around the word 'miracle', which Meillassoux employs only to distance himself from the mainstream religious sense of the term. For let there be no mistake: miracles *are* a considerable part of Meillassoux's philosophy. Whatever his caveat about how the laws of playing cards (or anything else) must 'factually re-emerge' in order for the Ten of Clubs to be a foreseeable, unsurprising result, there *is* such a thing as a law of playing cards; it is simply one that could change at any moment for no reason. In this way Meillassoux ends up with an ontological dualism similar to that found in Badiou's *Being and Event*,[6] in which the dull situation is interrupted now and then by miraculous truth-events not based on sufficient reason. The more radical step of denying the existence of laws altogether is not attempted, nor apparently even desired.

Now, it is true that in *L'Inexistence divine*, Meillassoux speaks of advent *within* the intra-worldly realm: 'It is necessary to draw a distinction between the advent of what I call a *world* and the advent of the *intra-worldly*' (DI 238). Whereas the advents of world are restricted to major leaps such as the emergence of life and thought, '"intraworldy advents" [are] those that are capable of occurring in the midst of a determinate World: for example, the advent of new species in the midst of the world of life, or advents of creative invention in the midst of the world of thought' (DI 238). While this passage may seem to challenge any strict division in terms of advent between the levels of world and the intra-worldly, it actually just shifts the problem to one side while making it even more complicated than before. After all, Meillassoux has two options here. Either he can say that remarkable intra-worldly events such as the emergence of new species or works of artistic genius are different *in kind* from banal incidents such as the yawns of a bureaucrat and the crumpling of tepid daily newspapers, or he can say that *all* intra-worldly happenings are advents. In the former case, we still have the two-world theory I have described in which advents *ex nihilo* are opposed to law-governed behavior; here, the principle of sufficient reason would continue to operate in cases of mediocre daily reality. The latter case would be more consistent, since here Meillassoux would have to abandon any notion of law, thereby turning absolutely everything that happens into an advent and a direct example of contingency. But the evidence of his published writings, as well as those unpublished writings that are known to me, suggests that he intends no such thing.

Here, as always, we find that *time* is what really interests Meillassoux: 'time thus conceived is not governed by any non-temporal principle – it is delivered to the pure immanence of its chaos, its illegality' (PV 73). He does celebrate Hume's view that 'from a determinate situation, one can never infer the ensuing situation' (PV 73). He also adds that 'the present is never pregnant with the future' (PV 73), yet he continues to fall back on a distinction between the normal and the miraculous:

> time might either, for no reason, maintain a universe of cases, a configuration of natural laws, within which it is possible to index a determinate set of recurrent situations constituting its 'potentialities' – or might, equally without reason, cancel the old universe, or supplement it with a universe of cases which were not at all pre-contained in the precedents, nor in any other Substrate wherein the possibilities of being would be ranged for all eternity. (PV 73)

These are two cases that do not have the same ontological status. Sufficient reason is suspended in those cases where laws change (or fail to change) suddenly and for no reason at all, but sufficient reason is perfectly applicable in synchronous cases 'within which it is possible to index a determinate set of recurrent situations' (PV 73). The danger for Meillassoux is that he gives us two ontologies; we might even call them a 'sublunary' and a 'superlunary', just as pre-Galilean physics was split in two. What makes this dangerous is that it allows him to transfer all key ontological problems over to the question of the sudden changes of laws. Rather than raising the question of why there should be laws at all, he simply questions whether laws are eternal and whether they have any reason for existing. As he puts it: 'I posit that *the law can be related to a universe of determinate cases*; I posit that there is no Universe of universes of cases; I posit that time can bring forth any contradictory set of possibilities' (PV 72, emphasis added). Emphasis is added to the first part of this sentence in order to show that there are such cases in Meillassoux's view of the world. He continues: 'I accord to time the capacity to bring forth new laws which were not "potentially" contained in some fixed set of possibles; I accord to time the capacity to bring forth situations which were not at all contained in precedent situations' (PV 72, emphasis removed). The fact that time has the 'capacity' to do this suggests that it is not doing so all the time, and this becomes even clearer when he adds that 'becoming is *not only* capable of bringing forth cases on the basis of a pre-given universe of cases' (PV 72, emphasis added).

In a beautiful passage, Meillassoux tells us that

> time creates the possible at the very moment it makes it come to pass, it brings forth the possible as it does the real, it inserts itself in the very throw of the die, to bring forth a seventh case, in principle unforeseeable, which breaks with the fixity of potentialities. (PV 74)

But for Meillassoux *time* is always the hero of these adventure stories of a chaotic universe. The six-sided die itself will not turn up the number seven, or explode into a shower of precious jewels, for as long as it belongs to a set of indexed cases with determinate potentialities governed by a law. Time must bring forth chaos in a way that dice and casinos cannot.

Subtraction and Contraction

Collapse III is perhaps most famous for its Appendix containing the transcript of the 2007 Speculative Realism Workshop. But earlier in the volume we find Meillassoux's article 'Subtraction and Contraction: Deleuze, Immanence, and *Matter and Memory*'. The method of this article is ingenious, and its content compellingly strange. 'Subtraction and Contraction' stands at the top of my personal list of articles I wish I had written myself. Like many great essays in philosophy, it begins in matter-of-fact fashion: 'We begin with a remark from Chapter 2 of *What Is Philosophy?* This book, of course, is by Deleuze and Guattari, but the text, in this case, clearly indicates a Deleuzian provenance' (SC 63).

Meillassoux then cites a passage about *immanence*, one of Deleuze's most celebrated terms. Deleuze praises Spinoza as 'the prince of philosophers': as the champion of immanence and perhaps the only philosopher never to have compromised with transcendence. Deleuze adds that this also happened with Bergson, but only *once*: at the beginning of *Matter and Memory*. It is here that Meillassoux adopts a strategy of staggering brilliance, one that continues to inspire surprise after multiple re-readings. Namely, he imagines that Deleuze was a pre-Socratic philosopher, and that the passage on immanence just cited is one of his few surviving fragments. He then proposes to reconstruct Deleuze's philosophy of immanence on the basis of this fragment alone. Meillassoux's discussion of this delicious strategy is worth savoring in full:

> let us decide to read Deleuze as a pre-Socratic, of whose writings we possess only a few rare fragments, including the text [just cited on immanence in Spinoza and Bergson], which we will call the 'Fragment of the Double Crown' since in it two philosophers are said to be princes. To these fragments we must add a 'life' of Deleuze by Diogenes Laertius, which teaches us little, apart from the fact that he was known as an original philosopher, rather than as a simple disciple of Spinoza or Bergson; and that his philosophy was known as a philosophy of immanence. This very term, in its banality, means no more to us than those terms such as 'water', 'air' or 'fire' which designate the first principle of this or that pre-Socratic. (SC 65)

Luckily, another of the conditions of the imagined scenario is that the works of Spinoza and Bergson have survived in their entirety, and thus we can read Deleuze indirectly by way of these two 'princes of immanence' who were taken by Deleuze as the model for an original philosophy.

We now imagine two schools of commentators. The first, which Meillassoux amusingly terms 'The Major Crown School' (SC 66), argues that interpretation of the Deleuzian fragment must begin with Spinoza, since he is praised as the greater of the two princes of immanence. But this strategy is more dubious than it might first seem. The problem is precisely that immanence is said to saturate the whole of Spinoza's philosophy, and this 'is to render it as difficult to perceive as a diffuse light: if it is everywhere, then it is nowhere in particular' (SC 66). Thus it will not be especially useful to opt for the more obvious, Spinozist route to Deleuzian immanence. This leaves us with a competing 'Minor Crown' school of interpreters. 'If for Spinoza's philosophy immanence is a state, for Bergson's it is an event' (SC 66). For not only did immanence happen to Bergson in just one book, *Matter and Memory*, but also, according to Deleuze, it did so only at the very beginning of that book. 'Now, this makes Bergson most precious in our quest to understand what Deleuze means by immanence; for it implies that in *Matter and Memory* is to be found that which is missing in Spinoza's philosophy, *viz., a differential of immanence*' (SC 67). Yet there is obviously an additional problem here, since Deleuze's opinion that something was lost after the first chapter of *Matter and Memory* is surely not an opinion shared by Bergson himself, and therefore not something highlighted in the text: 'Obviously, Bergson never wrote anything like "immanence came to me once, but only once– and then, nevermore!"' (SC 67). But even if Bergson would never admit to such a thing, we may be able to detect a relapse 'from the point of view of the *aspiration to be* Bergsonian. Something must be lost from a point of view immanent to the text: and thus from the point of view of a Bergsonian, if not from that of Bergson himself' (SC 68). We must therefore show how the ensuing chapters of *Matter and Memory* fail to live up to the rigorous and radical standards set by the first chapter. The result will be what Meillassoux calls a 'fictional system' of philosophy that does not fully resemble even Deleuze's philosophy, let alone Meillassoux's own. In this way Meillassoux gives birth to a possible new genre: 'philosophy fiction', after the model of science fiction. So far, all great philosophers seem to have sincerely *believed* in their published ideas. But it could have been most useful if Kant or Heidegger had devoted several books to developing systems in which they do not literally believe, just as Dickens and Proust did not literally accept the existence of their fictional characters. One hopes that this portion of Meillassoux's legacy is secure, and that a tradition of philosophical fiction will soon emerge from 'Subtraction and Contraction'.

After the opening scenario in which Deleuze is read as a pre-Socratic thinker, Meillassoux provides a quick summary of *Matter and Memory*, setting the table for the delightfully bizarre closing section of his article. Bergson's preface to the seventh edition of the book seems to suggest 'that a fundamental objective of *Matter and Memory* was to render Kantian critique unnecessary, and thereby to deny the need for limiting the applicability of metaphysical knowledge. This is a project one might call immanentist' (SC 70). Indeed, despite the use of the word 'metaphysical', Bergson's project resembles Meillassoux's own in this respect. For Bergson, as all readers of *Matter and Memory* know, reality is a matter of 'images', which are neither concealed things-in-themselves nor mere pictures in the mind, but something in between. The gulf between reality and knowledge is denied, but so is idealism: reality itself is made up of images. 'In thus maintaining that matter exists in itself just as we perceive it, Bergson explicitly undertakes to circumvent, and even to render unnecessary, Kant's Copernican Revolution' (SC 71). This is another point of similarity with Meillassoux, though their resemblance will cease soon enough.

Meillassoux calls Bergson's theory of perception a *subtractive* theory. For 'images, Bergson tells us, act and react upon one another according to constant laws, which are laws of nature' (SC 72). All images perceive all others; the body is just a special sort of image. Matter is an aggregate of images, and the material realm has an infinitely greater perception of reality than we do. 'To perceive is to come to rest on the surface of images, it is to impose upon the latter a superficial becoming, far removed from the infinite profundity of material perception' (SC 73). Living beings '[suppress] all the parts of the object that are without interest for their functions' (SC 73). This happens in two separate steps: the body selects, and then the mind chooses. 'The body is like a continuous emission of an infinite matter, whose particles constitute the terms of the choice offered to the mind' (SC 74). The body creates finitude. It is a 'massive interruption, carried out within the infinitude of communications' (SC 74). Even more colorfully, 'the body is like a windscreen for the mind against the infinite,' for 'whereas in every parcel of matter, however minute it might be, we can envisage an infinity of information, the body conquers finitude through the power of refusal' (SC 74). In other words, 'the living is not primarily the emergence of a power of interested choice, but the emergence of a massive disinterest in the real' (SC 74). The second selection, that made by the mind on the images provided by the body, is less impoverishing; while the mind simply chooses one image from a finite number, the body 'selects a finite number of options, at the expense of an infinity of images which pass through it without trace' (SC 75). Perception is a form of *ascesis*: 'It does not enrich matter. It impoverishes it' (SC 75).

With all of this, we are still in a world of immanence. Matter and sentient perception are still on the same ontological level. Yet we now seem to be approaching the point where, according to the Fragment of the Double Crown, immanence is betrayed. This happens at the point when Bergson moves to the topic of memory. The coincidence of perception with what it perceives is true 'in principle rather than in fact' (SC 76), for the simple reason that *memory* adds a great deal to every perception. Bergson draws a distinction between two kinds of memory, but Meillassoux follows a different distinction that he also finds in Bergson, and uses the term 'contraction-memory' for the kind that interests us here. 'For however brief a perception might be, it always occupies a certain duration and thus necessitates an effort of memory which prolongs a plurality of moments one into the other' (SC 77). To use Bergson's own image, memory covers perception with a cloak of recollection. Immanence has now broken down. The great achievement of the beginning of *Matter and Memory* was that 'our perception seems . . . to join directly with matter in itself,' or that 'matter contains no depths, no hidden aspect' (SC 77). But once memory is introduced, 'matter becomes what remains of perception once one has retracted that which memory . . . continually introduces into it' (SC 78). Meillassoux cites Bergson's example that red light vibrates 400 trillion times in a second, which would take 25,000 years for the human brain to process if we had to notice each vibration consciously. Instead of this ridiculous Herculean labor, 'we carry out an incredible contraction of material reality when we perceive in one moment what includes within itself an immense number of events. Now, it is this work of contraction that gives rise to qualities' (SC 79). Matter is composed of homogeneous, quantifiable vibrations, and it is our contraction of these that gives rise to heterogeneous qualities.

Meillassoux now redeploys a Bergsonian term with a new meaning, when he uses 'detension' as his term for the process of decontracting the work of memory to arrive once again at the image plain and simple. Given that contraction 'has always already taken place, since its effect is supposed to reach the elementary components of perception' (SC 82), Meillassoux holds that such detension is impossible. For 'we cannot see any convincing way to take the *reverse path*, so as to rediscover matter in itself not yet affected by our subjective duration' (SC 82–3). The consequences of this are clear: 'memory-contraction seems to abolish the principal result of the theory of pure perception, namely that of the cognisability of the in-itself' (SC 82). Perception is no longer an *ascesis* that merely subtracts from an infinity of relations and limits itself to a finite range of them; instead, it is now a *synthesis* in which our human perception distorts the direct image, producing a rather Kantian distinction between the in-itself and the for-us. Given that an inaccessible thing-in-itself would undercut any philosophy of immanence, the question becomes: 'can one envisage a theory of perception-ascesis which avoids passing via the synthetic moment of contraction?' (SC 85). Meillassoux proposes that Bergson can answer the question fairly easily by simply extending the subtractive theory of perception found in the opening of his book. The human perception of red light, for instance, need not be viewed as a synthesis that distorts an inaccessible homogeneous vibration. Instead, red light as we experience it is simply a selection of one of all the many possible ways it *could* manifest itself at various possible scales. In this way, it remains the case that 'the thing in itself is all the points of view it is possible to take on that thing' (SC 86). We find that 'human perception [is] not the *contraction* of material quantity, but the *selection* of one of the rhythms of a matter-image which contains each and every one of them' (SC 86).

We now come to the concluding section of this strange and ingenious essay. What emerges from its twenty-page sprint to the finish is a strange simulation of Deleuzian philosophy that often seems to border on Meillassoux's own, though he privately denies that the views of 'Subtraction and Contraction' should be literally identified with his own position. It is clear from our earlier discussion that what Meillassoux wants to develop is a model of subtraction *without* contraction. The subtractive model would be an immanent one in which all things are present to all other things, but with some of these relations simply closed off from view, without any difference between reality as perceived and reality as it is; this is what any philosophy of immanence demands. By contrast, contraction would return us to the bleak Kantian bias that tainted Chapter 2 of Bergson's *Matter and Memory*, in which the perceiver actually distorts reality in some way, thereby placing transcendent things-in-themselves at an inaccessible distance from us.

The world of matter is a world of images, or so Bergson tried to teach us. Meillassoux gives this global communication between images the name of 'flux' (SC 87). For Bergson the world prior to contraction is homogeneous, or purely quantitative. In Meillassoux's modification of his system, there is a *heterogeneous* landscape that consists not just of qualities for an observer, but of quality *and* quantity. Both of these are collapsed back onto an immanent plane where both are simply possible images among others; the trillions of vibrations of red light are images, but so is red light as seen by a human. The latter is no longer a mournful prison from which humans cannot reach the images themselves. But since not all images are accessible to us at any moment, we must also say that the primordial flux (in which all images are present to all others in what Meillassoux terms 'flows') is broken into districts by way of what he calls 'interceptions' (SC 87). As he puts it,

> rather than saying that the rarefaction of images in perception is due to the fact that the living being allows itself to be traversed by most images only to retain a few of them, we say that this rarefaction is due to cuts, barrings, which only permit certain flows to penetrate into consciousness. (SC 87–8)

Perception distorts nothing; it simply closes off many images in order to allow some to appear as they are in themselves.

Now, flux in its own right already contains all relations between all images, and since they are connected through laws we should in principle be able 'to determine the present, past, and future movement of all the others', with the devastating result that 'the very difference between the three dimensions of time is erased' (SC 88). As Meillassoux correctly concludes, the perfect immanence of a relational system of images thus results in a frozen monism, 'analogous to that of a powerful jet of water, in which the continuous jet of matter gives rise to a continuous immobility of form' (SC 88). Left to themselves, the supposed 'flows' of relation are immobilized. Thus, interruption is required in order to turn the cosmic frozen block of all past, present, and future relations between images into something able to *change*. And this obviously means that 'there must exist a becoming of interceptions themselves. It must be that the interceptions change' (SC 89). There is a flux of images, which does not move, and a flux of interceptions, which does. Becoming can arise only from the latter.

Having established this general standpoint, Meillassoux proceeds to derive many of the key terms of Deleuzian philosophy, which can be summarized briefly. The distinction between time as *Chronos* and time as *Aion*, famous to readers of Deleuze's *Logic of Sense*,[7] is shown to arise from the two kinds of flux already described. *Aion* is shown to be linked with *eventuality*, or the process by which interceptions are displaced, in a manner that '[excludes] every form of material explanation' (SC 91). In a manner reminiscent of Meillassoux's own philosophy, eventuality is a non-probabilizable becoming, 'the result of a unique throw of the dice, launched from all eternity upon the immutable table of fluxes' (SC 91). But the disconnections of *Aion* cannot be different in kind from the flux of *Chronos*, or immanence would be undermined and *Aion* would be reduced to an appearance over against reality-in-itself. Thus, the interruption that creates discrete forms amidst the otherwise global system of relations among images can only be viewed as a 'detour' of flux, or as a 'retardation effect' imposed upon it (SC 92). 'A break is a local accumulation to the *n*th power of detour of flux. We therefore find ourselves *within a strictly continuous ontology*' (SC 92).

Chronos, also known as the system of images in which past, present, and future are strictly simultaneous since no breaks are present, can be considered as a 'wave', meaning 'a material movement whose past as well as its future can in principle be reconstructed, in a deterministic or probabilistic way. To be pregnant with its past, if one might so speak, as well as with its future' (SC 93). What resists the wave through displacement, Meillassoux calls *the virtual*, and the virtual is linked with the theme of *the fold*. And while he admits that this model derived from Bergson may not succeed in clarifying the virtual of Deleuze, it does allow us to modify the Bergsonian virtual in a manner free of the quantity/quality opposition. Unlike for Bergson, 'quality ceases to be in itself the mark of novelty' (SC 95), since the fluxes in the subtractive model are always both quantitative and qualitative. Rather than a qualitative virtual there is a topology or geology of the virtual, marked by a becoming defined in terms of folds that are not produced by material causes.

Meillassoux introduces another change to the Bergsonian model as well.

> In [his] theory of pure perception, Bergson gives himself an indetermi-nate centre of action, that is to say a free being: it is such a freedom that is at the origin of selection, amongst images, of those alone which interest the living. (SC 96)

Strangely, Bergson thus continues a traditional dualism in which one or more entities stand sufficiently distant from the world as to be able to make free choices. But from Meillassoux's stand-point, 'the refusal of all dualism constrains us, for our part, not to concede existence to beings endowed with freedom' (SC 96). Freedom cannot be pulled from a hat as a magical exception to the laws of becoming, but must be conceived in a *subtractive* manner just as perception had to be. Living beings are a 'local rarefac-tion' of flux, meaning that they amount to a subtractive selection from an infinitely larger initial pool of global relations between all images: 'I mean by "rarefaction" any localized impoverishment of fluxes' (SC 97). But this selection is 'primary': it is 'a selec-tion anterior to all free choice, and one which offers us the terms from which a freedom might potentially be chosen' (SC 96–7). A living being turns out to be a citadel shielded from universal flux, a place where only certain forces pass through while others are blocked off. But the walls surrounding a living being must be discontinuous, since otherwise nothing could pass inside and life would be extinguished. Yet these bodies themselves must be involved in eventual becoming, since otherwise the living being would be nothing over and above its material conditions, or its organs. Meillassoux thus draws another famous Deleuzian term into his essay: 'we need a non-organic past of the living being, an inorganic becoming of bodies. Or further, we need a *body without organs*' (SC 98). We would follow the life of bodies along a line of folds of the virtual, 'and thus isolate a *typology* of vital becom-ings, becomings which cannot be identified with organic fluxes'

(SC 98). Let science deal with the states of organic flux; philosophy is concerned instead with virtual becomings.

Whereas Bergson allows for unfree selection imposed by perception, followed by a free perception stemming from the free action of the living being, Meillassoux allows only one kind: 'we gave ourselves *only* the first selections – unfree selections, that is – and then constituted the living being as a configuration of those selections' (SC 99). And 'these selections are then endowed with an unforeseeable becoming, alone capable of producing a novelty, thus making possible a distinction between two regimes of selection – active and reactive' (SC 100). This duality between active and reactive now carries Meillassoux all the way to the end of his astonishing essay. The living being must be closed off from the global flux of relations, but not *too* closed off. Its two options are either to narrow its interests and close in on itself, or to increase its openness to the world and let the fluxes rain down on its core. The narrowing movement can be called *reactive*, and the opening one *active*. Reactive becoming closes itself off from the world in the name of self-preservation, and in this respect can be identified with *bêtise*, stupidity. As Meillassoux puts it: 'stupidity, the stubborn stupidity of the proverbial mule, is for the living being always a way of conserving itself in its being, without opening onto exteriority' (SC 100). By contrast, active becoming is concerned with what is *interesting*.

> So the categories of interesting and uninteresting are, for us, substituted for those of freedom and unfreedom. For the two becomings – active and reactive (or stupid) – are both anterior to all free choice: they affect the space of choice, prior to all choice being made. (SC 100–1)

Thus, becoming is passive, 'a way for [the living being] to register an increased affectivity to a number of external fluxes' (SC 101). The body's 'increase of force does not come from an autonomous decision of a constitutive subject, but from an experience that is always undergone, an affective test in which a radical exteriority gives itself' (SC 101).

But if life is a question of openness to exteriority, 'how does the living being succumb to reactivity?' (SC 101). Or, as Deleuze and Guattari ask in *Anti-Oedipus*, 'are all forces doomed to become reactive?' (SC 101). Given that living things tend to increase their interactions with the world, it might be wondered why the opposite ever happens at all, even to the point that 'a reactive being can propagate its reactivity to other bodies' (SC 102) and drain the most revolutionary experiences of energy. The reason this can happen, says Meillassoux, is because the subtractive model teaches us 'that there exist two types of death. *And it is because there are two types of death that there are two types of lives*' (SC 102). The reason for this is fairly clear from the rift in living beings between closing themselves off from the world and opening themselves up to it. In identical fashion, reactive death closes itself off from the world, while active death opens itself to forces that overwhelm and destroy it. Reactive death is described quite vividly by Meillassoux:

> death by diminution of the surface [of the living being] is equivalent to a monadological death, a death by vanishing: folded in upon itself, the body shrinks more and more, until completely annihilated. The *reactive* power of death might well be conceived in this way: for the reactive tends toward a death by narcosis, by exhaustion, by an ever-increasing indifference to the world. And we could name as the *priest* the conceptual persona heralding such a regime of death. (SC 103)

But another name is needed for the opposite kind of death, which comes from a widening of one's contacts with the world. And here Meillassoux insinuates that he was personally horrified by this second sort of death the first time he read *Matter and Memory*. Despite his love for Bergson's work, upon first reading its words on the global play of images he 'felt, however, at the same time, a vague terror' (SC 104–5). As a materialist he was always satisfied that death means a return to the conditions of matter. But if Bergson is right about matter being a play of images, then death is nothing dark and peaceful, but rather 'an infinite madness' (SC 104, emphasis removed). Meillassoux now shares in vivid detail the terror felt by his younger self upon first reading the book:

> to make an image of death, we would have to conceive what our life would be if all the movements of the earth, all the smells, the tastes, all the light – of the earth and elsewhere, came to us in a moment, in an instant – like an atrocious screaming tumult of all things, traversing us continually and instantaneously. As if the nothing of death could not be understood as a simple void, but on the contrary only

as a saturation, an abominable superfluity of existence. Death, thus understood, is the triumphant reign of communication. (SC 104)

The communicator thereby joins the priest as a new conceptual persona – the herald of death by 'atrocious screaming tumult'. The reign of advertising and marketing is perhaps 'the terrifying continuation of authentic creation in the inconsistent and insignificant tumult of information' (SC 105). Deleuze's famous horror at debate and discussion in philosophy is linked by Meillassoux to horror in the face of the philosopher's own possible death: that is to say, 'degradation in the uninterrupted flood of communication, and not somnolence in the reinforced mutilation of affects' (SC 105). Kant is wrong about the regulative power of ideas, because 'there could be nothing worse than to achieve that towards which we tend' (SC 106, emphasis removed). Or stated differently, 'one tends towards chaos when one invents, when one creates, but there is nothing one intends less than actually catching up with it' (SC 106). As philosophers we must *tend* towards chaos, but it is not *regulative* since we must also guard against falling into it.

And here, at last, we find the secret to the success of reactivity and the priest in the kingdom of living beings. For 'the priest can at least promise us *a nice easy death*, a death that reinforces infinitely the process of birth, which was already originally a process of disinterest with regard to flux' (SC 106). Reactivity defends life against the perils of communication; narcosis prevents madness. The dual task of the philosopher is now clear: 'to maintain oneself in the Outside, but to hold oneself close, thus to some degree closed, and thus to discipline into writing a chaotic experience' (SC 107). This is how one of the strangest and most beautiful philosophical essays of the young millennium comes to a close. While 'Subtraction and Contraction' may tell us little about Meillassoux's own system, it tells us a great deal about his power of imagination.

Speculative Realism

The third volume of *Collapse* also contains the full, lightly edited transcript of the memorable Speculative Realism Workshop at Goldsmiths College on 27 April 2007. It would be no exaggeration to say that Speculative Realism has so far been the most visible of the new movements in continental philosophy in the twenty-first century. Even more importantly in the present context,

Speculative Realism was the decisive event in the reception of Meillassoux's philosophy in the Anglophone world, which to this point has been more widespread than in his native France. For this reason, it will be useful to record a brief history of the movement, in which he has played such a crucial role. While to some it might seem unusual to engage in misty-eyed reflection over events less than six years old, Meillassoux's high profile in Anglo-Saxonia is intertwined with that of Speculative Realism as a whole.

On 14 April 2005, I lectured to the Department of Philosophy at Middlesex University (London) at the invitation of Ray Brassier, who was then on the faculty there. The lecture was entitled 'Heidegger's Thing and Beyond', and was later published in *Space and Culture* in shorter form under a new title.[8] In January 2006, I was on vacation in Nice and suddenly needed to travel to Barcelona as quickly as possible, which turned out to be possible only on an EasyJet flight through London that included an overnight stop. I contacted Brassier in hopes of having a discussion on my way through London, and he unexpectedly offered me lodging. During the afternoon of 11 January, we had a discussion in his kitchen in which he briefly mentioned an excellent lecture at Middlesex by Iain Hamilton Grant that had occurred some months before my own – in November 2004, I believe. I said that I was not familiar with Grant, though in fact I knew of his published translations of Baudrillard and Lyotard, and had simply forgotten the name at the time. Brassier then vaguely suggested that Grant and I be paired for some future event, and this was the first embryonic hint of Speculative Realism.

In late March or early April, Brassier returned from vacation in Paris. He wrote with news of a book purchased while there that he had not yet had time to read, but which looked as though it would be right up my alley. The book in question was entitled *Après la finitude*, by a young French thinker named Quentin Meillassoux, who was said to be close to Alain Badiou. Brassier had heard of Meillassoux several years earlier from Nina Power, who must have been among the first in the Anglophone world to take note of him. Immediately I ordered the book from Amazon.fr; it arrived in Cairo on 9 April 2006. Two days later I left for a conference in Iceland, taking the book with me. On the morning of 12 April, I went on a whale-watching cruise in the bay near Reykjavik but saw no whales, thereby earning an automatic refund on the hefty ticket price. In the afternoon I returned to my hotel room and pulled out *Après la finitude*. I will never forget the impression left by the first sentence of the French: '*La théorie des qualités premières et secondes semble appartenir à un passé philosophique irrémédiablement périmé: il est temps de la réhabiliter*' (AF 13 in French version). Naturally, I could only salute this endorsement of the theory of primary and secondary qualities, and saluted all the more when I came to the passages on 'correlationism', a crisper version of my own term 'philosophy of access'. By 14 April, still in Reykjavik, I had finished the book in a spirit of admiration mixed with delighted puzzlement.

The next day I left for Akureyri on Iceland's northern coast. That afternoon, on 15 April, I was emailing Brassier from the hotel lobby with glowing reports on Meillassoux's book, summarizing the argument of a work that Brassier would soon translate into English himself. He quickly reintroduced Grant's name into the discussion as well, and impatient communicator that I am, it was only one day later that I emailed both Grant and Meillassoux, thereby putting Brassier's idea of a joint event into action. Meillassoux responded first, on 21 April; the tardy bohemian Grant followed suit three days later. Once the event took shape in the minds of all four participants, Alberto Toscano offered to host it at his home institution: Goldsmiths College, University of London. Toscano later stood in ably for Meillassoux at the 2009 follow-up event in Bristol. On 26 July 2006 I met Meillassoux in person for the first time, in the company of the Australian anthropologist Stephen Muecke, at the well-known café Le Rostand near the Jardin du Luxembourg. (Meillassoux himself had suggested the location.) Here I was immediately struck by his kind and modest personality, as well as his intellectual force. At my suggestion, Bruno Latour then hosted a salon on Meillassoux's book, in February 2007, where the young philosopher was well received by the audience despite their not being inclined to accept his ideas. As mentioned in the Introduction to this book, Latour described Meillassoux as a forceful speaker who could easily have gone on for hours if not halted by participant fatigue.

As noted, the Speculative Realism Workshop took place on 27 April 2007. Some months earlier we still had no name for the group, which had rallied around 'correlationism' as the shared enemy unifying four philosophical projects with little else in common. At first it seemed as though we might settle on 'Speculative Materialism', Meillassoux's name for his own system, despite my own rejection of materialism. No better alternative emerged until Brassier offered 'Speculative Realism'. The name had such appeal that it was adopted immediately by all members of the group, though Brassier (who disliked 'speculative') and Meillassoux (who preferred 'materialism' to 'realism') eventually distanced themselves from the term. Grant has since taken a turn in the direction of British Idealism, which leaves the author of the present book as the only original Speculative Realist who still endorses the term wholeheartedly. 'Speculative Realism' has since become a familiar phrase in continental philosophy circles in the Anglophone world, the subject of numerous university courses and ceaseless discussion in the blogosphere. It has served as a rallying point for the young, and has helped focus continental philosophy *for the first time* on the realism/anti-realism dispute, which was formerly dismissed as a 'pseudo-problem' by the overly reverent disciples of Husserl and Heidegger.

When the day of the workshop arrived, none of the four members had met all of the others. Only Brassier had met Grant, and only I had met Meillassoux, so that we all took the stage with at least one stranger that day. The speakers went in alphabetical order, which put Meillassoux fourth and last for the day, speaking in the shadows of late afternoon. His lecture, alone among the four, was a forceful defense of the inherent *strength* of the correlationist position, phrased even more strongly than in *After Finitude* itself. Due to illness and fatigue I failed to register just how surprising his lecture was at the time, and was struck with astonishment for the first time only later, when reading the printed version in *Collapse*.

By introducing the term 'correlationism', Meillassoux tried to pre-empt the usual response of those who claim that they are not idealists: Kant is not an idealist because he refutes idealism in the *Critique of Pure Reason*, phenomenology is not idealism because intentionality aims at an object outside itself, Heidegger is not an idealist because *Dasein* is always already immersed in the world. The point is that even these positions

> can't deny, without self-refutation, that the exteriority they elaborate is essentially relative: relative to a consciousness, a language, a *Dasein*, etc. No object, no being, no event, or law which is not always-already correlated to a point of view, to a subjective access – this is the thesis of any correlationism. (SR 409)

And although it is already fashionable to claim that the critique of correlationism is 'the least interesting part' of Meillassoux's philosophy, the reason this mere term was able to catalyze an entire movement is because it nailed so perfectly the basic problem with all continental philosophy (and much analytic philosophy) since Kant. In most post-Kantian circles, any talk of reality in its own right tends to be viewed as the clumsiest of intellectual gaffes. The critique of correlationism remains highly relevant today, its work not yet completed. And even now we see Heideggerians, Husserlians, Derrideans, and Kantians lining up to claim that their heroes were never correlationists to begin with, that the entire charge is a 'straw man', and so forth. But as far as I am concerned, this is merely a symptom of how devastatingly they have been struck by the correlationist charge.

As concerns the critique of correlationism, Meillassoux's views resemble my own. But in his Goldsmiths lecture he subtly pivoted and took issue with my own approach to the problem. 'By the term "correlation", I also wanted to exhibit the essential argument of these "philosophers of access", as Harman calls them; and – I insist on this point – the exceptional *strength* of this argumentation, apparently and desperately implacable' (SR 409). In Meillassoux's eyes the correlationist argument is simple and exceedingly powerful:

No X without givenness of X, and no theory about X without a positing of X ... To be is to be a correlate, a term of a correlation ... That is why it is impossible to conceive an absolute X, *i.e.*, an X which would be essentially separate from a subject. (SR 409)

And finally, 'we can't know what the reality of the object in itself is because we can't distinguish between properties which are supposed to belong to the object and properties belonging to the subjective access to the object' (SR 409). Meillassoux turns to Fichte as an example of this correlationism, perhaps surprisingly given how hard he worked in *After Finitude* to distinguish the strong correlationist position from truly idealist positions of the Fichtean sort. In the interview contained in the present book, Meillassoux reacts negatively to the question of whether his own position resembles that of the German Idealists. As he points out, the strength of the correlationist argument is merely a starting point for him, since the existence of things independent from us is eventually proven along the path of factiality. But as I will argue in Chapter 4, the thing-in-itself is not just something that exists even if all humans die, but must also be something different from our knowledge of it even when humans *have not* all died. In short, the problem of realism arises not from ancestral eras or lonely country houses, but from a reality in the things that escapes us even when we are *staring directly at* those things. To this extent I do not find the correlationist argument powerful at all, and also hold that Meillassoux's proof of the existence of things-in-themselves fails to recover the full pre-correlationist depth of those things. But this can be left to Chapter 4; for now, we simply follow Meillassoux's way of looking at the problem.

As he sees it, it is Fichte who gives 'the most rigorous expression of the correlationist challenge to realism' (SR 410). Meillassoux rejects the strange but long-dominant French reading of Fichte by Alexis Philonenko,[9] who held that the basic principles of the *Science of Knowledge* were not literal claims about how the world is, but ironically posited illusions that Fichte then set out to deconstruct. Against this odd reading, Meillassoux endorses the more recent French interpretation by Isabelle Thomas-Fogiel.[10] Her far more plausible claim is that Fichte is 'a thinker of the pragmatic contradiction: Fichte is a thinker who intends to evaluate every philosopher by his capacity to do what he says and to say what he does' (SR 411). To say 'I think and I do not think' would be a logical contradiction. But to say 'I do not think' is not a logical contradiction but a *pragmatic* one; after all, I cannot speak without thinking. 'What is a philosopher really doing when he claims to have access to a reality independent of the I? He posits, says Fichte, an X supposed to be independent of any position. In other words, he posits the X as non-posited' (SR 412). It is impossible to understand Meillassoux if one does not grasp that he is quite *persuaded* by this Fichtean argument. Though he will later differentiate himself from German Idealism by proving the existence of an in-itself, he has much more respect for the rigor of Fichte's point than he does for mainstream realism, which merely posits a reality without running the unavoidable gauntlet of a simple, inescapable problem: by thinking the unthought, we thereby turn it into a thought. 'To be a contemporary realist means, in my view, to directly challenge the Fichtean fatality of pragmatic contradiction . . . If you think X, then you *think* X' (SR 413).

This point leads Meillassoux on an interesting twelve-page

detour that we need not consider in detail. The detour amounts to a confrontation with the increasingly popular 'non-philosophy' of François Laruelle, and indirectly with Meillassoux's fellow speculative realist Brassier, who was among the first commentators on Laruelle in the Anglophone world. 'Brassier, who is a first-class reader, tries to show that Laruelle's "transcendental realism" is a more reliable and rigorous way to root out the philosophy of correlationism than that which I propose' (SR 414). And further, 'Brassier claims that Laruelle, with his non-philosophy, works out a non-correlationism more radical and sure than my own version, burdened as it is by intellectual intuition' (SR 416). In response, Meillassoux begins by saying that we need to distinguish between objectivity and reflection. 'The reason is: if you want to think the circle of objectivity [as Laruelle does] . . . you need a point of view outside of this circle' (SR 416). Kant described the structure of the world in terms of space, time, and the categories, but in Fichte's view Kant never explained how he was able to stand outside these structures in such a way as to gain knowledge of them. 'This operation needed, according to Fichte, another faculty which was almost described by Kant: the faculty of reflection' (SR 417). Like every philosopher, Laruelle also needs reflection, but Fichte was the first to include reflection explicitly as part of his own philosophical position. Meillassoux warns that 'if you want to escape from the circle of correlationism, you must not only escape from the circle of objectivity but also from the larger circle of reflection, which is outside Laruelle's circle and includes it' (SR 417–18). If you posit a Real outside our access to it, as Laruelle does, then it will still be a Real *for me*, '[b]ecause it will be a posited Real: a Real posited by reflection outside of representation' (SR 418). In the end, 'we shall see clearly . . . why I think that Laruelle doesn't really escape from the circle of correlation' (SR 418).

We now summarize quickly. Laruelle claims that the Real 'is radically indifferent to and independent of the circle of objectivity' (SR 418). Thought is dependent upon the Real, but not vice versa. But if we look at what Laruelle actually does, he *posits* the Real: 'he begins by thinking, and especially by thinking what philosophical thought is, and then progresses to the Real' (SR 419). In short, Laruelle's Real is just a Real *of thought*, despite all his efforts to the contrary. This 'is manifest in the very name of Laruelle's theory: "non-philosophy" . . . [since] the name "non-philosophy" can only be constructed from the name "philosophy" together with a negation' (SR 419). 'But of course,' Meillassoux mock-ingly adds, 'this contradiction, this pragmatic contradiction, is far too trivial to worry Laruelle' (SR 419), and he tries to evade it by proliferating a series of new concepts. Meillassoux tries to show that all of these new concepts never succeed in escaping from the correlational circle; Laruelle's radical autonomy, sufficiency, and Real-in-the-last-instance turn out to be autonomous, sufficient, and real only *for us*. With further light mockery, Meillassoux says that there is only one solution for every modern realism against the correlational or idealist circle: namely, 'to disqualify what you can't refute' (SR 421). After a brief and humorous com-parison of modern realists to Captain Haddock in a Tintin comic strip, Meillassoux tells us that there are two separate methods of 'disqualifying what you can't refute'.

The first is what he suggestively calls the 'Rhetoric of the Rich Elsewhere' (SR 423). According to this method, the correlation-ist point that we cannot think an unthought X without turning it into an X that is thought is simply a boring, formalistic waste of time. It traps us in a sterile paradox where we spin our wheels while ignoring all the fruitful diversity of the world. In this way, 'the realist disqualifies the correlationist argument as boring, uninteresting, producing arid idealities, boring academics, and pathological intellectuals' (SR 423). Meillassoux even gives us one name by way of example. 'Latour, sometimes, severs all links with correlationism, and does so with much talent and humour', but rather than an argument, this means of fighting the correlational circle is merely 'a disqualification of he who argues: the sickly and boring correlationist' (SR 423).

The second method of disqualifying what one cannot refute turns out to be simply a more brutal version of the first. Here, the realist proceeds directly to attack the *motives* of the correlationist: 'It is the well-known logic of suspicion that we find in Marx, with the notion of ideology, or in Freud, with precisely the notion of resistance. The realist fights every form of idealism by discover-ing the hidden reasons behind these discourses ... class-interest, libido, etc.' (SR 424). Every attack on correlationism is treated as the symptom of a disease, including 'the Nietzschean suspicion of the sickly Kantians of the university' (SR 424). Laruelle receives even harsher treatment: his supposed autonomy of the Real is said to be nothing more than Laruelle's own autonomy from discussion with correlationists (SR 425). Laruelle merely secedes from philosophical dialogue with a correlationist argument that is too strong for any realism to conquer. But correlationism is an argument, and can only be defeated by a better argument.

As we have seen in *After Finitude*, Meillassoux aims to provide that better argument. The correlationist first refutes the realist by appealing to the correlational circle, then refutes the idealist by saying that just because the in-itself is unthinkable does not make it nonexistent. And then the correlationist is refuted in turn by the Speculative Realist (a rare use by Meillassoux of this term) when it is observed that the correlationist would slip into idealism if not for relying on an absolutization of facticity rather than an absolutization of the correlate. Our supposed ignorance of the true nature of things is converted into a *knowledge* of the absolute contingency of all that exists. This line of argument is already familiar to us. The new things here are mostly details: the correlationist mistake is termed 'a pragmatic contradiction' (SR 432), and Brassier is charged with effacing the difference between Kant and Hegel when he identifies Laruelle's term 'philosophy' with Meillassoux's 'correlationism' (SR 428). The latter point is a matter of life and death for Meillassoux, whose entire philosophy will fail if it cannot distinguish between correlationism and outright idealism. He also defends his notion of 'intellectual intuition' against Brassier's critique of this concept in *Nihil Unbound*.[11]

But as we have seen, what remains more vivid in the Goldsmiths lecture than anywhere else in Meillassoux's work is his glowing admiration for the correlationist argument. Laruelle fails to escape correlationism, since his Real is nothing more than a *posited* Real, one that is therefore always already recuperated by thought. Whereas Laruelle *begins* by positing the Real, Meillassoux believes 'that you must begin with correlationism, then show that correlationism must itself posit the facticity of the correlation, and demonstrate in this way that this facticity is absolute contingency. Then, finally, you will accede to an independent Real' (SR 433). But Meillassoux seeks realism, not just a Real. In his view recent philosophy has had too much Real and not enough realism. The problem is that 'this Real, as a non-conceptual residue of the concept, separates itself from any realism, because it forbids any possibility of a conceptual discourse about the Real in itself' (SR 434–5). The Real becomes that which resists conceptualization, but we are left unable to conceptualize the Real. In short, realism for Meillassoux is a philosophy in which the Real can be known absolutely: 'I refuse [the] "Real without realism", because if I don't have a rational procedure to discover specific properties of the Real, those properties threaten to be arbitrarily posited' (SR 435). The real challenge of thinking is a Real *with* realism, 'and that's why I think the title of our day – speculative realism – was perfectly chosen, and is in itself a sort of event' (SR 435).

Spectral Dilemma

The last of Meillassoux's four articles to appear in *Collapse* so far was 'Spectral Dilemma'. This brief piece gave the Anglophone readership its first taste of the major themes of the unpublished *L'Inexistence divine*, and it remained the only taste until the Appendix of the present book. The epigraph at the top of the article ('Mourning to come, God to come', SD 261) sounds more Derridean than Meillassouxian in style, but the content to which it refers is of deep importance to Meillassoux's speculative aspirations.

A specter is a person who has not been properly mourned. But there are also those who cannot be mourned: 'a dead person the horror of whose death lays heavy not only upon their nearest and dearest, but upon all those who cross the path of their history' (SD 262). What Meillassoux has in mind are the most miserable atrocities of our history: 'premature deaths, odious deaths, the death of a child, the death of parents knowing their children are destined to the same end – and yet others' (SD 262). His seriousness about this theme is reflected throughout this essay, as throughout the whole of *L'Inexistence divine*, by some of his most poignant writing: 'These are not necessarily shadows who declare their revenge, but shadows who cry out beyond all vengeance. Whoever commits the imprudence of lending an ear to their call risks passing the rest of his life hearing their complaint' (SD 262). Meillassoux calls such cases *essential* specters, and says that they require a kind of essential mourning. There turns out to be an extremely high threshold for achieving it: 'To accomplish essential mourning would mean to live with essential spectres, thereby no longer to die with them' (SD 262). After a twentieth century packed with odious deaths, the question presses heavily upon us. Strange as it may sound, it will turn out that essential mourning can only take place if the dead are resurrected. This thesis may sound retrograde amidst the obligatory atheism of cutting-edge European thought, but it is given a very strange twist by Meillassoux, whose ideas about God would qualify him as a heretic in any religion in human history so far.

Either God exists, or not. But both alternatives lead to despair when we think of those who died odious deaths: 'both are paths to despair when confronted with spectres' (SD 263). For if God does not exist, there is no redemption for the victims of injustice and atrocity. And if God does exist, then what a horrible God to have allowed these things to occur! 'Thus the dilemma is as follows: either to despair of another life for the dead, or to despair of a God who has let such deaths take place' (SD 265). *Spectral dilemma*, as in the title of the article, is the name Meillassoux gives to this deadlock: 'we oscillate between the absurdity of a life without God, and the mystery of a God who calls "love" his *laissez-faire* and production of extreme evil' (SD 265–6). Thus, the only way to resolve the spectral dilemma is to adopt a position that is neither religious nor atheist. And this is precisely the position Meillassoux develops, both in this article and in *L'Inexistence divine*, with a daring picture of a God who does not yet exist but might exist in the future.

To solve the spectral dilemma, we need to combine the religious insight that the dead must be resurrected with the atheist insight that God does not exist. Without the first, there is no hope; without the second, we are faced with a detestable God who allows evil things to occur or even commits them himself. To solve the dilemma requires the thesis of *the divine inexistence*, the very title of Meillassoux's still withheld major book. In a useful play on words, he notes that this phrase has two meanings. It refers to the inexistence of the divine, but also to the divine character of this inexistence, for 'what remains in a virtual state in present reality harbours the possibility of a God still to come, become innocent of the disasters of the world, and in which one might anticipate the power to accord to spectres something other than their death' (SD 268). With striking originality, Meillassoux notes that theism and atheism falsely claim to exhaust the field of possibilities, since both are committed not only to the truth of their position, but also to the *necessity* of its truth. 'To be atheist is not simply to maintain that God does not exist, but also that he *could not* exist; to be a believer is to have faith in the essential existence of God' (SD 268, emphasis added). And thus, in order to make headway against the useless trench war between the atheist and the theist, we must 'shift the battle to the terrain of modalities' (SD 268). We do so by saying that the existence of God is *possible*: not in the sense that God might exist right now, but in the sense that he does not exist now but might exist in the future. To speak more properly, however, God is *virtual* rather than possible – as we have seen, the possible for Meillassoux refers to a whole of indexable possible cases, whereas God belongs to the same non-totalizable, transfinite virtual realm that makes the laws of nature susceptible to sudden and groundless change.

We must also avoid the exaggerated forms of both theism and atheism that provide false answers to the spectral dilemma. The exaggerated theism says that there is a hidden God who is already in motion towards a Providential resolution of all the odious deaths. The exaggerated atheism takes on Promethean form, claiming that we are well on the way to a mastery of death through hyper-technological means. The problem is that both of these stances have faith in some sort of hidden process.

> In both cases, one maintains that an occult law exists upon which all hope must rest: a natural law not yet known, of the resurrection of bodies, a providential law of progressive emergence of the divine – indemonstrable, even fantastic theses, incapable in any case of supporting any serious hope. (SD 270)

But the God sought by Meillassoux is not only inexistent and possible, but also contingent and unmasterable. Contingency is the key. After all, what is it that immediately makes Meillassoux's theory of God sound so absurd even to those who otherwise admire his books? *The sheer improbability of it*. There seems to be no way that a God could appear from out of nowhere for no reason at all, given that we believe in the laws of nature, and given further that the laws of nature seem necessary (SD 271–2). We have already seen Meillassoux's reasoning as to why these laws are not necessary at all, and need not cover the same ground again. We should only repeat his familiar point that speculative philosophies (which he supports) are those that allow thought the capacity to reach the absolute, while metaphysical philosophies (which he rejects) are those based on the principle of sufficient reason. And '[any] speculation which founded itself on the radical *falsity* of the Principle of Sufficient Reason would describe an absolute which would not constrain things to being thus rather than otherwise, but which would constrain them *to being able not to be how they are*' (SD 275, emphasis added). Therefore, the resolution of the spectral dilemma must proceed 'by way of the speculative, but non-metaphysical, resolution of Hume's problem' (SD 275, emphasis removed).

We might still have many questions about the virtual God. For what does this God allow us to hope? Will it finally be a God worthy of admiration rather than the evil mastermind who sends us plagues and wars? Will it be a personal God? Meillassoux closes the essay with the following answer: 'We believe that precise responses to these questions can be envisaged, and that they determine an original regime of thought, in rupture with both atheism and theology: a *divinology*' (SD 275). In Chapter 4, for the first time in any language, we will examine the basic principles of Meillassoux's divinology, since we have been granted access to his unpublished book on the topic.

New Speculative Essays

We now turn to those writings of Meillassoux that were not yet available in English at the time this book was originally completed. This opening section will consider the following two essays: 'The Immanence of the World Beyond' (IW) and 'The Contingency of the Laws of Nature' (CL). The reason for grouping these pieces together is that both begin with a compact review of *After Finitude* before adding some extra twist to the themes of that book. For reasons of space I have omitted any account of 'Metaphysics, Speculation, Correlation' (MS), which does not cover as much new ground as the two articles just mentioned, but is still recommended for enthusiasts of Meillassoux. We begin with 'The Immanence of the World Beyond', whose title wrongly suggests a concern with refuting the Kantian thing-in-itself. The essay travels in a different direction, passing through Nietzsche's famous theory of the eternal return of the same.

As we will see below when discussing the unpublished manuscript of *The Divine Inexistence*, Meillassoux envisions four regimes of existence: matter, life, thought, and justice. Given that the fourth world of justice may or may not arrive, and given as well that it seems entirely disconnected from our present-day actions, it might be wondered whether this world of justice is a useless notion both ethically and politically. Meillassoux is well aware of this possible objection, and spends the remainder of his essay trying to put it to rest:

> Our intention . . . is to make the fourth world a possibility which can enhance, *in our own world*, the subjectivity of human beings living in our day by profoundly transforming the private lives of those who take seriously such a hypothesis. (IW 462–3)

The atheist is a creature of despair, locked in the hopeless view that the unjust deaths of history can never be redeemed: 'Despair is that which results from the irreducible separation of justice and being which is operative in *all* atheisms and through *every* transcendence . . .' (IW 464). Nor can any hope be found in the ethics of Kant, with its categorical imperative, for which 'the end is to make life simply livable, coherent for the subject, subordinated to universal principles in spite of the phenomenal disjunction of the moral law and the given society . . .' (IW 464). Against this 'major Kantian dead end' (IW 464), which results from Kant's commitment to finitude, Meillassoux appeals instead to human *illimitation*. In *After Finitude*, the 'speculative materialist' was the one who stepped forth and rescued us from our supposed limitations in the ontological sphere. Now that we enter the ethical and political sphere, our new rescuer's name is the 'militant universalist':

> For the fourth world, universal justice cannot be conceived as independent of our acts and thus should not be passively awaited. Because this justice can just as well not arrive . . . it thus imposes upon us an injunction to act in the present in order to hasten its approach and to make some live in its existence, in such a way as to be worthy of this hypothesis that exceeds our capacities but gives meaning to our aspirations. (IW 465)

Meillassoux now draws a distinction, introducing the term 'desperate subject' to describe atheistic humans who view 'universal justice as an impossibility for the living and the dead' (IW 465) and 'nihilistic subject' for those humans who *accept* the claim that universal justice is possible, but who '[consider] this sudden arrival of the future as *non-desirable*, and in truth an *appalling possibility*' (IW 465). Though the term 'nihilist' has been around at least since

Turgenev's *Fathers and Sons* in 1862, Meillassoux reconstructs the term in a new form dependent on his own speculative wager: 'the nihilist is thus a *new* figure, a subjective type who never before existed until now, who is produced by the conceptual possibility present in the hypothetical renewal [brought about by the world of justice]' (IW 465).

He now directs our attention to the Eternal Return, one of the most famous and least believed of Nietzsche's ideas: the notion that everything that has ever happened will repeat itself an infinite number of times without variation. The recent trend is to assert that Nietzsche could not have meant this doctrine literally. Since it looks like a bad 'metaphysical' thesis about reality, it is habitually modified in the readings of text-centered postmodernists, as well as by Deleuze in his widely read *Nietzsche and Philosophy*. Thus it is refreshing to discover that Meillassoux does not follow this trend: 'I reject all these subtle reinterpretations of Nietzsche. [T]he most interesting interpretation of the Eternal Return is, on the contrary, that which gives it the most immediate and direct interpretation, as . . . has just been stated: everything returns eternally to the same, yourself included' (IW 466). The broader point here is that 'one cannot transform a body, invent a new subjectivity, without a speculative proposition about the world. One has really to think that one returns eternally . . . in order to face the experience of the *Übermensch*' (IW 467).

This brings us to the key word 'immanence' in the title of Meillassoux's article. As he comments: 'I believe that with the Eternal Return, Nietzsche reveals a formidable paradox of immanence, one he is undoubtedly the only one to grasp with such acuity. I think we can state this paradox as follows: immanence is not of this world' (IW 467–8). This point is missed by the usual partisans of immanence, who want to overcome the present either with death, or with ceaseless and novel mutations. What Nietzsche shows instead is that

> there is no longer anything like the All-Other – the coat-of-arms of religiosity and transcendence. And there is no longer anything like the More, the more and always, the coat-of-arms of all immanentist philosophy. If the two great accounts of immanence – Nietzsche's and Spinoza's – are conceptions, not of finitude, but of immortality conceived as the endless perpetuation of existing life (or some aspect of existing life), then this is so because the only genuine meaning of

the immanent consists in upholding its continuation to infinity. (IW 468–9)

Despite its recent association with philosophies of otherness and becoming, immanence is not immanence unless it amounts to 'a future becoming in which life is no longer open onto itself, without any hope of escaping from it for another "place" [that] will be incommensurable . . .' (IW 469). Our will is tested by its readiness to envisage 'perpetual imprisonment in our present life – this existence without glory that is our life in the "here and now"' (IW 469).

At stake for Meillassoux is not just a reading of Nietzsche, but a way of interpreting his own proposition about the possible World of Justice, which shares some features with the eternal return despite their obvious differences:

> The main difference is that we are dealing with the real possibility of bodily recommencement which is not open to an eternal cycle of the same but to a non-defined linearity: a life open to the novelty of its recommencement and not always and evermore a life that is identical down to its smallest details. (IW 470)

Nonetheless, Meillassoux's World of Justice also imposes a terrible test on the one who thinks it. The danger of the test is not atheism, since the atheist never properly confronts the spectral dilemma of terrible deaths, and merely laughs off all mention of a World of Justice. The danger, instead, is *nihilism*. Just as one might easily be terrified by the Nietzschean thought that the most mediocre everyday events will recur eternally, we might also be scared by the prospect of endless boredom in a World of Justice, devoid of the entertainments of our everyday scheming and plotting. What we now face, as Meillassoux puts it, 'is not the test of despair, but the test of nihilism. Not the test of a dissociation between being and justice, since the link between the two has been restored, but the test of disgust with universal justice as such' (IW 471). For it seems that we now face a perilous contradiction. Whereas the hope of a World of Justice was supposed to inspire our lives with a kind of 'eschatological vectorization', the actual arrival of that World would put an end to our activist longing for it. For the World of Justice 'seeks the *accomplishment* of justice, [and] hence *the end of the struggle and the vectorization towards such a justice*' (IW 472).

It might well seem that the Fourth World offers nothing more than 'a world of egotism and disengagement in which life would no longer find the meaning of its existence in the generous gift of itself in political or individual engagement in favor of emancipation' (IW 472). It may sound like hell for fervent seekers of justice and a paradise for mediocrities. Hence the temptation of nihilism, 'the hatred of universal justice insofar as it is accomplished' (IW 472). To evade this temptation would require that we 'overcome our violent desire for a life entirely dedicated to the perilous, and sometimes mortal, struggle for justice. For this desire risks, when taken to the extremity of its potency, the intimate assuming of hatred into its hypothesis of victorious justice' (IW 473). This amounts to a strong criticism of many of Meillassoux's fellows on the Left, whose ardor in struggle risks loving itself more than it loves the thought of ultimate success. Nonetheless, Meillassoux finds a precursor of his own hope in the writings of Marx himself:

I believe that what remains once the advent of justice has occurred is precisely what Marx had promised – and perhaps this is in truth his most extraordinary promise, even if today it is held in contempt even by his most inventive heirs: there will be a *communist life*, that is to say, *life finally without politics*. In other words, life without the balance of power, ruse, war, bloody sacrifice for the sake of a universal and also life without the unspeakable enthusiasm which proceeds from all these things in those generous souls. To love life beyond war, violence, and sacrifice – and this even in a world of war, violence, and sacrifice – that is what is at stake in the ultimate transformation of the eschatological subject. (IW 473–4)

For this reason, militants must clarify their own relation to the revolutionary task: 'Certain militants portray their existence as made up of sacrifice, but they do not sacrifice anything at all: they are nihilists who love the war, ruse and violence which are intrinsic to political struggle. The others do not love it, but they do not flee this existence if it is necessary' (IW 476). Meillassoux cautions each of us not to become 'a bureaucrat who loves his files, a party secretary who adores administration, a leader who loves purges, an agent who worships intelligence, etc.' (IW 476). But the abolition of politics cannot itself take place through political means: 'To deny this and to affirm – as was the case in the Soviet

Union – that politics has no place left because it has dissolved itself in the accomplishment of Socialism is in truth to conduct a totalitarian politics that prohibits any politics of opposition' (IW 477).

We turn next to 'The Contingency of the Laws of Nature', beginning with the conclusion of the article, where Meillassoux gives a lucid account of the aims of his intellectual career:

> And so, my general project is as follows: I seek to develop a style of argumentation that establishes the nontrivial consequences of the absence of reason. In other words, I seek to prove that there do indeed exist necessary properties of being but that these properties are the very consequences of the contingency of being ... This is what I call the project of a speculative non-metaphysics: renouncing the principle of sufficient reason, without renouncing a thinking of the absolute. (CL 334)

He does this in the present article by beginning with Hume's problem: 'What is Hume's problem? Classically formulated, the problem is posed as follows: is it possible to prove that, in the future, the same effects will follow from the same causes, all other things being equal, ceteris paribus? In other words, can it be established that, in exactly identical circumstances, future concatenations of phenomena will be identical to present concatenations?' (CL 322). Readers of *After Finitude* already know Meillassoux's highly original way of responding to the problem: 'rather than affirming like Hume that reason is incapable of proving a priori the *necessity* of laws, I propose to show that, quite on the contrary, reason proves to us a priori the *contingency* of laws' (CL 325). Since Meillassoux makes the same arguments for contingency in the article as he does in *After Finitude*, we will focus instead on one of the peripheral points of Meillassoux's article that is not treated in such detail in that book. As he puts it, there have been three basic sorts of response to this problem: metaphysical, skeptical, and transcendental. The metaphysical strategy consists in attempting to prove that some necessary entity exists that governs our world, as Leibniz did with God a century before Hume. The skeptical response can be found in Hume's own writings: 'since one cannot prove the necessity of causal connection, one must cease to ask why laws are necessary, and instead ask where our *belief* in such laws comes from' (CL 324). As for the transcendental response,

Kant considers that the hypothesis of the contingency of laws is refuted by the fact of representation ... [He] does not say that it is *absolutely* impossible that causality should cease to govern the world in the future; he says that it is impossible that such an event be *manifested* – and this because, if the world ceased to be governed by causality, nothing would any longer have any consistency, and therefore nothing would be representable. (CL 325)

As different as these three approaches may seem, Meillassoux claims that all share the same underlying supposition, and that his own position is original precisely through his rejection of it:

One can see, therefore, that these three approaches, although they may lead to very different, and apparently opposed, solutions, all begin with the same postulate: causal necessity is an incontestable fact. My starting point consists in refusing to admit this presupposition, common to all three theses, and in wagering on a fourth option, neither metaphysical, nor skeptical, nor transcendental; an option I call – and we shall see why – speculative. In what does the speculative response to Hume's problem consist? Very simply, rather than affirming like Hume that reason is incapable of proving a priori the necessity of laws, I propose to show that, quite on the contrary, reason proves to us a priori the contingency of laws. (CL 325)

This is the same argument Meillassoux made in *After Finitude* to radicalize strong correlationism into his own 'speculative materialist' position. Rather than Hume's problem leading to an epistemological *limitation on our knowledge* of causality, it gives us a *positive ontological certainty* that anything could happen at any time without reason. To repeat an earlier citation: 'rather than affirming like Hume that reason is incapable of proving a priori the necessity of laws, I propose to show that, quite on the contrary, reason proves to us a priori the contingency of laws' (CL 325).

Yet there are two points worth noting here, both of them already covered briefly in our discussion of *After Finitude*. The first is that Meillassoux does not get rid of necessity so much as assign it a place in a new division of labor. For all the contingency he ascribes to the *laws* of nature, he does retain causal laws in his system to the extent that events occurring *within* any given regime of natural laws have a bond of strict necessity with those laws. For example, Meillassoux would contend that the laws governing collisions in the CERN collider in Geneva may change suddenly without reason. But he could never allow for occasional 'fluke' results that violate the current laws of nature. I have mentioned that this twofold ontology of exceptional changes in the law of nature on the one hand and banal, everyday, lawlike events on the other is probably indebted to Badiou's distinction between rare truth-events and the insipid everyday 'situations' in which nothing really changes. We can credit Meillassoux with bravely extending Badiou's twofold theory from the human sphere into the arena of nature itself; alternatively, we can ask why such a twofold split is needed at all. Stated in the form of a question: what is the purpose of keeping contingency a relatively rare event? One suspects that this gesture is useful in maintaining some degree of scientific plausibility for Meillassoux's theory. Yet since he has already played the card (against Jean-René Vernes) of saying that contingency does not entail *frequent* change, why not make the same play when it comes to local events? Why not say: 'just because local events are contingent in the same manner as laws of nature, it does not mean that they must violate the current laws of nature *frequently*'? It is simply not clear why Meillassoux feels the need to quarantine contingency at the level of laws themselves, given that this requires him to ascribe flat-out lawlike necessity to the everyday course of things. Though Meillassoux is known as a bold philosopher of radical contingency, it would be more accurate to describe him as a bold dualist philosopher of contingency on one side and necessity on the other.

This leads us to a second point worth mentioning. We have seen that Meillassoux defines the originality of his position against those of Leibniz, Hume, and Kant by saying that all three accept the necessity of causal laws. But in fact, Meillassoux's speculative approach actually shares a deeper assumption with all of these thinkers: namely, the prejudice that necessity and contingency are the only two options. In other words, Meillassoux presents us a world of *hyperchaos* on the level of laws combined with *hypernecessity* on the level of individual events subordinated to those laws. For any event E, the only two options he leaves us are that E is utterly contingent and governed by no reason whatsoever, or that E is fully determined with mechanical rigidity. It is perhaps easiest to see the flaw in this model by considering human life. We take it as a truism that no human being chooses equally at every given moment from all possible actions. The sphere of possibilities is severely limited by our geographical and historical position, our physical capacities, our current place in the social structure, our knowledge, our character, our specific history of traumas and disappointments, and so forth. Hence, we would not be immediately inclined to accept hyperchaos as a valid model of human biography, and any possible 'proof' by Meillassoux to this effect would at least be running against the wind. But neither are we usually inclined to think of human life as mechanistically determined down to its tiniest details, as seen from the fact that no one will accept our pleas of innocence for malevolent acts on the grounds that we are mere machines not in control of our actions.

These two extreme opposite ways of looking at human life, which seem to be the only two ways Meillassoux would allow if he were to reflect on the problem, are simply the same two poles found in Kant's famous antinomy concerning freedom and necessity. What is missing from the picture is any notion of sufficient reason short of outright mechanistic determinism. The possibility should at least be considered, though Leibniz ignored it, that every event has reasons without being fully determined by them. In fact, we should not speak only of *temporal* reasons, since we have seen that causal relations do not merely unfold over time, but also pertain to the composition of an entity in any given moment. Rather than dissolving the opposition between contingency and necessity into the latter term in the manner of Leibniz, rather than transforming it into a problem of knowledge and belief as Hume does, and rather than making it an unknowable antinomy like Kant, Meillassoux simply preserves both contingency and necessity and assigns each of them a different half of the job: contingency governs the laws of nature, while necessity controls those events that unfold according to currently extant laws. In this way, Meillassoux fails to account for reasons that would not be mechanistic reasons: links that are *loose* rather than non-existent (contingency) or all-powerful (necessity).

The April 2012 Berlin Lecture

In the spring of 2012, Armen Avanessian and others organized an imaginative repetition of the inaugural 2007 Speculative Realism event, this time in Berlin. Rather than assembling all of the participants simultaneously as with the first event, the method was to invite one Speculative Realist to Berlin at a time, with the prominent young Swedish philosopher Martin Hägglund added to the mix as a fifth speaker. As it happened, Hägglund led off the series on 11 March 2012. My own lecture took place on 11 April, followed by Meillassoux's on 20 April, Brassier's on 4 May, and Grant's on 10 May. The lecture by Meillassoux was entitled 'Iteration, Reiteration, Repetition: A Speculative Analysis of the Meaningless Sign', but today it is more often known by its short-hand description: 'The Berlin Lecture'. This important document is the topic of the present chapter. Given that the text of the lecture has entered circulation without Meillassoux's permission, he has asked me to note that the version I will discuss was not intended for publication. But since the lecture is already the subject of widespread discussion, and since it directly discusses my own work, Meillassoux has allowed me to cite from it for purposes of response.[12]

The written form of the Berlin Lecture is split into two parts of roughly equal length – the first concerned with something called 'subjectalism' and Meillassoux's disagreement with it, the second devoted to an intriguing analysis of the meaningless sign as grounded in the necessity of contingency. Given that the second part is uncompleted by Meillassoux's own admission, and given my need to respond personally to Meillassoux's critiques in the first part of the lecture, this section will focus entirely on the first part of the Berlin Lecture. For obvious reasons, we can ignore those portions of Part One that merely repeat or add nuance to the main arguments of *After Finitude*. Meillassoux begins with a candid statement of his philosophical program: 'My thesis (which may sound bizarrely classical) comes down to saying that thought is capable of the "absolute", capable even of producing something like "eternal truths" . . .' (BL 1). By this stage no one will be fooled by the scare quotes, since we know that Meillassoux *literally maintains* that his philosophy can deduce absolute eternal truths. This is what makes his philosophy both so refreshing, and so appealing a target for critical engagement. It also signals his lineage within the basic style of philosophy represented by Badiou, whatever their differences on other points.

Meillassoux's Berlin discussion of the correlational circle argument – we have already seen he *supports* it – makes use of a revealing formulation. I refer to the following fragment: 'If metaphysical materialism seemed basically untenable after Berkeley . . .' (BL 1). This half-sentence is revealing in two important ways. First, it implies that the enemy of Berkeley and his purported lineage is not realism, but *materialism*. Indeed, in Meillassoux's philosophical lexicon we find that 'materialism' is always a more important term than 'realism'. Second, there is his initially quiet mention of the claim that Berkeley is a decisive turning point in modern philosophy – and not in a good sense. Berkeley's philosophy, in which mountains and rivers do not exist outside their being perceived, is generally treated either as a cautionary tale of argument run amok or as an intellectual freak show fit for ridicule by common sense. Meillassoux treats Berkeley instead as a Pied Piper who led most later philosophers down the wrong fork in the road, including Maupertuis, Diderot, Hegel, Schelling, Bergson, Schopenhauer, Nietzsche, and Deleuze (BL 3), not to mention myself and Iain Hamilton Grant (BL 7). Furthermore, we have already seen that Meillassoux treats Berkeley as an *enemy* of materialism but a *friend* of realism: 'So every materialism is a realism, but not every realism is a materialism (. . . Berkeley is a realist of the spirit and of ideas.)' (BL 6). The words in parentheses are simply untenable, since under this extremely generous definition of realism, we fail to see who *would not* count as an ontological realist.[13] They remain untenable even when we follow Meillassoux's own Berlin definition of realism: 'I call "realism" every position that claims to accede to an absolute reality – every speculative position, then' (BL 6). As for speculative positions, he had earlier defined them as follows:

> I call 'correlationism' every form of de-absolutization of thought that, to obtain this result, argues from the closure of thought upon itself, and its subsequent incapacity to attain an absolute outside of it. I call 'speculative' every philosophy that claims, on the contrary, to attain such an absolute. (BL 2)

Please note that under these definitions, neither Kant nor Heidegger – who both think we cannot attain the absolute – could be considered realists. Although some commentators would be perfectly happy with that restriction, few would be happy to contend (as Meillassoux does) that *Berkeley* is a realist while Kant and Heidegger are not. For it is difficult to see how a philosopher most famous for saying *to be is to be perceived* could be taken for more of a realist than two philosophers who defend a thing-in-itself *beyond* all perception and a Being that *withdraws* from all presence. I mention this point not to challenge Meillassoux's command of the history of philosophy, a field in which he has much erudition. Instead, I call attention to the way that Meillassoux purposely deflates the importance of realism in Berlin while laying great stress on materialism. Speaking of which, we should also quote his definition of materialism: 'I call "materialism" . . . every thought acceding to an absolute that is at once external to thought *and in itself devoid of all subjectivity*' (BL 2; emphasis added). Pay attention to the phrase I have placed in italics, since it will prove to be the ambiguous pivot of Meillassoux's argument against 'subjectalism'.

In *After Finitude*, Meillassoux spoke of correlationism in both a narrow sense and a broad one. At times it seemed to refer only to a *skeptical* position about our ability to access the in-itself (as in Hume, Kant, and their various heirs), while at other times 'correlationism' combined this skeptical view with very different views that *absolutized* the subject (as in Hegel and the later Husserl). Meillassoux now laments that 'this created a regrettable air of confusion to which I intend to put an end' (BL 4). Yet this is not the fault of the readers of *After Finitude*; Meillassoux concedes that his own exposition did not use 'correlationism' in a sufficiently precise sense. Starting with the Berlin Lecture, however, the terminology becomes perfectly clear. 'Correlationism' now stands exclusively for the skeptical view that we cannot reach an absolute, given that we are forever trapped in the mutual correlation of human and world. The broader term that includes both the skeptical and the absolute positions will henceforth be called the 'Era of the Correlate', with Berkeley identified as its regrettable founder.

As we have seen, full-blown idealism tries to escape correlationism by doubling down on its apparent weakness. Whereas a naïve realist would tell the correlationist 'I can escape the correlate by making true statements about a world outside the mind,' the idealist would join the correlationist in viewing this as utterly impossible, since we cannot think a reality outside thought without turning it into a thought. Yet the idealist pushes things even further by saying that the human-world correlate *is itself* the absolute. As we saw when discussing *After Finitude*, Meillassoux claims to reject idealism no less than correlationism, and tries to wedge his own 'speculative materialist' position midway between the two. But what interests us here is how Meillassoux places Berkeley at the head of an unexpectedly long list of successors, though Berkeley is normally viewed as a sort of fascinating dead end, incapable of further development. Meillassoux discusses the idealist position as follows: 'If thought cannot exit from itself, this is not because it runs up against gnoseological limits, but because it discovers a form of existence that is intrinsically necessary: the subjective' (BL 3). He continues:

> Of course, the most elementary form of this belief would be solipsism: I can believe that it is my subjectivity, qua psychological individual, that is absolute, and therefore believe myself entirely alone in the world. But in the history of philosophy, no one has ever sincerely taken this path; and the metaphysical reply to correlationism consisted rather in absolutizing the subjective in general – according to a trans-individual modality in which every human, and indeed every living or inorganic being, participates at its proper level. (BL 3)

In short, Meillassoux argues that idealism and vitalism are intellectual allies, and even that they are genetically interrelated. Though at first glance it might seem that idealism leaves us stranded in our thoughts while vitalism breaks free into a wild arena of cosmic speculation, what both share in common is that they 'absolutize thought'. This is why Meillassoux now groups both idealism and vitalism under a common name: *subjectalism*.

> Why this term 'subjectalism'? Because we need a term that allows us to encompass at once all forms of idealism and all forms of vitalism, so as to contest the apparent opposition between these currents – in particular during the twentieth century; and so as to emphasize instead their essential relatedness and their original anti-materialist complicity. (BL 3)

And as we read a bit later:

> The critical force of this word 'subjectalism' is to put together *into the same camp* these currents that claim to be radically opposed, to put them all together – Hegel, Nietzsche, and Deleuze included – into the camp of Berkeley himself. For Berkeley, inventor of the argument of the correlationist circle, was not a correlationist, but a subjectalist . . . (BL 6)

Meillassoux offers several variations on this critique of subjectalism and its motives. For instance, 'the strangest moment came when various vitalisms – Nietzsche, Deleuze – participated in the radical critique of consciousness and of the subject' (BL 4). The supposed strangeness came from the fact that Nietzsche, Deleuze, and others criticized the idealist subject even while spreading consciousness throughout the universe at large, by '[hypostatizing] one or several traits of human subjectivity – even with regard to inorganic reality. This enterprise thus produced typically subjectalist concepts such as "will to power", or "the inorganic life of things"' (BL 4). Instead of eliminating subjectivity, the subject was found everywhere one looked, 'but not at all in the same sense that these terms took on when referring to their human instantiation. But in that case, why use the *same words?*' (BL 4–5). Why, that is, should we view the difference between rocks, plants, animals, and humans merely as a difference in *degree* rather than as a series of radical leaps? Meillassoux is aware that some wish to end the anthropocentrism of modern philosophy, yet he sees a different danger arising from this wish: 'this refusal of anthropocentrism in fact leads only to an *anthropomorphism* that consists in the illusion of seeing in every reality (even inorganic reality) subjective traits the experience of which is in fact entirely human, merely varying their degree (an equally human act of imagination)' (BL 5). Later, his patience finally wears thin: 'To free oneself of man, in this strange humanism-in-denial, was simply to disseminate oneself everywhere, even into rocks and particles, and according to a whole scale of intensities' (BL 5). This critique has grave consequences for the history of philosophy as well, since where others see a series of original advances, Meillassoux sees only three centuries of spinning our wheels:

> Once you reopen the materialist struggle against every form of hypostasis of the subjective ... you see only *variants* where we have been told there are radical, vertiginous *ruptures*. Every subjectalism is a variant of Berkeleyanism – each time a new, reinvented way of inhabiting its formidably effective anti-materialist gesture. Berkeley, Hegel, Nietzsche and Deleuze prosecuted, according to diverse strategies, *one and the same combat*: that of abolishing the idea of de-subjectivized matter. And from this point of view, there is no essential difference between one of these thinkers and another. All make their home, in a more or less original way, on the Berkeleyan continent. (BL 6)

This is certainly a daring interpretation of modern philosophy, especially since it leaves Meillassoux and a handful of 'materialists' to fight a veritable army of great correlationists (Hume, Kant) and subjectalists (Berkeley, Hegel, Nietzsche). Since Meillassoux also links Badiou with Berkeley – as we will see in the next section – he even seems to place his own potential forerunner in the repetitious post-Berkeleyan camp. And when it comes to Meillassoux's Speculative Realist colleagues there is no need for guesswork, since two of us are identified by name as covert Berkeleyans without knowing it:

> the appellation 'speculative realist', designating the movement (in itself important) with which I have become associated, does not quite correspond to my enterprise, since it also comprises the option that I seek to counter – subjectalism. If this term, nevertheless, was quite the correct one to choose to designate the set of projects of four philosophers who are indeed anti-correlationist, it is because two of them are, to my mind, anti-materialist, that is to say subjectalist – namely, Iain Hamilton Grant, who is (Deleuzo-)Schellingian, and Graham Harman, who hypostatizes our subjective relation to things by projecting it into the things themselves. Harman, in particular, develops a very original and paradoxical subjectalism, since he hypostatizes the relation we have with things that, according to him, withdraw continually from the contact we can make with them. But the implicit form of this withdrawal is given by *our relation* to things. To make of our subjective relation to things that withdraw from their (full) contact with us, the universal relation of things to things – this is a typically subjectalist gesture, carried out in a new and brilliant form, but which still belongs to what I have called the 'Era of Correlation'. Now, it is this era that I wish definitively to escape . . . (BL 6–7)

To this long passage we must affix a medium-sized one of the same general tone:

> Harman designates with the expression 'philosophies of access' philosophies that base themselves upon the relation between humans and things, and which consider that we have access only to this access, not to the things themselves. But Harman, to my mind, does not escape from this 'access', since on the contrary he hypostatizes it for the things themselves: there is no longer any chance of our escaping from access, since from now on, it is everywhere. Only the materialist can escape from it, for he makes of this human access to things something that belongs only to the thing–human relation, and absolutely does

not exist in things, *a fortiori* between things. If we are to keep the promise of escaping from access towards the thing itself, we must not rediscover access (to a greater or lesser degree of intensity) *within* the thing itself. (BL 7)

This first portion of the Berlin Lecture closes with a reminder of the supposed kinship between idealism and vitalism: 'Hegelian idealism is obviously the paradigm of such a metaphysics of the Subject thought as the Absolute – but vitalism obeys the same logic, *even if it does not always do so in full consciousness of its fundamental argument*' (BL 8). What is new here is the introduction of a sort of hierarchy, according to which idealism is superior to vitalism insofar as it is more aware of its own aims and methods.

I will now explain why I find Meillassoux's argumentation so far to be unusually weak by his standards, and will argue as well that he invents a concept ('subjectalism') that has no basis in reality. That which enables Meillassoux to link idealism and vitalism under the single heading of 'subjectalism' is his claim that both idealism and vitalism 'absolutize the subject', insofar as they think that everything in the world is a subject, with no 'dead matter' to be found anywhere. Hence the need for 'materialism', as the only philosophy that can prevent wholesale subjectivization of the world. Yet there are serious problems with this line of argument. In the first place, the phrase 'absolutize the subject' is hopelessly ambiguous. For what does it mean in the case of Berkeley and Hegel, members of the 'idealist' camp of subjectalism? Here it at least means that there is no thing-in-itself beyond our grasp, and in Berkeley's even stronger version of idealism it means that nothing exists but *perceptions*, whether those of people or of God. This, then, is the first meaning of 'absolutizing the subject': the elimination of any thing-in-itself. But this is not necessarily what all vitalists say, even if some of them do. All it takes to be a 'vitalist' (or rather, a *panpsychist*; Meillassoux wrongly interchanges the terms) is to say that everything thinks in some way, including inorganic things. But if this amounts to 'absolutizing the subject', then this is not meant in the same sense as Hegel's and Berkeley's. For here, the supposed 'absolutization' is merely a *democratizing* in which all things are said to think to some degree. If the idealists hold that everything is just an appearance to the subject, vitalists hold that everything is a subject. The difference is that idealists cannot possibly be realists, whereas vitalists can be.

How so? Let's invent a philosophical position called 'Maximum Vitalism'. The Maximum Vitalist candidly holds that everything has consciousness, even full-blown human consciousness. The moon sends poetic messages to dust, which whisper them in turn to blades of grass. Chairs have nightmares, while tables form conspiracies against birds and reptiles but are simply too weak to carry them to fruition. The position sounds ludicrous to common sense. But we know that Meillassoux cannot appeal to common sense against vitalism, not even rhetorically, given his own uncommonsensical commitment to the absolute contingency of the laws of nature and the possible advent of a future God, to be preceded by a temporary Messiah (as we will discuss soon enough). Meillassoux gives *arguments* for his own unusual results, and thus he needs to give *arguments* against the evidently crazy philosophy we have called Maximum Vitalism.

What are those arguments? For my part, I see only two, and cannot accept either of them. The first argument is really just Meillassoux's assumption that a non-subjective reality must be established in *taxonomical* fashion, with two basic *types* of entity in the world: humans who think, and dead matter which does not (leaving aside his underdeveloped intermediate term 'life'). Yet there is no reason to create such a taxonomy. For even the Maximum Vitalist does not need to say that 'everything is subjective'. Quite the contrary: the Maximum Vitalist might easily say that the moon, dust, chairs, tables, and all other things are divided between a thinking part and an extended part, in a democratized version of Cartesian ontology. In short, Meillassoux's category of 'dead matter' is entirely unnecessary if the goal is simply to make room in the world for a non-subjective reality. In the case of the Maximum Vitalist, that non-subjective reality is adequately provided by the *bodies* of the thinking moon, dust, chair, and tables. Thus we see that the Maximum Vitalist has nothing to do with Berkeley, who never could have ascribed genuine physical bodies to these entities any more than to humans or God. To summarize, there are no rational grounds for insisting on something called 'dead matter' as a means of putting a brake on idealism. The taxonomical remedy for Berkeleyan idealism is not the only one, and hence it would need to be justified in its own right – something Meillassoux never really attempts, but merely inherits without comment from the Cartesian tradition.

That leaves Meillassoux with just one argument against the

Maximum Vitalist, the 'anti-anthropomorphic' argument. As we have seen, that argument runs roughly as follows: 'We only know the features of thought by looking at our own thinking, and hence we should not project those features onto nonhuman entities. To do so may seem innovative, but it is really just a sad projection of human subjectivity onto the entire cosmos. In the attempt to escape *anthropocentrism*, the vitalist runs headlong into *anthropomorphism*.' But this last sentence merely amounts to a belated reversal of Jane Bennett's formula: 'We need to cultivate a bit of anthropomorphism – the idea that human agency has some echoes in non-human nature – to counter the narcissism of humans in charge of the world.'[14] We may now seem to be locked into a sort of Kantian antinomy, with Meillassoux saying 'anthropocentrism is needed to counter anthropomorphism' and Bennett simply saying the reverse. Is the antinomy undecidable? Or shall we side with Meillassoux simply because it makes a better fit with the common presuppositions of modern philosophy and science? Neither of these. We must side instead with Bennett, since the real asymmetry in the two statements favors *her* position rather than Meillassoux's.

Namely, Bennett's 'anthropomorphism' is simply a metaphorical rhetoric designed to challenge the timeworn prejudice that the obvious differences between humans and nonhumans must be embodied in a difference of *ontological kind*. By contrast, Meillassoux does not use anthropocentrism metaphorically, but *actually adheres* to a doctrine that treats human thought as so uniquely special that it deserves half of a 50–50 split, in an ontology consisting of humans on one side and all the trillions of species and categories of nonhumans on the other. To use a different example, when Bruno Latour speaks of nonhuman actors 'negotiating' with each other, it is simply idiotic to accuse him (and some do) of 'anthropomorphizing' speed bumps, peaches, or robotic arms. Latour is not making the Maximum Vitalist claim that these entities hold discussions and strike deals just as humans do. Instead, he is simply drawing on the richness of metaphorical description to draw our attention to some underlying features shared by human negotiations and nonhuman interactions. We must not give way to a puritanism of metaphor that warns of the dangers of describing anything in terms of anything else, for then we would simply be left with a series of arid propositions, in keeping with the usual bias of analytic philosophy that metaphors have no cognitive value and simply muddy the waters.

This brings us to Meillassoux's critique of my own position, which he describes as a 'typically subjectalist' position despite its 'brilliance': a brilliance that will apparently not save me from being Berkeley's unwitting prisoner on the wrong side of the history of philosophy. The first problem with Meillassoux's critique is that by no means do I project human psychological traits onto nonhuman things. I am not the Maximum Vitalist described above. My point, rather, is as follows. Human experience shows, through the surprise and disruption that are the topic both of Heidegger's tool-analysis and the analysis of finitude by Kant, that we only deal with caricatured versions of things rather than encountering them directly in the flesh. But whereas Heidegger and Kant leap to the inference that this is a special tragic feature of finite human beings alone, I have argued that nonhuman objects must do the same to each other as well. Instead of calling my version a 'projection' of human finitude onto nonhuman entities, it could be stated instead that Heidegger and Kant impose an artificial *narrowing* on such caricature, limiting to the human sphere what can be deduced to belong to *all* relations. Stated more briefly, my claim is that there is a broader category – *relation* – that covers both human thought and nonhuman collision. I will not contest, like the Maximum Vitalist would, that there are apparently great differences between how humans react to raindrops and how the roofs of houses react to them. But what we must contest is the groundless claim that this evident difference between humans and nonhumans needs to be *built into the very foundation of philosophy*. This is simply Descartes's (and Meillassoux's) version of what I have called the Taxonomical Fallacy: the notion that different modes of being must be embodied in different *kinds* of entities, so that people have thoughts and stones have dead physical mass. A much more fundamental distinction is that between the pre-relational character of all entities (human or otherwise) and their caricatured models as found in any relation. The difference between relational and non-relational is much deeper than that between thought and matter, and thus is a much better basis for a philosophy.

Perhaps these considerations will help explain why Meillassoux's conception of modern philosophy seems so impossible to me. Let us assume he is right that Berkeley is the chief figure of one axis of modern thought (with Hume and Kant leading the other, more skeptical axis). Berkeley's signature phrase, we know, is *esse est percipi*: to be is to be perceived – an anti-*realist* maxim if ever there was one, and not just an anti-*materialist* principle as Meillassoux claims. How are we to reverse Berkeley – assuming that this must be done to establish a new path of philosophy? Meillassoux seems to hold, like the seventeenth-century rationalists, that the opposite of 'to be is to be perceived' is this: 'to be is to be *knowable*'. His profound trust in mathematics – so reminiscent of Badiou's – goes hand in hand with his view that thought can reach the absolute. Hence his definition of realism as the view that we can *reach* an absolute reality, which conflates an epistemological definition of realism with an ontological one. By mathematizing the things, thereby obtaining their primary qualities, we supposedly reach the thing-in-itself despite our fated initial entrapment in the correlational circle. But as argued earlier, this gives us an insufficient conception of the things-in-themselves, which are defined by Meillassoux merely as *that which outlasts our lifespans*, not as that which cannot be mastered or exhausted even while we are still alive and staring directly at the things.

This is why I would contend that Berkeley needs to be reversed in a different manner, since perceiving and knowing are equally unable to make absolute contact with the things. Namely, when reading Berkeley's *esse est percipi*, we should interpret *percipi* as just one form of relation. In other words, the ultimate claim of Berkeleyanism is 'to be is to be *in relation*', whether that relation take the form of a thought, a perception, or a brutal inanimate collision. Alfred North Whitehead and more recently Bruno Latour have developed relational ontologies of precisely this sort. But if the deeper meaning of *esse est percipi* is 'to be is to be in relation', then the proper way to reverse Berkeley is to demand that we take account of the things as non-relational cores that can enter differently into many different relations. I call these *objects*, and it will immediately be seen that they are the exact opposite of anything that Berkeley could have endorsed, since they are defined by complete autonomy from any kind of relation, including any relation – whether perceptual or cognitive – to a human or divine mind.

This brings us to a final disagreement with Meillassoux. He claims that I complain about the 'philosophy of access' even while leaving all entities in the cosmos trapped in nothing but access, unable to reach each other as things-in-themselves. But here Meillassoux is simply judging me in accordance with his own priorities. As he is well aware, my phrase 'philosophy of access' is simply an abbreviation for 'philosophy of *human* access'. Whereas

Meillassoux opposes Kant because of his insistence on finitude and the impossibility of absolute knowledge, I oppose Kant on a different point: his assumption that finitude is a solely human drama. If Kant had been reversed on this point instead of the point about things-in-themselves, we could have seen an era of 'German Realism' rather than the German Idealism that ensued, and with far greater damage to the 'Berkeleyan' tradition than was accomplished by Hegel. By offering up a 'mathematized' version of the thing-in-itself, Meillassoux sacrifices the real to *knowledge* of the real, as in his backwards definition of realism as a philosophy that claims to *reach* reality, to *reach* the absolute and eternal. Though I have already shown that 'subjectalism' does not exist, we can now introduce the term *epistemism*, whose critical point consists in including under the same heading both overtly idealist philosophies (such as Berkeley's and Hegel's) that allow for no things-in-themselves, and mathematist philosophies (such as Meillassoux's) which reduce the things-in-themselves to a mathematical model presentable to consciousness. The fact that both Berkeley and Meillassoux support the argument of the correlational circle while I reject it outright should have been sufficient for Meillassoux to recognize, gratefully, his own deep kinship with Berkeley. To fight Berkeley we must fight *epistemism*, which really exists as a unified trend, and not 'subjectalism', which does not.

We conclude by noting that Meillassoux's *taxonomical* approach to escaping subjectalism has further consequences. Near the end of the first part of the Berlin Lecture, Meillassoux boasts that he, unlike some philosophers, does not try to tell scientists what to do. When he tells us that he is only interested in necessity, and that the sciences do not offer any (BL 16–17), this may initially sound dismissive of the sciences. But Meillassoux insists that what it really means is a hands-off attitude to the sciences, which deal with domains where philosophy has nothing to offer. He then draws an explicit contrast between his own attitude and a more meddling philosophical attitude that he calls 'hyperphysics', in the manner of nineteenth-century Romantic philosophies with their wild *metaphysical* theories of electricity, magnetism, geology, even medicine. Yet Meillassoux also claims to detect this very attitude in at least one of his contemporaries:

Contemporary hyperphysics (which, to my mind, includes Graham Harman's philosophy) can no longer deduce according to an absolute necessity that the object is such and such (subjectivity, made of will, etc.). They can only *postulate*, and observe the greater or lesser adequation of this postulate to reality . . . Thus, even if a hyperphysics is deployed, it can no longer maintain the old metaphysics' arrogance in relation to other discourses bearing upon what is . . . its proposition is postulative, hypothetical, and without any foundation in necessity. Its interest is ultimately heuristic, without any possible assurance of being definitively true, for it touches upon nothing eternal within beings. (BL 14)

Throughout Meillassoux's work, we find the assumption that the task of philosophy is *deductive*, and that it must attain the necessary rather than merely describing. He frequently asserts this claim as if it were an obvious truth about the nature of philosophy. Yet this is so far from an obvious truth that it is not even a truth. In the second half of my book *Prince of Networks*, I allied myself with Whitehead's contrary claim that philosophy *is not* primarily a labor of deduction from unshakable first principles. Instead, it is closer to what Whitehead calls a 'descriptive generalization' that can fail through internal inconsistencies or simply through failing to account sufficiently for known aspects of experience. It is hard to see what is shameful in the prospect of a philosophy that 'can only *postulate*, and observe the greater or lesser adequation of this postulate to reality', since this is precisely what philosophy does. Meillassoux seems instead to be bewitched by the Cartesian assumption that the whole of philosophy must proceed by deduction from clear and distinct ideas, as if philosophy were basically the same sort of thing as geometry. But this is not how Socrates saw it, nor even (contra Badiou) how Plato saw it. We can aspire to *philosophia* (love of wisdom), but not to *sophia* (wisdom itself). And given that 'materialism' is the sort of philosophy that replaces the real with a specific prejudiced *model* of the real (as taxonomically composed of 'thought' and 'dead matter'), we need a realism without materialism, or more generally a realism without epistemism.

Returning now to the concept of 'hyperphysics', this new polemical term is perhaps the worst consequence of Meillassoux's approach. For what he really intends here is an all-too-familiar taxonomical division of labor: science deals with inanimate things, and philosophy deals with what can be deduced from the structure of thought itself. Given his commitment to this division of labor, he will naturally be inclined to see any discussion by philosophers of inanimate nature to be either an arrogant or ludicrous trespass on the kingdom of organized science. If we characterize the post-Galilean sciences as an account of reality through the mathematization of their physical properties (though this is already a poor description of biology, for instance) we can all agree that metaphysics need not meddle in this enterprise, which science is doing well enough without us. It does not follow that philosophy must remain silent about inanimate things, or that it has no right to speak about the relations between stone and stone in the absence of any human – a surprisingly Kantian prejudice on the part of the anti-Kantian Meillassoux. For there is a specifically philosophical way of treating the theme of inanimate contact (by way of withdrawal) that has nothing to do with any purely physical discussion. Rather than permitting philosophy and science to speak about the same world in different ways (the latter yielding *knowledge*, the former unable to do so), Meillassoux chooses to carve up the world and give one part to science and the other to philosophy. And though Meillassoux seems convinced of his own originality by comparison with the post-Berkeleyan schema, his twofold taxonomy of matter and thought, that crushingly common dogma of the modern world, is surely the *least* original point in his otherwise deeply imaginative thinking.

Two Articles on Badiou

The article 'History and Event in Alain Badiou' (HE) was originally delivered as a conference paper in Paris in February 2008, and appeared in English translation three years later. Though it is mostly expository in tone, it will help prepare us for the more daring claims of a second article. Meillassoux begins by sizing up his relation to Badiou:

> I do not speak as a disciple of Alain Badiou, because I develop positions distinct from his: but it seems important to me, that if one seeks to enter into a conceptual contemporaneity with the Marxist and post-Marxist demands of politics and history, that one do so with the full scope of Badiou's system in view, a system now built around his two principal works *Being and Event* and *Logics of Worlds*. (HE 1)

Meillassoux is in fact not a disciple of Badiou because he is something much more dangerous for both: a potential *heir*. The statement just quoted is proof that Meillassoux knows this, and Badiou's laudatory words on *After Finitude* indicate that the older philosopher sees it this way as well. Despite Meillassoux's love for *ex nihilo* emergence, he would surely agree that no philosophy truly appears *ex nihilo*. The philosopher spends years of preparation that involve a great deal of reading, with feelings of strong kinship or strong dislike for much of what is read. Ultimately, a few prior figures settle in one's mind as models, and anyone inspired to create original philosophy will feel that there are certain points in those models that must either be remedied, expanded beyond their previous bounds, or even reversed. The tensions between the older and newer philosophy in any lineage are all the greater when both authors are still alive, even in cases where personal relations remain warm and supportive. It is also a fact that no one in intellectual life has the power to determine their own heir: Kant would never have chosen the German Idealists as his successors, nor would Freud have chosen Lacan. What all of this entails for us is that we need to take any remarks by Badiou and Meillassoux about each other with the greatest possible seriousness. These remarks contain almost limitless stakes for both.

The method of 'History and Event in Alain Badiou' is to explain Badiou's rather complicated philosophy through the two concepts named in the article's title: history and event. 'I will thus explain a nodal and seemingly paradoxical thesis of Badiou's: *that there is only a history of the eternal, because only the eternal proceeds from the event*' (HE 1). In arguing thus, Badiou rejects both the classical notion of eternal truths apart from history and the historicist conception that all truth belongs to a specific context and are valid in that context alone. Badiou's major 1988 work *Being and Event* contends that 'there are eternal truths, but . . . they are not unifiable in a metaphysical system, because they are distributed among four truth procedures: science, art, politics, and love – philosophy itself not having the capacity to produce truths' (HE 1). And moreover, 'these truths . . . are the result of an undecidable event and of a fidelity of subjects that attempt to investigate the world in light of it' (HE 1). As for the belated 2006 sequel, *Logics of Worlds*, it adds the notion that 'all processes lacking truth are not historical in the true sense, but have been reduced to a simple temporal modification without the capacity for truth and the subjects who adhere to it' (HE 1). While none of this is controversial or surprising as a reading of Badiou, no two commentators will simplify a thinker in exactly the same way; hence it is useful to see where Meillassoux's own emphases lie.

Most hardcore Badiouians prefer the austere rigors of *Being and Event* to the sensual concreteness of *Logics of Worlds* with its witty descriptions of countryside evenings and protests at the Place de la République. Meillassoux himself will later tell us that he prefers *Being and Event*. Nonetheless, in the present essay he spends a mere handful of pages summarizing *Being and Event*, though the pages in question are lucid enough to be worth hundreds by a less focused and invested commentator. As Meillassoux sees it, there are three chief lessons to be drawn from *Being and Event*. First, 'it is, and always has been, mathematics, *and only mathematics*, that constitutes according to Badiou, the discourse of being-qua-being ... For Badiou, the "Platonizing gesture" consists in mathematizing and not poetizing being' (HE 1–2). The implicit target here is obviously Heidegger. Second, 'ontology, for our time, is thus identified with set theory, in the sense that this theory reveals to us that any entity can be thought of as a multiple' (HE 2). Badiou is therefore an opponent of the One, not just in the sense of an all-encompassing One, but also in the sense of the many *different* ones that we call individual entities: 'Being is not therefore composed of stable and ultimate unities, but a multiplicity that is in turn composed of multiplicities' (HE 2). The multiple for Badiou is therefore an inconsistent multiplicity not made of definite units, as opposed to those consistent multiplicities of experienced units that always result from a *count*. Third, since philosophers have lost their discourse on being to the mathematicians, what they are left with 'consists in thinking being's exception – that which happens and not that which is' (HE 2). Philosophers must now think the *event*, not being. The event is an exception not allowed by the current situation, '*a multiple belonging to itself*: a reflexive multiple counted among the number of its elements' (HE 2). Events are produced according to four 'truth procedures': art, science, politics, and love, with philosophy conspicuously absent from the list.

Take a political event such as the May 1968 Student Revolution in France, honored by Badiou and Meillassoux as by so many recent French thinkers. May'68 can be viewed as an event, insofar as it was no mere bundle of facts: 'student demonstrations, the occupation of the Sorbonne, massive strikes, etc.' (HE 2). Indeed, May '68 'earned its name: that is to say that May '68 produced not only a number of facts, *but also produced May '68'* (HE 2). More generally, 'the event is that multiple which, presenting itself, exhibits the inconsistency underlying all situations, and in a flash throws into a panic their constituted classifications' (HE 2). Thus the event 'imposes another kind of procedure on whomever admits that, right here, in this place, something hitherto unnamed really and truly occurred' (HE 2). By the same token, an event can always be rejected 'by one who only believes in brute facts: is there political revolution, or merely an accumulation of disorder and crime? Amorous encounter, or merely sexual desire? Pictorial novelty, or shapeless mass and imposture? Etc.' (HE 3). Since the event immediately disappears upon occurrence, 'the fragile being of the event [is] therefore held in a trace that only a militant discourse – and not an erudite one – can draw out . . . the subject is thus the name of the faithful operations of an eventual trace, i.e. having wagered on the existence of the event, and having decided to follow out its consequences' (HE 3). Since a truth always has infinite consequences, 'a truth is the bearer of theoretical movements that form among themselves a historicity both profound and discontinuous' (HE 3). This means that it is 'capable of being extended to historical moments in profoundly different contexts' (HE 3). In turn, this entails that

> there is . . . no novelty that does not try to forge a previously unknown historical depth, by bringing together a series of ideas previously dispersed in common consciousness, in order to herald a new lineage of the present. There is no truth, as new as it may be, which does not claim to be realizing an idea that was not already germinal in a largely unknown, or misinterpreted past. (HE 3–4)

This explains the dual character of truths as both

> eternal and historical, eternal because they are historical: they insist in history, tying together temporal segments across the centuries, always unfolding more profoundly the infinity of their potential consequences, through captivated subjects, separated sometimes by distant epochs, but all equally transfixed by the urgent eventuality that illuminates their present. (HE 4)

To give full consideration to how truths always appear in a specific context, we must turn to *Logics of Worlds*, which is devoted explicitly to this theme. *Being and Event* had defined being as a pure multiplicity without totality, and even without discernible units:

> A building is a multiple of bricks, that in turn are multiples of molecules, made of a multiplicity of atoms, themselves decomposable into a multiplicity of quarks – and so on to infinity, since Badiou's ontology does not abide by the givens of contemporary physics – making of all entities a pure multiple such that one never encounters any fundamental unity. (HE 4)

Yet our experience presents us with unities of all possible kinds, and this creates a tension between the inconsistent multiplicity of being and the consistent multiplicities of appearance. Hence we must ask: 'how is it possible to have an order of appearance that does not proceed from being itself?' (HE 5). The Kantian solution holds that the subject structures the world rather than the reverse. But Badiou, as a self-described materialist, must claim instead that the subject is constituted rather than pre-given. We must also keep in mind that unlike most philosophers, Badiou does not use the term 'subject' to refer to all individual thinking humans, but gives it the special restricted sense of an individual *or* collective that remains faithful to a truth. In any case, the subject itself is not what constitutes the ordering of appearance:

> if appearance can have a consistency, it can therefore only be the result of an asubjective order, that is on the one hand connected with being – for it is always being that appears – and yet distinct from it – insofar as its order does not itself result from multiple-being. (HE 5)

This results in a theory 'of how a truth appears in a world – and in particular how the same truth – transhistorical, transworldly, and ultimately eternal – can appear in distinct worlds' (HE 5). And unlike the theory of being, in which an element either belongs or does not belong to a given multiple, the theory of appearance must account for degrees of intensity of appearance, which

> according to Badiou, is far from always obedient to the law of the excluded middle: the colorful richness of the given imposes upon us weighted judgments, of 'more or less' truth, of complex degrees

of probability, and all that faces these realities escapes the strict disjunction between affirmation and negation. (HE 5)

Despite these variations of intensity, Badiou speaks of 'invariants' that occur in different situations: whether it be the insight into prime numbers that remains the same despite different detailed understandings of them throughout history, or the invariant form of a horse in both primeval cave paintings and Picasso. But one of Badiou's clearest examples of an event, discussed repeatedly in *Logics of Worlds* and again in Meillassoux's article, is the slave revolt led by Spartacus in ancient Rome.

> The slaves united in an army constituted from then on a new type of *subject-body* tied to the production of a previously inexistent present, characterized by that which the event suddenly foresees as *possible*: this very day, to stop being slaves, and return home. (HE 6)

The fidelity of the subject-body of slaves proceeds, for Badiou, by way of *points* that mark yes/no decisions, thus leaving the kingdom of appearance and its gradations while turning back to the binary yes/no of being itself: '"Is it necessary to march to the south, or attack Rome?", "Is it necessary to confront the legions, or evade them?"' (HE 6). Yet these points also require a specific *organization* of the body in the realm of appearance, one appropriate to its concrete tasks at each moment. As a result, 'it is divided into an efficacious region, an organ appropriate to the point being treated, and, "a vast inert component"' (HE 7). Yet along with the faithful subject-body of the rebelling slaves, two other subjects are produced. There is the *reactive* subject that *denies* the rebellion: for the most part, these are slaves who come up with reasons not to participate in the revolt. And then there is the *obscure* subject who *occludes* the rebellion, denying that it has any reality at all, treating it as a mere criminal outburst. Yet there is also a fourth subject, the one who repeats the Spartacus-event as an eternal truth in a new context:

> whether it is Toussaint-Louverture, the leader of the Saint-Domingue slave revolt who was dubbed 'the black Spartacus', or whether it is Karl Liebknecht and Rosa Luxemburg, leaders of the Spartacist revolution, the Spartacus-event never ceases to be reborn, as an eternal truth, in different worlds, according to radically different contexts ... (HE 7)

For this reason, Meillassoux considers Badiou to be 'the one who was the first to understand the militant nature, and not the erudite nature, of truth' (HE 10). He also sees this as the secret to a possible Badiouian rereading of Marxism, insofar as Badiou 'isolates from Marxism its eschatological part, separates it from its pretensions – which he judges to be illusory, based on economic science – and delivers it, ardently, to subjects distributed among all kinds of struggles, political as well as amorous' (HE7).

But these fine explanations of Badiou's system merely pave the way for a less expository account in Meillassoux's 'Decision and Undecidability of the Event in *Being and Event I* and *II*'. The claim of Meillassoux in this article is that there are not just minor discrepancies of standpoint between Badiou's two major books, but a profound difference. For 'as with every genuine philosopher, Badiou made progress in his thought as he elaborated it. The thought of an authentic philosopher does not consist in submitting new domains to ready-made concepts, but simultaneously submits its own concepts to such domains, transforms them upon contact' (DU 22). The chief transformation found in *Logics of Worlds*, according to Meillassoux, is Badiou's newfound embrace of *objects*: 'The pivot on which I will support my inquiry will be the introduction of the notion of "object" into a philosophy that, up till now, refused to add it to its constitutive categories: the event, the subject, and truth' (DU 23). It should be noted that Meillassoux is no great supporter of this move. As he has it, *Being and Event* is dominated by what he calls an 'arch-anonymous' approach, and *Logics of Worlds* by an 'arch-engaged' attitude: 'Badiou, I believe, privileges henceforth the arch-engaged line of [*Logics of Worlds*]; but I will plead for my part in favor of the arch-anonymous line that seems to me to still be that of [*Being and Event*]' (DU 23).

Meillassoux considers the turn to the object to be a 'veritable rupture' (DU 23) in Badiou's thought.

> For Badiou, subject and object are two notions that can be thought without each other. And in fact, the subject was thought by Badiou for more than ten years without any correlation to an object – and it is still thought in this way in Book I of [*Logics of Worlds*] – while the object is conversely thought in an autonomous fashion in Book III, without any relation to a transcendental subject. (DU 23)

He even goes so far as to suggest that the objectless Badiou of *Being and Event* occupies a subject-centered position so strong that only Berkeley can rival it. Truth is entirely dependent on the subject alone: 'For Badiou, the rejection of the object signified above all that the event – whence originates a subjective process of fidelity through which a generic truth is hatched – must depend on the choice, the wager, the militant gesture of the subject' (DU 23). Indeed, in this period the object seems to be the very opposite of the event: 'In [*Being and Event*], it seems clear [in fact] that Badiou considers the object as that to which postivism . . . reduces presentation. The object is thus at that moment the site of a veritable foreclosure of the event' (DU 24). In short, Badiou's use of the term 'object' here is closer to Heidegger's than to my own: the object entails the reduction of reality to measurable, knowable properties. It is little wonder that a philosopher of indeterminate events would reject such a conception.

The remainder of Meillassoux's essay tries to show that there is in fact an object-turn in *Logics of Worlds*, but one that cannot be interpreted in 'positivist' terms, and hence does not sacrifice the evental indeterminacy characteristic of *Being and Event*. The turn to objects is nothing less than a 'spectacular turnaround' in which even 'the event itself can be given as an object' (DU 24), in such a way that this objecthood alone makes possible the typology of events ranging from the rather weak 'fact' to the powerful 'strong singularity'. Thus we must ask: 'has the event become the object of knowledge, and no longer of militant wager, at the same time that it has become an object? In other words, does the objectivation of the event engender what I will call a *positivization* of the event, i.e., its submission to a positive knowledge?' (DU 24). The question is rhetorical, since Meillassoux is already convinced that the object-turn implies no positivization of the object as a set of knowable properties. In order to show this, he adopts the strategy of first spelling out a positivizing interpretation of Badiou, then following up with a refutation of that interpretation.

Meillassoux has a special dramatist's talent for giving words to hypothetical adversaries, and we now see it in action once again. He introduces a new dramatic character that we will call 'the Positivizer' who argues that the event loses all of its undecidablity in *Logics of Worlds* and becomes just another scientifically knowable object. In the Positivizer's own words:

Badiou has manifestly abandoned the idea that the event is undecidable. For the event, henceforth, forms a part of knowledge in the same way that facts could do so in [*Being and Event*]. That the event in its lowest degree in [*Logics of Worlds*] is named a 'fact' is indicative of its evolution, since the fact in [*Being and Event*] designated precisely the possible object of knowledge. (DU 25)

Facts include such minimal events as 'the pathetically triumphant declaration of the [Central Committee of the Paris Commune] the very day it was crushed [in 1871]' (DU 25). At the other extreme from the fact, we find the 'strong singularity', which 'brings into existence what Badiou calls the proper inexistent of the object that supports the event, i.e., of the site' (DU 25). An example would be the Paris Commune on the date of its founding, referring to 'the political capacity of workers [which] exists maximally in the consequences of the founding act of 1870. Consequences that will inspire revolutionary struggles for a whole century' (DU 25). Midway between the fact and the strong singularity, we have the 'weak singularity':

such is, according to Badiou, the founding of the [French] Third Republic, which relies on a real popular movement, but is rapidly confiscated by politicians already evidenced by the epoch, and does not thus reveal the proper inexistent (the political capacity of workers) of the object-site. (DU 25)

Missing from all these examples is the concept of *nomination* found in *Being and Event*, a book in which 'the event required, in order to be effective, what we could call a "co-participation" of the multiple and the subject' (DU 25). Stated more clearly, in *Being and Event* 'the subject intervened not only in the labor of fidelity to the past event, but in its very constitution, since without nomination, the event itself could not occur' (DU 25). By contrast, in *Logics of Worlds* 'the event has become an object, but an object *independent* of the subject; and it occurs according to a power, an intensity of existence about which the subject can do nothing' (DU 26). In other words, it is not the subject's fidelity that determines whether the Paris Commune is crushed or the Third Republic is hijacked by mediocre career politicians. In the case of the Commune's pathetic declaration, we have 'an event whose intrinsic weakness stems from the fact that it is *uniquely* supported

by the voluntarism of the subject – and which, therefore, in no way
has the power to introduce into the world the least consequence of
its being' (DU 26). In short, 'a fact will remain a fact, whatever the
subject's ulterior intervention' (DU 26). And finally, 'the evental
object is – like every object – independent of every activity of the
subject: *there are subjectless events* – and therefore, events whose
power the fidelity of the subject cannot modify' (DU 26). Although
the subject certainly intervenes in the world in important ways, 'it
only intervenes once the event is constituted as a strong singularity
capable of producing these consequences in a world' (DU 26).

The Positivizer now closes his case. The event in *Logics of Worlds*
ceases to be indeterminate, since unlike in *Being and Event* 'there
is a possible knowledge of the event as an object entering into a
determined typology [i.e., fact, weak singularity, or strong singular-
ity], and this is indeed why we can henceforth affirm its guaranteed
existence' (DU 26). The subject's former role in lending ambiguity to
the event, given that an event 'could always be suspected of existing
solely as an arbitrary decision of nomination' (DU 26), gives way to a
subjectless field of objectively existing events that might be discerned
by knowledge. In *Being and Event*, we can never 'be assured – in
the manner of a knowledge – that there has ever existed a single
truth in the whole history of humanity' (DU 26). Yet in *Logics of
Worlds* it seems that positivism has taken command: 'an orientation
of thought capable of perturbing the history of knowledge by never
discovering therein anything other than a certain and methodical
progressison of knowledge, to the exclusion of every evental interruption' (DU 26). So, if *Logics of Worlds* really does '[suppose]
truth to be as guaranteed in its existence as an empirical fact, then
we should conclude that the event, which is its conditioning source,
has in its turn also become an equally decidable object' (DU 26).
The Positivizer finds further evidence for this in the opening pages
of *Logics of Worlds*, in which Badiou famously agrees with the
'democratic materialist' (his stated enemy in the book) that 'there
are only bodies and languages', *except* that there are truths. Badiou
then goes on to speak of truths in terms of 'empirical evidence' while
also distancing himself from the contingency of Mallarmé's thinking
by crossing out the poet's word 'perhaps' (DU 26). The later Badiou
might now seem to be on a positivist roll:

> We can thus affirm that Badiou has abandoned the romantic and vol-
> untarist sphere of [*Being and Event*], in which evental undecidability

proceeded from the creeping subjectivization of the taking-place, that is to say, from the coparticipation . . . of the subject in the event; and that Badiouianism follows henceforth the certain path of a science of the event. (DU 27)

As a result, the militants who dominated the pages of *Being and Event* now seem to be left with a clean-up mission, merely pushing events a little bit further once their existence has been confirmed by knowledgeable experts (DU 27).

Meillassoux now mounts his expected counter-attack against the Positivizer. The key point is that 'if we maintain Badiou's anti-positivism, we must still explain how the objectivization of the event does not imperil its undecidability' (DU 27). Meillassoux's strategy is even a bit reminiscent of object-oriented philosophy: 'a major originality of the theory of the subject in [*Logics of Worlds*] resides in the elaboration of a possible non-positivating objectivation, which I formulate with the statement: *there are unknown objects*' (DU 27). We saw earlier that in *After Finitude* Meillassoux lends surprising *support* to the correlational circle: the notion, lying at the basis of German Idealism, that we cannot think a thing outside thought without thereby converting it into a thought, leading to a pragmatic contradiction. Yet Meillassoux now takes the *opposite* tack in defending Badiou from the positivist: '[the fact that] the object-site, i.e., the objective event, cannot give place to a positive knowledge does not mean that it cannot be thought' (DU 27). This is obviously more Kant than Fichte, and it is perhaps more object-oriented philosophy than speculative materialism. Meillassoux concedes to the objectivist that in *Logics of Worlds* 'Badiou takes care to exclude from [the] typology [of events] every co-participation of the subject . . . this point is a major novelty of [*Logics of Worlds*] with respect to [*Being and Event*]' (DU 27). Nonetheless, Meillassoux adds, 'I diverge from the objectivist when he concludes that the subject can thus solely intervene *downstream* from the event, once the event is fully constituted, in order to faithfully, or in an unfaithful manner, deploy its consequences' (DU 27–8). For this would assume that events could occur in nature even in the absence of thinking beings. And Meillassoux is perfectly correct to note that 'there is in [*Logics of Worlds*] no example of purely "natural" events, radically foreign to every human intervention, to every subjective intervention in general. For example, there is in Badiou no description of the evolutionary emergence of species in terms of events – no evental Darwinism' (DU 28).

Meillassoux's attempt to rescue Badiou from the charge of positivism hinges on two points. First, there is the fact that an event by definition cannot exist in the sense of something stably and durably knowable: 'its paradoxical being implies that the event remains a scintillation that vanishes as soon as it appears, an ontological impossibility that can only exist as always-already abolished, about which the subject is uncertain, and about which it must decide' (DU 28). Second, Meillassoux deploys Badiou's a distinction between the 'being' and the 'existence' of an event. In short, he creates a division of labor in which the *being* of an event is undecidable or unknowable, yet in which its *type* (fact, weak singularity, or strong singularity) is perfectly knowable.

> Badiou attempts to formulate what we could call a 'militant objectivity' ... It is thus an objective knowledge, which is not a pseudo-science, since it does not pretend to be a positive science, but knows how to take its origin in the risk of a decision. (DU 28)

Badiouian truths, in other words, exist in a kind of 'unwavering fragility' that 'exempts them from every positivist reduction' (DU 28). In perhaps the most helpful formulation of the entire essay, Meillassoux notes that 'the undecidable, in Badiou, is not what *cannot* be decided, but quite the contrary, what *must* be decided' (DU 29). Or stated differently:

> [the] undecidability of the event requires the subject to decide *by itself* the existence of the event, and if it engages in it, to *resolutely* decide its existence. In reality, once the choice is made in favor of the taking-place, hesitation is not appropriate as soon as the being of the event is too weak to suffice for its own perduration in time. The event is *uniquely* sustained by the resolution of the subject ... Maxim of the event: the undecidable, yes – but not indecision. (DU 29)

Meillassoux closes the essay with further reflections on the differences between Badiou's two major systematic books. In a sense, we can say that they differ due to the character of their chief adversary. *Being and Event* fights the positivist, or the dogmatic metaphysician, and thus in this case

Badiou insists ... on knowledge's inability to reduce the undecidability of the event ... thinking the event *as such*, in its undecidable essence, before thinking it as such and such an event, effectively
engaged in a determined truth procedure. We must, then, think the
general and meta-ontological categories of eventuality – pure multiple,
subject, fidelity, truth – as properly philosophical categories. (DU 29)

Yet the philosopher is not a subject for Badiou, not being governed
by one of the four truth procedures of politics, art, science, and
love. The philosopher is instead a 'quasi-subject,' and 'we can thus
say that there is an anonymity peculiar to the philosopher, insofar
as he is the non-subject who establishes the ephemeral taking-
place of the event as such, in order to preserve it from positivist
inspection or dogmatic absolutization' (DU 30). Here Meillassoux
returns to what he called the 'arch-anonymous' perspective of
Being and Event, in which the philosopher 'speaks of the already-
anonymous event, the event that did not receive a name and is not
destined to receive one, the event as such, through a figure of non-
engagement, a retreat outside of truth, which alone enables him to
speak of truth in general, without producing it himself' (DU 30).
And again, 'maxim of the philosophical pole: do not give way on
the evental undecidable, hold fast to your necessary hesitation to
pronounce the event' (DU 30).

By contrast, the adversary of *Logics of Worlds* is 'not positivism, but *relativism* – postmodern, democratic materialism that
opposes to the tyranny of the true the indefinite and ludic plurality of historical and linguistic contexts' (DU 30). For this reason,
'the discourse of [*Logics of Worlds*] is produced from the viewpoint of the unwavering subject and no longer the philosopher
quasi-subject; or rather, from the viewpoint of ... unwavering
resolution, whose maxim would this time be: do not give way
on your decision about the undecidable' (DU 30). If the arch-
anonymous standpoint of *Being and Event* makes a good match
with the poetry of Mallarmé, the arch-engaged attitude of *Logics
of Worlds* makes a better fit with the writing of Fernando Pessoa,
who writes in the voice of countless characters other than himself.
Unlike the arch-anonymous subject, the arch-engaged subject
'thinks itself as the unity not of a single truth, but of a multiplicity of truths belonging to a multiplicity of truth procedures (DU
30). As Meillassoux sees it, this explains the sudden eruption of
autobiographical references by Badiou in the notes to *Logics of*

Worlds, a procedure that had otherwise appalled Badiou in the case of such melodramatic authors as Rousseau, Kierkegaard, or Nietzsche (DU 30).

In the wake of *Being and Event*, which insisted so stridently on the undecidability and heterogeneity of truths, Badiou wrote against terror:

> namely [against] the barbarity that does not proceed from the rejection of philosophy, but from philosophy itself, as a disaster inherent in the propensity to confound the multiple and subtractive being of truths with the plenitude of a True of which it would be the unique custodian. (DU 31)

But following *Logics of Worlds*, the reverse emphasis is made:

> the engaged voices, fully engaged in their multiple procedures, become the unfailing support of truths. To the point that Badiou no longer insists, in [*Logics of Worlds*], on the rejection of lowercase-terror, but on the legitimacy of Terror – this time in uppercase ... Thus, insistence in [*Logics of Worlds*] on uppercase-terror, in Robespierre's legacy, through which Badiou does not hesitate to convoke the necessity of an eventally extreme violence, including and above all in politics, in order to defend a truth. (DU 32)

Meillassoux finds passages in two other books of Badiou that emphasize this wavering between two attitudes towards terror. In *Conditions* (a satellite work of *Being and Event*) he defends Socrates against the terror that put him to death, while in *The Century* (a later work) he tells us not to be so sure that Fouquier-Tinville was wrong to condemn the great chemist Lavoisier to the guillotine. Meillassoux greatly favors the first of these poles: 'one of the maxims of the twenty-first century needs to be: do not give way *on* truth, do not give in *to* T/terror' (DU 33). There follows another interesting claim: 'But I add that I have always read Badiou as an essential viaticum for thinking this decoupling of truth and T/terror – for I believe there is in his System something to counter every barbaric drift of the true' (DU 33). This is to be found, he holds, in the distinction in *Logics of Worlds* between the faithful, reactive, and obscure subjects. For example, when speaking of the grisly confrontation between Fouquier-Tinville and Lavoisier, we are faced with a political truth – Robespierrist Terror – whose operator of fidelity ends up negating *another* truth procedure, that of science, of chemistry for which Lavoisier is an authentically revolutionary subject. Put differently, we discover that a same subject, supposedly faithful for one given truth procedure, *can be an obscure subject for another truth procedure.* (DU 33)

Thus, the faithful subject heads to disaster when plowing over all other truths in the name of the one that animates that subject with fidelity.

For there indeed exists aesthetically iconoclastic revolutionaries, politically reactionary brilliant authors, audacious scientists incapable of love, and timid lovers who detest the asceticism of scientists. A whole world of subjects who are simultaneously faithful and closed-minded, or worse, towards the fidelity of others. (DU 33)

This leads to a new task for the philosopher: to embody the *prudence* that would prevent each of the four truth procedures from destroying each other. 'How to decide between the exigency of political violence, which is ultimately legitimate in certain circumstances, and the incalculable destruction of amorous relations, scientific inventions, and artistic creations that this violence risks occasioning?' (DU 34). The Badiouian philosopher, according to Meillassoux, is the one 'through whom truths not only insist at the expense of opinions, but coexist at the expense of their reciprocal violence' (DU 34).

Mellassoux's account of a possible tension between different truth procedures adds a new dimension to Badiou, who too often leaves us with the impression of a simplistic conflict of faithful subjects versus reactive mediocrities and obscure oppressors. Yet there is something still missing even from Meillassoux's own account: the possibility of strife between two *different* truths within the *same* type of truth procedure. In art we have rivalries such as that between Picasso and Matisse, without it being clear that only one of these subjects was faithful – or even that both belonged to a larger subject, as Badiou tries to portray in his intriguing history of atonal music (Schoenberg/Berg/Webern) in *Logics of Worlds*. In science we have rivalries such as that between Newton and Hooke, and basic disagreements such as that between Einstein and Bohr, without it being clear that Einstein was merely 'reactive' in his misgivings about quantum theory. In the sphere of love it is even more obvious how two or more truths might and do lead to conflict. That leaves us with politics, the truth procedure where Badiou often comes across as the most dogmatic, because the most impoverished in his commitment to a single truth: 'the communist invariant', recurring across the millennia. Is it possible, instead, to develop a Badiouian politics that could take two positions seriously at the same time?

Notes

1. Levi Bryant, Nick Srnicek, and Graham Harman (eds), *The Speculative Turn*.
2. Martin Heidegger, *What Is Called Thinking?*, p. 50.
3. Slavoj Žižek and Glyn Daly, *Conversations with Žižek*, p. 41.
4. For one fascinating account of all the finely tuned physical constants needed for human life to be possible, see Martin Rees, *Just Six Numbers*.
5. For a discussion of the debate see Leonard Susskind, *The Cosmic Landscape*.
6. Alain Badiou, *Being and Event*.
7. Gilles Deleuze, *Logic of Sense*.
8. Graham Harman, 'Dwelling With the Fourfold'.
9. Alexis Philonenko, *La Liberté humaine dans la philosophie de Fichte*.
10. Isabelle Thomas-Fogiel, *Critique de la représentation: Étude sur Fichte*.
11. Ray Brassier, *Nihil Unbound*.
12. Quentin Meillassoux, personal communication, 26 March 2014.
13. Berkeley is often called a 'realist' in the theory of knowledge, since he is not a 'representationalist' in the manner of Locke, but we are speaking here of ontology.
14. Jane Bennett, *Vibrant Matter*, p. xvi.

3

The Number and the Siren

Stéphane Mallarmé is widely regarded as one of the greatest figures in the illustrious history of French literature, and is also a key figure in the writings of Badiou and Meillassoux alike. As we have seen, Meillassoux's hypothetical opponent the Positivizer interprets Badiou's distancing remarks from Mallarmé at the beginning of *Logics of Worlds* to amount to a full-blown distancing from his own concept of the undecidable event. But on top of Meillassoux's arguments against the Positivizer summarized above, he does not even agree that Mallarmé's term 'perhaps' marks the same sort of undecidability as Badiou's event. The interested reader can read the full argument for this in Meillassoux's typically lucid article 'Badiou and Mallarmé: The Event and the Perhaps' (BM).

But here we will focus instead on *The Number and the Siren*, Meillassoux's magnificent book-length treatment of Mallarmé's difficult major poem, *Un coup de dés jamais n'abolira le Hasard* (*A Throw of the Dice Will Never Abolish Chance*). Born in Paris in 1842, Mallarmé lived an improbable double life: one life as an almost comically inept schoolteacher, and another as the lionized captain of a star-studded Paris literary salon, which he hosted for many years on Tuesdays at his home near the Gare Saint-Lazare. Initially Mallarmé's most ambitious project was the plan for a new secular religion, a surprisingly common aspiration in the post-Christian nineteenth century – as seen for instance in the philosophy of Auguste Comte and the operas of Richard Wagner. The project was known as 'The Book', aptly described by Jacques Polieri as 'an absolute book, the quintessence of all literature and all reality – the Total Book. The world exists to arrive at a book, [Mallarmé] said. This book would be proclaimed by a sacred ceremony of predetermined detail, a proof as well as a communion.'[1]

The Book would be characterized by precise numerological configurations. Polieri continues:

> four books, which can be ordered as two pairs, make up The Book. Each book is subdivided into five volumes ... Each volume of each book is made up of three groups of eight pages – 24 pages in all. Each page is discrete and may be further broken down, having 18 lines of 12 words.[2]

This should suffice to indicate the rigid numerical formulae of The Book, which extend as well to the ceremonials surrounding it and the number of participants in each ceremony. The Book was also to be read according to various non-standard spatial methods:

> Mallarmé even proposes that each page be read not only in the normal horizontal way ... but backwards, or vertically, or in a selective order of omissions, or diagonally ... [Also,] the five volumes form a block. The reader looks *through* the pages, and reads according to depth. Each line of each page helps form a new vertical page. Paging is therefore three-dimensional.[3]

As to the contents of The Book, the following will give some idea: 'poem of outcry, poem of death by starvation, poem of the two women, poem of the feast.'[4] Though the project was eventually abandoned by Mallarmé, replaced by *Un coup de dés* as his destined major work, we must always remember the ambitions of The Book when trying to understand Mallarmé's greatest poem.

Meillassoux reads *Un coup de dés* as an attempt to address two crises in Mallarmé's time: the collapse of traditional French meter in the wake of the free verse invasion, and (like The Book itself) the collapse of monarchy and Catholicism. Though the poem looks at first like the wildest piece of free verse, with its strange typographical arrangement and often puzzling syntax, Meillassoux sees it as governed by the strictest numerical necessity, and hence as the heir to the failed project of The Book. His manner of showing this may be surprising, and is introduced in the very first words of the book:

> Let us come straight to the point: This book proposes to bring to light a procedure of *encryption* housed within Stéphane Mallarmé's *Coup de dés*. This procedure, once deciphered, allows the precise determination of the 'unique Number' enigmatically evoked in the poem. We thus claim:

a) that Mallarmé's poem is coded;
b) that the ability to read this code is a condition of the true comprehension of *Coup de dés*, since it elucidates one of its essential components, namely the Nature of the number. (NS 3)

More specifically, Meillassoux will demonstrate that the number 707 is the 'unique number' spoken of in the poem itself, thereby saving us (or so Mallarmé hopes) from the arbitrariness of both modern secular life and modern free verse. This claim might easily provoke laughter, since secret codes are usually viewed as a trifle for pre-adolescents. More than this, almost all Mallarmé scholars have concluded that there is no code hidden in the poem. Consider the philosopher Jacques Rancière, for instance: 'Mallarmé is not a *hermetic* author, he is a difficult author' (NS 4).[5] But Meillassoux does in fact argue that Mallarmé *is a coded author*, leading to an analysis that is nothing short of a masterpiece. As Meillassoux notes, 'it would hardly be surprising if [Mallarmé's] calculating obsession had been propagated from one text [The Book] to the other [*Coup de dés*]' (NS 7). Indeed, it is Meillassoux's opinion that Mallarmé scholars deny this obvious link precisely because they hope that Mallarmé repudiated The Book (NS 8), a visibly extravagant project that can cause embarrassment just as the quasi-religious projects of Comte and Wagner sometimes do. But Meillassoux contends that Mallarmé never really abandoned The Book, and that the existence of a code in his greatest poem proves that its spirit lived on.

As with much of Mallarmé's poetry, it can be difficult even to grasp the literal scene depicted in *Coup de dés*. There has been a shipwreck, though the ship itself is no longer visible. Someone called the 'Master' is still afloat, holding a pair of dice in one fist, hesitant as to whether or not he should throw them. The Master then disappears beneath the sea, with only his cap and its plume left behind, moving towards a whirlpool. A Siren appears from this vortex and uses her tail to smash the rock that caused the shipwreck. At the end of the poem we still do not know if the Master threw the dice or not, but once the feather of the Master's cap is swallowed by the sea, we *perhaps* see a constellation similar or identical to the one known in French as the Septentrion: in the Anglophone world this is called *Ursa Major* (the Great Bear), of which the famous Big Dipper forms one part. The constellation that we *perhaps* see 'seems to be set in motion as if by a celestial

Throw supplementing that of the Master, with an outcome described as "consecrated" – the stars being identified with the points of a nocturnal Die' (NS 17–18). Also worthy of note is that the final seven words of the poem, which seem to be set off from the others, run as follows: *Toute Pensée émet un Coup de Dés* (*Every Thought emits a Throw of Dice*). Furthermore, there are two mentions in the poem of the 'Number', which Meillassoux will slowly conclude should be identified as 707.

One of the few other commentators to have argued for a secret code in Mallarmé's poem was Mitsou Ronat, a prominent opponent of the Kristeva/Sollers *Tel Quel* group, who died tragically in a car accident in 1984 while still a young woman. It is fairly clear that Mallarmé's plans for The Book were dominated by the number 12, and Ronat claimed to observe this dodecaphilia in *Coup de dés* as well. Yet Meillassoux and others reject this claim, since it relies too heavily on claims about pagination that cannot withstand scrutiny of the poem's manuscript – not yet available during Ronat's lifetime. Meillassoux continues: 'If Ronat's thesis had been correct, it would have placed the *Coup de dés* in strict continuity with *Igitur*, that unfinished tale composed in 1869 and published in 1925, well after the poet's death' (NS 28). In this story, Igitur enters the family tomb, 'there to carry out, at midnight, a decisive act: a throw of dice whose intent is to see whether it will yield a 12' (NS 28). Like the Master in *Coup de dés*, Igitur is hesitant about the throw, thereby establishing an obvious link with the later poem, as does the link between *Igitur*'s midnight and the 'midnight cap' of the Master in the later poem. Yet Meillassoux regards the number 12 as a failed solution to define a unique number, as seen from the non-completion of the story. As a lucky victorious dice-throw, 12 cannot live up to the *infinity* of chance, which ought to encompass both the usual mediocre results of the dice as well as dramatic winning throws. Furthermore, 'to affirm resolutely the value of 12 is still to dream of the perfect alexandrine' (NS 33), the classic 12-syllable French poetic meter, which given *Igitur*'s association of the number 12 with a lucky throw means that 'this alexandrine would be but the result of chance, and not its negation' (NS 33).

Yet Meillassoux amasses ample evidence that a numerical code does exist in the poem, evidence that is hard to reconcile with any theory of mere coincidence. Following the evident failure of Ronat's search for a hidden code in the poem, we seem to be left with what Meillassoux calls an 'ironist' reading of the poem, in which the Master's hope of a unique number was necessarily fruit-less. This seems to be bolstered by words in the poem that run as follows: 'anxious expiatory and pubescent mute laugh that if it was the Number it would be Chance' (NS 35), apparently meaning that even the number could only be the result of chance, and there-fore not a truly *unique* number. But there is an internal textual reason why this ironist reading fails: given that the shipwreck is what triggered the Master's *hope* for a unique number, it could not also trigger ironic resignation in the abandonment of such hope. As Meillassoux emphatically puts it: '*it is the shipwreck – the very ruin of classical verse – that, for him, holds out the promise of the Number*' (NS 37). The fact that both the ironist reading and Ronat's search for a code seem to fail 'brings out the core of the difficulty: *The title of the poem* [*A Throw of the Dice Will Never Abolish Chance*] *. . . contradicts the Master's inference*; but there is nothing to justify us in affirming that one or the other of them is false' (NS 37). The only possible solution is to find some way in which *both* claims – the cryptographical and the ironic – are true. Meillassoux finds just such a solution by re-reading the words 'mute laugh that if it was the Number it would be Chance' more literally than before. It is not that the number would be the *effect* of chance, and hence purely arbitrary, but that the number itself would *be* chance. 'In other words, if we obtain the Number that can be identified with Chance, *it would possess the unalterable eternity of contingency itself . . .*' (NS 39).

The value of constructing the poem around a unique number is that, in fusing the evidently wild free verse of *Coup de dés* with the non-arbitrary rigors of a unique number, Mallarmé will have constructed an actual poetic synthesis of regular and free verse, rather than simply recommending a division of labor of the two. In this way, *Coup de dés* will have achieved a 'performative' dimen-sion, enacting the solution of the crisis of verse rather than merely referring to it. If we look at the last page of the poem, only one number is mentioned: in the reference to the constellation of the Septentrion, '*Sept*' (French for 'seven') obviously refers to the seven stars in the constellation. And given that the Septentrion contains what we in English call the Big Dipper, which points in turn to the North Star, the number 7 seems 'destined to become the new North of modern poetry' (NS 43). There are other beautifully sig-nificant associations as well. There is the ironic fact that whereas the 12 of *Igitur* is (along with 2) the rarest result of a dice-throw, 7 is the most common. Also of interest is that '7 is the number of rhymes in a sonnet, undoubtedly the most perfect poetical form in Mallarmé's eyes, since the most continually practiced by him' (NS 45). There is also a remarkable indication in Mallarmé's notes for The Book. We have already seen that 12 is the dominant number of The Book, though not (despite Ronat's expectations) of *Coup de dés* itself. Yet 5 is also a prominent number in the unpublished drafts for The Book. Why this prominence of the number 5, so apparently unrelated to the parameters of known verse structures in French? 'Mallarmé, in his Notes, responds indirectly to this question: *The Number internal to The Book will be the reciprocal of 5 to obtain 12*. In other words, one need only take the 5 from the 12 to give the result: 12 − 5 = 7' (NS 48). Before responding with skepticism to all these claims about numbers, it should be remembered that the poet 'is precisely [the] one who submits language to a count, and more especially to the count of syllables so as to guarantee their meter' (NS 49).

There is still more evidence available testifying to the importance of the number 7. The final line of the poem seems to be special, in its simplicity and its lack of interpolations. Note that this line contains exactly seven words: '*Toute Pensée émet un Coup de Dés*' ('Every Thought emits a Throw of Dice'). If this final phrase is the key to the poem, then it must somehow stands outside of it, not included in the word count. Given the length of the poem, we can estimate that its total of words will run into three digits. Will the poem – up through the word '*sacré*' or 'sacred', not including the final seven-word 'key' – total exactly 777 words, then? We should also remember that the number 0 also plays a role for Mallarmé, as 'an obvious symbol of Nothingness or of the night upon whose ground the Septentrion appears' (NS 51). For this reason we should also consider 700, 707, and 770 as candidates for the unique number. At the same time, we should not confine our argument to a mere word count, since this could always amount to a mere coincidence. For this reason, we need to obtain 'a *twofold* verification of the Number, and thus of the code: once through the count, and once through the text' (NS 53).

Meillassoux notes that the theme of decapitation runs throughout Mallarmé's career, from an 1864 prose poem that ends with the decapitation of a young child, to the *Noces d'Hérodiade*, 'whose prelude sees the head of John the Baptist intoning a victory song at the very instant that the executioner separates it from his body' (NS 56). Shifting now to *Coup de dés* itself, we find nothing less than a *symbolic decapitation* of the Master: for other than his fist clutching the dice, only the Master's head is visible above the waves, and later his hat with its feather (a writer's quill) floats above the water, as if to emphasize the solitude of the head. Meillassoux now makes startling use of a passage from Bertrand Marchal's commentary on Mallarmé, which points to a three-fold meaning of the French word *si* (the English 'if'), so pivotal in both *Coup de dés* and the *Noces d'Hérodiade*. In one sense it simply means 'if,' just as in everyday French. Yet *si* also evokes the musical note of that name (*Do Re Mi Fa Sol La Si Do*) in which Si is the *seventh* note of the scale. And what is the etymology of Si as the name of the musical note? Marchal tells us it is well known that Si stands for *Sancte Ioannes*: John the Baptist. In other words, the key phrase *comme si* in *Coup de dés* can be literally read to mean 'as if', but can also be read as meaning 'like the seventh musical note' or 'like John the Baptist'. Above all, we must not forget that *si* is both the central word of Mallarmé's greatest poem (*Un coup de dés*) and the first word of his final poem (*Les Noces d'Hérodiade*).

According to Meillassoux, the two occurrences of the phrase *comme si* ('as if') in the poem should both be read as meaning 'like 7', referring to the first and last digits of the number 7–7. The missing digit in the center remains in doubt: should it be 0, 7, or some other number? By looking to what happens in the poem between the two instances of *comme si*, we find our answer: 'what the central text speaks of is the whirlpool or "vortex", the "gulf" that carries away everything, situated as it is in the abyssal folding of the Poem at its center' (NS 67). This clearly suggests that 707 is the very number we seek. Meillassoux also invites us to perform a reading trick that would seem preposterous if not for Mallarmé's obvious obsession with the typographical organization of his major works. If we look at page viii of the French text of the poem, we will notice the word *SI* in larger type than any other word on the page. If we then turn suddenly to page ix, we find at the top other words in a similarly large typeface: *C'ÉTAIT LE NOMBRE*. The effect of this trick is that the poem tells us 'SI: IT WAS THE NUMBER', or rather 'SEVEN: IT WAS THE NUMBER'.

From all of this Meillassoux concludes that 707 is the number, is chance itself. Both beginning and ending with 7, 707 'rhymes'

the number 7, or acts (in Hegelian fashion) as the 'negation of
the negation' of 7. In one of several moments of glowing self-
confidence in the book, Meillassoux finishes off his analysis with
words we might expect to find in a religious text: 'Thus it is illuminated' (NS 77). And indeed, *sacré* ('sacred') proves to be the 707th
word of the poem, followed by the final seven-word 'key': *Toute
Pensée émet un Coup de Dés*. But more evidence is already on the
way. There are two other poems by Mallarmé preceding *Coup
de dés* that seem to be closely related to it, given their concern
with shipwrecks, sirens, and the undecidable hypothesis: 'Salut'
and 'À la nue accablante tu . . .' (NS 81). A word count yields the
remarkable result that 'Salut' contains exactly 77 words (NS 81),
and we also discover that this poem was first read at the *seventh*
banquet of *La Plume* (NS 84). As for 'À la nue accablante tu . . .',
since this poem is much darker in tone than the other, we are not
surprised when our count yields exactly 70 words (NS 82–3). For
those readers who still suspect a mere coincidence, let it be noted
that both poems retain their word counts (77 and 70, respectively)
in *all* draft versions despite textual changes in both (NS 87). Thus
it is illuminated. Thus ends a *tour de force* of poetic decoding.

We now have less time to cover the fascinating Part Two of
Meillassoux's book, which partially undercuts the certitude of Part
One even while increasing our appreciation of it. As Meillassoux
will amusedly note after complicating the results of Part One, 'it
may be that the reader, having resisted the idea that the *Coup de
dés* could be coded, now resists the idea that the code could be
seriously put in doubt by such trifles' (NS 213). What then are
these 'trifles' of which he speaks? We confine ourselves to the most
significant. First, imagine for a moment that *Coup de dés* had
instead been blatantly entitled 'Ode to the Number 707', perhaps
accompanied by a Mallarmé essay explaining why 707 must be
the unique number that saves us from the crisis of free verse. The
effect of this could only be ridiculous. Some find a similar ridicu-
lousness in the rather less overt operas of Wagner, which have
an equally hubristic ambition to save music, and indeed German
culture as a whole. In Meillassoux's own words:

> To figure upon a scene the relation of humans and their gods, to render
> visible to the masses the principle of their communion with the aid of a
> narrative embellished with song – in short, to *represent* to a people its
> own mystery: such is for Mallarmé the Greek heritage upon which art,

including Wagnerian art, continues to feed. But according to the poet, *it is precisely representation that art must break with* if it would claim to go beyond Christianity. (NS 108)

But in attempting to go beyond Christianity, Mallarmé seems to draw on that religion's own foremost weapon:

Christianity has handed down to us a ritual superior in power to those of paganism – namely the *real convocation of a real drama*. The drama is, of course, that of the Passion, taken as historical by Christians, and which the Mass, 'prototype of ceremonials,' does not represent as would a piece of theater, but of which it claims to produce the true, effective Presence, to the point where the host is absorbed by the faithful. Now here is what [Wagner's headquarters] Bayreuth could not offer, since in view of forging a new political unity, it offered only the 'Greek' compound of (Nordic) legend and scenic devices. This is why the office of the Mass can never be replaced by the communions of total art . . . (NS 108–9)

Yet the presence of Christ in the Mass is not that of the presence of the Norse god Wotan in Wagner's Ring Cycle. For 'the Eucharist . . . even if it is a real Presence of the Son of Man in the course of the Mass, is not his full presentation . . .' (NS 111). Meillassoux continues: 'The Eucharist is thus a paradoxical mode of "presence in absence" . . . It gives itself according to a sufficiently withdrawn mode of reality to leave room for both remembrance (the Passion) and expectation (of Salvation)' (NS 111).

Now, it would also be ridiculous for Mallarmé or others to continue the theme of 707 in a series of further poems. The unique number needs to be *unique*, occurring just once in one poem only. In the same fashion, the Passion of Christ needed to occur just once in order to retain its power by splitting history in half: if Christ were to return to earth and somehow be crucified a second time, this would approximate a Monty Python comedy sketch; 707 must have a kind of withdrawal, a presence-in-absence, and this is precisely what it has thanks to Mallarmé's act of encryption. Though no message in a bottle appears in Mallarmé's poem,

he *actually threw such a bottle . . . Coup de dés . . .* [is] not just a text but an *act*. The Poem . . . acquires . . . a performative dimension, in becoming the very act that it describes. And this act is of a very precise nature: It is a *wager*. The Number is thrown, beyond Mallarmé's death, into the chaotic seas of historical reception. (NS 116)

But rather than entrusting his Number to God, he entrusts it to *chance*, inaccessible to any rational deduction. For there is no other way to discover the code, Meillassoux, claims, than through chance: 'Our knowledge of the poet was of no use whatsoever in decrypting the poem' (NS 121).

The mystery we discover through our discovery of the Number is nothing less than Mallarmé's own personal drama, characterized by two fundamental risks. First, there was a very good chance that his code would never have been discovered, if not for Meillassoux's book. In this way, Mallarmé sacrifices not his *body* in the manner of Christ, but the very *meaning* of his work (NS 122). The second risk was that the code would be discovered and ridiculed by a more cynical critic than Meillassoux: 'The denunciation by future readers of a bogus mystery ("so it was only that . . .") was an intrinsic possibility of an encryption that, in itself, is indeed but a puerile thing' (NS 123). The fact that the content of the poem (secret number 707) is so impoverished separates Mallarmé from 'those gimcrack spiritualities that had flooded the literature of his time' (NS 124). Nor is Mallarmé's secret a *hermetic* one in the strict sense, given that 'its transmission is not assured by a continuous line of initiates, but instead implies a (potentially definitive) discontinuity between its author and his successors' (NS 124–5).

The usual reading of the poem is that the Master is ultimately unable to decide whether or not to throw the dice (NS 131). But Meillassoux puts a different spin on the problem, one strikingly reminiscent of his method in *After Finitude*, where he converted our epistemological uncertainty about whether anything was necessary into an ontological certitude that everything must be contingent. Namely, Meillassoux displaces the uncertainty from the drowned Master onto the unique number itself. He does this by rereading the number 707 as a *quavering* 707 that blurs into its neighbors (NS 138). 'The solution is simple: it would suffice that the code elucidated above should *contain an indeterminacy*' (NS 141). Meillassoux now takes a long but interesting detour concerning Mallarmé's position on whether or not to pronounce the silent *e* in French verse (NS 167–85), a point that will soon become crucial in his discussion of the Siren in *Coup de dés* (NS

186–98). Just as we needed an *internal* confirmation of the code 707 in the text rather than a mere word count, we also need an *internal* confirmation of the quavering of this number and not just a count that slightly misses the mark, which could always be the result of trivial mistakes on Mallarmé's part or our own (NS 186). Meillassoux claims to find such internal evidence in the episode of the Siren. In the first place, page viii, where the Siren appears, is nearly plastered with words ending in silent *e*. But even more tellingly, the word *muet* (or 'silent') appears midway down the page. Meillassoux thus concludes that 'the episode of the siren, placed under the aegis of the "veiled" letter, suggests that it is the question of the strict rule and of its relaxation that is going to be broached' (NS 192). He argues further that both the Master and the Siren are Mallarmé himself: a beheaded John the Baptist returned as Christ (NS 196–7).

Having seen these *internal* references to a 'quavering' unique number, we should ask if the quavering can be found in the word count itself. Indeed it can. Meillassoux shares a bit of his own authorial story with us:

> During the first few months of our investigation, we regularly recounted the words of the Poem to assure ourselves that we had not been mistaken about the code. Now, to our perplexity, it happened that we did so one day and failed to arrive at the 'correct' count. In its place, we found a number hardly more or less than 707: 708, 706, 705 . . . We did eventually find our error and find the required Number again. But this episode also unveiled for us the most profound dimension of the poem. (NS 198–9)

The misfired counts did not result from sloppiness or inattentiveness on Meillassoux's part, but from the presence of exactly *three* compound words in the poem. Oddly, two of the three have no hyphen, even though they normally have one in contemporary French: *par delà* and *au delà*, both of which might be translated as 'beyond', giving them an implied cosmic significance (NS 199). Also strange is that *au delà* is used not as a preposition but as a substantive, in the sense of *the* beyond – yet no definite article is present. The poem says *au delà*, not *l'au delà*, which makes the lack of a hyphen seem rather deliberate, as if Mallarmé were drawing our attention to this irregularity as the key to some secret (NS 200). But given that *au delà* and *par delà* are not hyphenated, and given that the third compound word *is* hyphenated, the method suggests itself of counting the first two as two words apiece, while counting the hyphenated third compound as only one. And this is the method that yields the expected 707.

What, then, is the third compound word, the one with the hyphen? It is none other than *peut-être*, the English 'perhaps', one of the key words of the poem given its reference to chance. 'And perhaps this was the secret ambition of the *Coup de dés*: to write the most beautiful *peut-être* in the French language, the cause of itself in its letters of fire' (NS 214). The book concludes with suitably weighty claims: 'Thus, modernity triumphed and we did not know it' (NS 221). All of the apparently failed efforts of the nineteenth century to '[extract] messianism from its Christian matrix ... all this would nevertheless have succeeded in making *one* breakthrough up to our times, one only, and at a precise point – a unique Poem that would traverse the twentieth century like a hidden gem, finally to reveal itself, in the following century, as the strangely successful defense of an epoch we had buried under our disenchantments' (NS 222).

Notes

1. Jacques Polieri, 'Le livre de Mallarmé: A Mise en Scène', p. 180.
2. Ibid.
3. Ibid., p. 181.
4. Ibid.
5. Jacques Rancière, *Mallarmé: The Politics of the Siren*, p. xiv.

4

The Divine Inexistence

In 1997, the same year in which he turned thirty years old, Quentin Meillassoux received his doctorate with an audacious thesis entitled *L'Inexistence divine*, or *The Divine Inexistence*. When Badiou refers to Meillassoux's *After Finitude* as 'a fragment from a particularly important philosophical . . . enterprise' (AF vi) this is the work to which he is alluding. But despite the term 'fragment', the pages of *After Finitude* are nowhere to be found within those of *The Divine Inexistence*. And despite the expected degree of conceptual overlap between two works by the same philosopher, the term 'correlationism' does not even appear in the longer work, and their respective range of subject matter is different enough that it would be better to describe both works as fragments of a longer philosophical trajectory. We should also emphasize the unusual status of *The Divine Inexistence*, which is probably the most famous work in present-day continental philosophy that no one has read, with the exception of a handful of dauntless archivists who may have consulted the microfilm resources of the École Normale Supérieure, and those shadowy figures who hawk the pirate edition online. But while the book has never been published, it has already become famous: through the printed remarks of Badiou, and the hypothetical public musings of Meillassoux's fellow Speculative Realists.

With the publication of the present book, the situation has changed. When arrangements for this book were being made with Edinburgh University Press, I asked Meillassoux for a copy of the most up-to-date version of his manuscript. This was no easy request: Meillassoux's notable perfectionist tendencies often lead him to withhold work from publication for years, with the admitted benefit that his published works always have a sparkling polish and precision that would meet the standards of the most ruthless

civil engineer. Somewhat to my surprise, Meillassoux agreed to let
me see the manuscript for the purposes of composing the present
chapter. However, he added a reasonable proviso that eventually
changed the shape of this book: namely, I was permitted to write
about *The Divine Inexistence* only on the condition that the relevant portions of that work be contained in my own book as an
appendix. And given the obvious absurdity of attaching a long
French appendix to a book published by Edinburgh University
Press, I found myself with a medium-sized translation project on
my hands.

The Appendix to this book contains approximately 27,000
words in English, translated from the 2003 version of
Meillassoux's manuscript. In all, it amounts to roughly one-sixth
of the total manuscript as of that date. But in the meantime, the
original project has been reorganized and expanded, with the
ultimate French version probably running to three volumes, and
still with no definite publication date. During the summer of
2010, I selected fourteen representative excerpts from the work
for translation. Given the large number of cuts that had to be
made, they are not always consecutive, though all occur in their
proper order in the Appendix. For the most part, I removed
those sections whose ideas were already familiar to readers of
Meillassoux's published works, though in the first few excerpts
there was no way to avoid striking a familiar note. Some of the
most painful cuts were of sections where Meillassoux reflects
brilliantly on figures from the history of philosophy; several
passages on Hegel and Heidegger were of especial interest. But
it seemed better to emphasize Meillassoux's own systematic
work than to focus on his historical commentaries, however
interesting.

Despite all this compulsory editing for reasons of space, it is
my view that the resulting selection *does* read somewhat like a
unified book. We encounter a satisfying development of themes,
a consistent vision of cosmic and human history as composed of
sudden leaps, and a conclusion even more stunning than that of
'Subtraction and Contraction', given that in this case Meillassoux
actually *believes* the conclusion. While many present-day readers
will find it hard to endorse the results of *The Divine Inexistence*,
it continues to develop a 'non-Euclidean philosophy' of a sort that
grows on the reader over time, and which is sufficiently interesting
to draw thousands of adherents once it is better understood. If we

remove all necessity from the laws of nature, thereby removing any question of probability or improbability, the world begins to look like a very different place. Rather than confining ourselves to likely events that might unfold within a framework of real necessity, we turn to the structural features of the framework itself, which turn out to be no more likely or unlikely than any possible modification of them. We surf along the contours of the logically possible, treat all such possibilities as equally likely, and then focus not on the ones that would be most 'probable', but on those that would be ontologically the most important. In the interview found in this volume, Meillassoux concedes that given the disappearance of sufficient reason, unicorns or flying spaghetti monsters might appear just as easily as the virtual God (QM 220). But such monstrous beasts would change nothing as to the nature of the real, while the virtual God would mark a next great step in the cosmos – indeed, the final great step.

Advent

The term 'advent' is a translation of the French *surgissement*, though I will occasionally use 'sudden advent' for purposes of emphasis. For those cases in which Meillassoux uses the related verb *surgir*, I have chosen to avoid the absurd English equivalent 'advene' and have generally chosen 'emerge' or 'arise' instead. The English word 'advent' already has the flavor of something that happens suddenly and with overwhelming force, as in the phrase 'the advent of Islam'. But Meillassoux's term pushes things even further, since for him it is always an advent without any reason at all, and hence something radically novel in comparison with what came before. Like the Bergson of *Matter and Memory*, Meillassoux is fully committed to immanence. Nothing is hiding outside the world or beyond the scope of human knowledge that could provide a cryptic causal depth for a world of appearances. Immanence 'implies a world with nothing outside that could limit its power of novelty' (DI 224). If anything other than the world itself were the source of novelty, 'time would essentially be poor, since what followed this Origin could be no better than a diminishing of it' (DI 225). There is no secret principle 'hidden away in the secret drawer of a demiurge' (DI 225), and reason teaches us that there is nothing illogical about sudden changes for no reason at all even if our senses proclaim the relative stability of the world.

Hence, 'if we think advent in its truth, it is an advent *ex nihilo* and thus *without any reason at all*' (DI 225).

Although Meillassoux glosses this principle as saying that there is more in the effect than in its cause (DI 226), he actually means a lot more than this; many philosophers would be willing to endorse an excess of effects over their originating causes, without enlisting in a Meillassouxian universe where there is no necessary link between effect and cause at all. To place the power of innovation in the hands of a transcendent God is to deprive the world itself of any such power. Good sense always 'wants the originary real to be richer than what ensues from it' (DI 226), but the inexistence of God allows us to secularize the forces of novelty. For 'the world is by no means the power of whatever arises within it, because this advent concerns the *sum total* of what belongs to it' (DI 226). The change or even stability of the world itself is '*without reserve* . . . [having] no substrate of becoming, no determinate substance that remains unchanged amidst change' (DI 226). There is no better example of a philosophy of immanence than these statements by Meillassoux. In a sense, the whole of *The Divine Inexistence* aims only to develop the conception of an immanent God, albeit one that does not yet exist and might never exist.

In *The Divine Inexistence* just as in *After Finitude*, the Cantor-inspired collapse of probability not only renders all sudden changes possible; it also entails that change need not occur at all. 'For to affirm that the transformation of laws *ought* to occur as long as it *can* occur is once more to subordinate the contingency of becoming to the necessity of a law that all possibilities must ultimately be actualized' (DI 226–7). In other words, 'a world that is capable of everything ought *also* to be capable of not accomplishing those things of which it is capable' (DI 227). The world has 'the eternal capacity to produce or *not* to produce new laws' (DI 227). Belief in the stability of laws is in fact *irrational*, since reason follows the law of non-contradiction, and there is nothing contradictory about sudden alteration of the laws of nature. In this philosophy, 'nothing is supposed concerning the world in its present, past, or future state: the contingency of laws forbids us to say what disruption (if any) has occurred or will occur, or whether the world exempted from all necessity might remain indefinitely stable' (DI 227).

Meillassoux's next concern is to demonstrate that there is no

mystery about the apparently miraculous appearance of life and
thought from material reality. This is not because he agrees with
the scientistic program of *reducing* life and thought to matter.
Quite the contrary: he sees the progression from matter to life to
thought as a series of sudden leaps not contained in germ in what
came before. He eliminates the mystery of life and thought not
by creating a tough-minded Empire of Matter beneath the gullible delusions of an autonomous biological or cognitive sphere,
but by saying that life and thought emerged for no reason at all.
Since Cantor's transfinite implies that possible universes cannot
be indexed as a list of possible cases of some wider Universe of
Universes, 'the emergence of these universes is an advent literally
ex nihilo, for it is irreducible to the actualization of some sort
of potentiality that would be pre-existent in the supposedly perpetual Universe-Whole of what is able to happen' (DI 228). Since
advent is *ex nihilo*, we arrive at an *irreligious* concept of pure
novelty. Many immanentist philosophers would want nothing
to do with the concept of the *ex nihilo*, but Meillassoux is not
troubled by their objections, since 'suspicions against the idea
of origin are always based on the same prejudice: the problem
of origin or of the originary advent of novelty is linked with the
religious theme of Creation. As such, it is viewed as meaningless
or uninteresting for a thinking of immanence' (DI 228). Disputes
over how life or thought originated quickly polarize into an
atheist camp that denies any problem, and a theist camp that cel-
ebrates its triumph over the atheist's inability to explain how life
and thought emerged. At bottom both camps are the same, since
even the atheist 'transposes the religious ban on thinking about
the origin into the sphere of rationality. The origin of novelty is
supposed to be unthinkable for a purely human understanding'
(DI 228).

The key problem, Meillassoux holds, is that rationality is
usually identified with a commitment to the constancy of laws
of nature. This makes it difficult to think about the origins of life
and matter, 'because it cannot be understood how the lifeless can
produce a qualitative multiplicity of affects and perceptions from
a certain "molecular geometry"' (DI 229). As he sees it,

[the] affective contents of living and thinking beings were obviously
not contained in the actually existing particles that presided at their
formation . . . This essential excess of life and thought beyond matter

implies a scission that ruptures all continuity, leaving the divine and the soul free rein to fill in the resulting chasm. (DI 229)

Novelty is not true novelty if it can be explained by what preceded it. Even if life and thought have a 'possibly regular concordance with material complexes [this] does not obliterate the radical excess found in the affective qualities of suffering or jubilation and the travails of life or consciousness' (DI 229). The only hope of accounting for novelty, in short, is to view it as advent *ex nihilo*. 'No affections . . . exist before they seize an organism, and no perception or thought haunts a matter supposedly sensitive enough to be myopic, and stupid enough to have confused thoughts' (DI 229). Life and thought are the first two major cases of advent from nothing, and Meillassoux will later add a third and ultimate advent: justice. This justice is the crowning notion of *The Divine Inexistence*.

In fact, we can say that *all* quality emerges *ex nihilo*, 'since none of its content refers to anything other than the advent *ex nihilo* of its being' (DI 230). It is absurd to ask why red is red: 'no material counterpart can ever tell us how this red is red' (DI 230). We cannot write a genealogy of red in terms of any physical basis. As Meillassoux puts it in one of his loveliest passages:

> there was *nothing* of this red in the world prior to its advent that would give us a reason by relating it to a pre-red where it had always been contained. For matter is not haunted by any potentiality of red, any pale pink specter, before the advent of red among the sensitive powers of the living. (DI 230)

In a sense, Meillassoux's entire philosophy can be read as a polemic against pale pink specters, as well as pale light brown trees, pale fleshy pre-humans, and pale transparent gods; entities exist only following their advent *ex nihilo*, and no sooner. 'If quality arises, it does so *from nothing*, not from the potentiality of a Universe-Whole where it would have lain in ambush for all eternity' (DI 230). Meillassoux pursues the point further. The usual materialist approach holds that life is a potentiality locked in matter, and that it necessarily arises from a certain configuration of that matter. 'This would amount to the claim that the affects are a possible property of matter in the same manner as nuclear fission' (DI 230). The claim is that life and thought lie dormant in matter, with certain 'tendencies' toward them later appearing in full-blown form. But for Meillassoux matter is purely lifeless, with no incipient life harbored in its depths, and this fact 'imposes a pure discontinuity between matter and vital content' (DI 231). Every consistent materialism soon turns into *hylozoism*. With life supposedly present in everything, the difference between full-blown life and dormant pre-life will be described in terms of 'intensive difference'. But Meillassoux is unimpressed by this claim: 'we know that no such monism of intensive differences has ever solved anything' (DI 231). For though we might claim that every difference is a difference of degree, the fact remains that 'despite what has been said of Rodin, there was nothing of intensified marble about him' (DI 231). The young Bergson of *Time and Free Will*[1] already knew that intensity was simply a way of '[masking] qualitative discontinuity by means of mathematical continuity' (DI 232).

But in addition to dissolving the supposed mystery of the emergence of sentient qualities from matter, we can push the problem back another level and note the apparent improbability that even the material structures associated with life would ever have emerged.

> Indeed, the advent of material configurations that could support life or thought now seem *highly unlikely* in the light of known physical laws, whether we are speaking of the appearance of the first constituents of life, of the evolution of species, or of the emergence and evolution of the human brain. (DI 232)

Chance apparently fails to explain such events, and the unfortunate result is that 'the need again seems to arise for some sort of enigmatic principle of finality, since religiosity continues to look like the only alternative to algebraic rationality' (DI 232). It might be assumed that science can explain the rise of material animal bodies and human brains, leaving only perceptual qualia and absolute thought as sudden, unpredictable emergences from otherwise calculable physical matter. But in fact, it might be the case that 'like all radical novelty, the advent of life ... *is accompanied by the simultaneous advent of material configurations that rupture with the physical laws in the midst of which they emerge*' (DI 232). Even further, it might be that the advent of life is *no different* from the advent of its proper material configurations. But this would simply indicate that matter itself does not obey any necessary laws.

Nature is no longer a riddle. 'Our astonishment in the face of the enigma of the constancy of laws, or of the sudden advent of life, ceases to point toward a mystery exceeding reason' (DI 233). It is immanence, or non-Whole. And it is not only immanence, but a *contingent* immanence. 'To identify rationalism with the eternity of natural, deterministic, or frequential laws is to render thought powerless before originary phenomena, and ultimately to resign oneself to acknowledging a transcendent foundation' (DI 236). By contrast, Meillassoux recognizes no transcendent law, but divides the world into several stages of advent, which he calls 'three *orders* that mark the essential ruptures of becoming: *matter, life*, and *thought*' (DI 236). For 'each of these three appears as a Universe that cannot be *qualitatively* reduced to anything that preceded it' (DI 236). We may be greatly impressed by the emergence of vertebrate species, the appearance of agriculture after the long hunter-gatherer era, or the first appearance of stars in the universe. But for Meillassoux the distinct orders of reality are strictly limited to matter, life, thought, and justice. Only the latter has not yet emerged, and indeed it may never emerge.

Immortality

We are now familiar with Meillassoux's theory of the immanent advent of new realities *ex nihilo*, in which no rock is contained in germ in some pale stony specter pre-dating the rock itself. He now introduces us to his immanent conception of ethics. All immanent theories hold that comprehensible truths are the only truths there are. By analogy, 'an immanent ethics is an ethics that *posits this life as the only desirable life*' (DI 236). Instead of promising immortality in heaven, immanent ethics wants our *present* life to continue forever. This will immediately strike the reader as an unrealistic aspiration, and of course human culture is saturated with poignant awareness of our mortality. But by now we are also familiar with Meillassoux's lack of concern for probability when dealing with matters of ultimate importance, and not out of carelessness, but for reasons connected with the very fabric of his ontology. While religious ethics points to a completely other and incomprehensible life, 'philosophical ethics *must* be an ethics of immortality: *that is to say, an ethics of life with no elsewhere*' (DI 237). The true concept of immortality is philosophical rather than religious.

And it is precisely because Spinoza and Nietzsche were the masters of irreligiosity that they were also the thinkers of immortality, though of an immortality such that I am not capable of expecting the renewal without end of what is here in this world. (DI 237)

Meillassoux coins the term 'divine ethics' for the kind of ethics that seeks immortality only for the present life. In fact, *The Divine Inexistence* ultimately hinges not just on immortality for those already living, but on resurrection for the dead as well.

In the Western context, the resurrection of the dead has previously seemed like a special doctrine of the Christian faith, and is usually among the first to be scoffed at by those who reject this religion. But Meillassoux revives the doctrine on purely logical grounds: 'since everything logically possible is really possible, then since *the rebirth of bodies* is not illogical it must also be possible. And not only is rebirth possible: it cannot even be deemed either probable or improbable' (DI 238). Such rebirth would obviously be of comparable importance to the emergence of life from matter or thought from life. 'It is an event that would be no more astonishing than these latter advents that *have* in fact *taken place*' (DI 238). Or as he says at the very end of Excerpt D, referring to an idea of Pascal: 'the surprising fact of humans' rebirth would never be as surprising as the fact that they had been born at all' (DI 242).

Meillassoux now draws a distinction which may sound Badiouian, but which predates his contact with the manuscript of Badiou's *Logics of Worlds*, a work that Meillassoux reports having first seen in manuscript in 2005.[2] I refer to the distinction between the worldly and the intra-worldly:

> I call 'worlds', or 'orders', the three categories of advent known as matter, life, and thought. I call 'intra-worldly advents' those that are capable of occurring in the midst of a determinate World: for example, the advent of a new species in the midst of the world of life, or advents of creative invention in the midst of the world of thought. (DI 238)

World with a capital 'W' refers to a specific World, while world with a lower-case letter refers to the 'non-Whole' of possible worlds. 'Worlds arise suddenly from the world, and if these have a right to a majestic capital letter for the first time, it is because there is more in a World than in the world, since there is more in what ensues than there is in the origin' (DI 238).

The reason for making this distinction between world and the intra-worldly is that Meillassoux does not believe that rebirth, meaning the immortality in this life for both the currently living and the already dead, is merely an intra-worldly incident. Instead, rebirth is a major World-changing event of the sort we encountered in the previous section:

> Following the three Worlds of matter, life, and thought, *the rebirth of humans ought to be distinguished as a fourth world* . . . [For] *if* a World were to arise beyond the three previous ones, this World could *only* be that of the rebirth of humans. (DI 238)

Another name for this fourth order is the World of justice, in which humans attain the immortality they richly deserve, given that they are entities capable of absolute, immanent knowledge of a thoroughly comprehensible cosmos. While the fourth World has not yet occurred, it '*[exists] already as an object of hope, of the desire of every human qua rational being*' (DI 238). If some new order is to appear, it must be something just as radically new compared with humans as human thought is in comparison with mere life. Meillassoux always displays a resounding sense of human dignity: 'we know that humans have access to the eternal truth of the world' (DI 239). Under the term 'human' he includes all 'rational beings capable of grasping the absolute truth of contingency, and not simply the bipedal species in which such a reality now happens to be encountered' (DI 239). Even a super-advanced rational species (such as a cone-shaped Lovecraftian monster of ingenious intellect) would not mark the advent of anything truly new. It would simply be a new permutation of the humans we already know: faster in calculation and surer in intuition, and certainly more repulsive in physical form, but not something new *in kind* in comparison with a Meillassouxian thinker of absolute contingency. To pass beyond this stage of ontological development, 'only a thought reaching a higher truth than that of contingency could re-enact the rupture inaugurated by thought with respect to animality' (DI 239). The only thing higher than the human, it turns out, would be the recommencement of the human, its immortality in the same world we already know. 'That is why the fourth World ought to be called the World of justice: for it is only the World of the rebirth of humans *that makes universal justice possible, by erasing even the injustice of shattered lives*' (DI 239).

Humans, rational beings, are so central for Meillassoux's philosophy that he even defines a World as '*the advent of an element that is constitutive for humans*' (DI 239). This is true of matter, life, and thought, and equally true for rebirth/justice.

> The [first] three Worlds thus represent the three constitutive orders of the human. Whatever might be the laws of matter, of forms of life, or of intellectual or artistic inventions ... the three Worlds remain the definitional invariants of the human as a being of reason. (DI 240)

But we are also defined by our relation to the fourth World, via 'hope as desire crossed by thought: the desire of humans torn between their present contingency and the knowledge of the eternal by which they reach the idea of justice' (DI 240). This idea teaches us the strict *equality* of all humans; eternal truths are '*indifferent to differences*' (DI 240) among humans. And this equality is the reason why 'humans, as long as they think, are *affected* by injustice whenever it strikes them, since nothing permits us to found an inegalitarian difference of humans from themselves' (DI 240). And as we already saw in 'Spectral Dilemma': 'of all ... injustices the most extreme is still death: absurd death, early death, death inflicted by those unconcerned with equality' (DI 240). Humans must be reborn under conditions of justice that outstrip the horrible deaths of our fellows. To those who think this sounds like too extreme a conception of justice, Meillassoux notes that this justice always means 'an extravagance towards the present world' (DI 241), and in fact 'we owe the dead nothing less' (DI 241). In short, justice refers not only to the living, 'but *also* summons our refusal of injustice for the dead, for recent or ancient deaths, for known and unknown deaths. For the universal is universal only when it makes no exceptions' (DI 241).

The World of justice is '*the sole* conceivable radical novelty following the human: the recommencement of the human in just form' (DI 241). Ethics thereby requires the astonishment at the world found in Greek philosophy, but also the hope for justice familiar from Jewish messianism. The bond between these two must remain immanent, referring to no other world than the present one. What makes the present world so astonishing is that the more has arisen from the less: namely, humans have arisen from sheer lifeless matter. But if God existed, the reverse would be the case, and the less would have arisen from the more: namely, humans from God. 'Thus the hope of rebirth is bound to the astonishing awareness of the inexistence of God' (DI 241). But hope is not faith, since faith pertains only to what exists or will exist. By contrast, the World of justice 'can be produced *or not* produced. No necessity, no probability, can guarantee its advent' (DI 241). The *non*-advent of the fourth World is perfectly possible. But the resulting attitude is far from nihilistic. As Meillassoux wonderfully puts it: 'the philosophical astonishment that we feel before an existence deprived of any "why" ceases to be identified with the shrill and desperate consciousness of a godless human condition that leads to no specific *act* other than perhaps suicide' (DI 242). The shrill, desperate, and suicidal *avant-garde* of those who endured the death of God is replaced by one that hopes for a purely contingent justice.

Symbolization

We now come to the concept of *symbolization*, which Meillassoux proclaims to be 'one of the basic and original features of the present enterprise' (DI 243). Symbolization must be distinguished from the related term 'foundation'. In the present world, Meillassoux holds, there is still no *foundation* for justice. And yet justice is truly possible, and not merely a vain hope in the way that ideals often seem to be in vain in comparison with the practical complexities of the world. But while this possibility is already interesting enough, it 'would be unable to found the *value* of the original requirement of justice' (DI 242). In other words, the mere fact that justice is *possible* does not make it a worthwhile goal: 'the fact that justice is possible does not tell us *why* it is necessary to be just' (DI 243). A rogue relativist might still insist that justice is an arbitrary personal choice arranged alongside other equally valid life commitments, whether it be the advent of pleasure or anarchy or the accrual of personal power. All we know is that 'the fact of living for justice, of living an unselfish relation to other humans, means living according to the truth of the ultimate ontological possibility of the world: namely, our rebirth' (DI 243). But already, the relation between being and value has been salvaged by the very possibility of justice. The atrocities that fill human history are no longer a mockery of the possibility of justice; they actually pave the way for it. There is 'an immanent rational link between being and the universal' (DI 243), and this is precisely what is meant by symbolization: 'the rational guarantee of a possible realization of the universal' (DI 243). If foundations are what give legitimacy to universal principles such as justice, symbols are what *incarnate* principles in immanent form.

Symbolization consists in understanding the relation of universal values with the actual world. 'It is a matter of discovering an agreement between the discourse of values and the discourse of truth, or between world and justice, whatever form this agreement might take' (DI 244). Values are not arbitrary inventions by free-wheeling human subjects untethered from any absolute. Instead, they are *'the discovery of a truth* concerning the world, concerning extra-human reality, and this truth ought to be shown by reason alone *without the intervention of a transcendent revelation'* (DI 244). A system of values requires some sort of concord between justice and being. Meillassoux does not claim that the values he defends are especially original: 'the elements of such systems . . . are often quite similar' (DI 244). And yet, 'their arrangement and general signification, the *basic coloring* taken on by the values in a specific accord between justice and being, vary in each case according to how these values are inscribed in the world' (DI 244). The question of how reality itself can serve as a foundation for justice is, in Meillassoux's view, 'the primordial axis of philosophical questioning' (DI 244). Or even more vividly: *'The goal of every philosophy must be the immanent inscription of values in being'* (DI 244). When there is despair at the failure of the world to make way for human moral ends, we should not take the easy route of religious transcendence. As philosophers, we should 'oppose both the tepidity of lucid despair and the obscurantism of faith' (DI 244). Morality is a site of truth, not of mere subjective positings. What philosophers really need is fervor (*ardeur*): 'the jubilation that results from rational knowledge of the ontological accord between the immeasurable requirement of justice and the absurdity of a world without God' (DI 245).

We now encounter the figure of the sophist, the flip side of Meillassoux's other great enemy: the priest. The sophist holds that value is not based on any reality at all, but is merely 'a profitable social convention' (DI 245), to be followed only when 'advantageous either for me or for whatever elite group I favor' (DI 245). By contrast, philosophy must be different 'both from the absurd and hopeless world of the sophist who sees value as nothing but convention, and from the transcendent world of the religious person who inscribes value in the world by the irrational means of a revelation, a tradition, an authority' (DI 245). What this requires is an 'immanent and comprehensible inscription of values in a world' (DI 245). Philosophers can actually be stimulated by the opposition of the sophist and the priest, since 'the great epochs of philosophy are the ones initially dominated by the nightmarish duel between the traditionalism of religion and the vulgar cynicism of sophistry' (DI 245). The philosopher must always counter by showing that justice is neither a social illusion nor a blind submission to an omnipotent God. The problem 'is not knowing the meaning of justice, but knowing what good it is to be just' (DI 245–6). The real danger comes from those who do know what justice means but who still wonder why it is worth the trouble.

Meillassoux then gives us the interesting etymology for the Greek word *symballein*. In the ancient world, in a situation when guests and hosts might not meet again for many years to come, or might return to find only the other's children still alive, some method of future recognition was necessary. This was done by breaking in half a small tablet made of bone, with each person keeping one piece. Years later, the two pieces could be rejoined as a means of verifying former friendships obscured by the passage of time. 'In this sense', Meillassoux says, 'the symbol is what permits the renewal of links of hospitality. And this is truly the task of philosophy' (DI 246). The hospitality to which he refers is that between humans and world, and just as the ancient Greek symbol showed that one friend belonged to another, so too the philosopher's symbol '[demonstrates] that moral aspirations are not absurd illusions or vulgar ideologies, but that they rest instead on the non-reflective, intuitive perception of the world in its ultimate truth' (DI 246).

The history of philosophy has been dominated by just three Symbols so far: cosmological, naturalistic, and historical. It is interesting to note that this must be a series of 'intra-worldly' advents, and hence it does not proceed by the same set of rules as the advents of Worlds themselves: matter, life, thought, justice. Yet just as we hopefully await a Fourth World, Meillassoux proposes a fourth symbol as well – the *factial* symbol, the first non-metaphysical kind.

The cosmological symbol 'was sought by Socrates, inaugurated by Plato, and accomplished by Aristotle' (DI 246). Astronomy abandoned myth through its mathematical description of the motion of planets. And yet myth remained dominant in the ethical sphere: 'it is possible for a cultivated Greek to explain courage by narrating the exploits of Achilles even after ceasing to believe in such discourses as concerns the movement of the planets or the nature of becoming' (DI 247). In this way, 'an unthought scission is produced between the science of phenomena and the representation of moral norms' (DI 247). The sophist takes the scission one step further by removing even the legitimacy of tradition from values, making them an empty play of opinion: 'Justice, courage, piety, and wisdom are assessed in terms of utility . . . But in that case, what is the point of following these virtues when they become personally injurious to me?' (DI 247). It was Socrates who tried to restore the bond between value and being by 'conceptualizing the discourse of values' (DI 247). In this way, philosophy is opposed 'both to the traditionalist reaction of the religious who view every adversary as a sophist, and the skepticism of the sophists who view every adversary as a priest' (DI 248). The philosopher is attacked from two sides for opposite reasons, which is generally a good sign that one is misunderstood by both groups of critics: 'Even today, the great philosophers are treated as sophists by the priests, and as priests by the sophists' (DI 248). Plato's doctrine of Ideas reinscribes justice in being: 'the Cosmos . . . becomes the literal and fascinating image of the Good itself' (DI 249). More generally, 'the Cosmos depicts the justice that guides the celestial world: the circular trajectories allow the planets to follow a course that is uninterrupted and devoid of conflict' (DI 249). By contrast, the human populations of the terrestrial world are doomed to strife and bloodshed. And yet 'the children of the Earth need only lift their eyes to consider the model of beauty and peace that ought to guide their existence' (DI 249). Meillassoux credits Isaac Newton with destroying the cosmological Symbol by decomposing planetary orbits into linear motions resembling those on earth (though perhaps a case could be made for Galileo and his telescope, with its revelation of a defective celestial realm filled with sunspots and craters on the moon). 'Justice, disjoined from the real, is unveiled once more as a useful artifice invented by humans, not as a veridical principle of the world understood as Cosmos' (DI 249). With the libertines of the eighteenth century we encounter a new tribe of sophists, who make it fully impossible to reconcile being and justice by pointing to the perfection of the sky.

The priests and the sophists 'have now become clerics and sceptics' (DI 250). Enter Jean-Jacques Rousseau, who transposes the cosmological opposition between superlunary and sublunary into a new difference: the natural versus the social. The new Symbol is the naturalist or romantic Symbol. No longer do we have a corrupt earth opposed to a majestic sky; it is now a corrupt society riddled with inequalities, which ruined the egalitarian state of nature. 'The affirmation that "man was born good" allows us to rediscover an inscription of the Good in the spontaneous being of the *living* and no longer in cosmic *matter*' (DI 250). We feel the good in the experience of pity, and in this way 'the Symbol passes from astral trajectories to compassionate bodies, from the unchangeable ether of celestial entities to the innocence of childlike organisms' (DI 250). Just as the Greeks were amazed by the sky, Rousseau is astonished by the beauties of the earth. (Meillassoux claims that 'Plotinus [was] the first Ancient who bothered to tell us that flowers are beautiful,' DI 250.) The Good is not separate from the earth, but only separate from human society, which *corrupted* the Good. This means that the Good is not just an illusion, as Sade and the other libertines hold, 'but something that teaches us a truth about being: no longer the being of dead stars, but that of living creatures and their tears' (DI 250). But just as the Cosmological symbol was doomed by the decomposition of celestial circles into earthly straight lines, the Romantic symbol crashes against the fact that 'pity is no more common in the living than are war, violence, or cruelty' (DI 250). Romanticism crumbles, lingering on 'only in the form of various irrational and amoral vitalisms' (DI 250).

This brings us to the historical Symbol, which has only begun its decline in our own time. *Historical process* now assumes the mantle of objective value. 'The principle that governs the world is no longer justice, but rather the human community as a whole' (DI 251). History as a disembodied process restores the meaning that was stripped from the sky and then from nature. 'The anarchic will of individuals seems to produce a result that none of these wills had ever desired individually' (DI 251). No individual guides history, yet a sort of Justice can be found in its outcome. The historic Symbol takes its ultimate form in *economism*:

For the liberal, every economic reverse amounts to a transient retreat amidst a larger movement toward a necessarily positive outcome. For the Marxist, the principle of social becoming occurs through a necessary auto-collapse of whatever alienates humans, and in this way their emancipation is attained. (DI 251)

But in our time, 'we have lost ... *the ultimate certainty of having the real on our side*' (DI 251), and thus the historical-economic Symbol has entered its decadence. And as always when a Symbol begins to die, 'we encounter the alternative nightmares reborn from their ashes: traditionalism and sophistical immoralism.'

Meillassoux holds that all of the Symbols have failed for just one reason: all were metaphysical, and for this reason all were dependent on a belief in real necessity, in a necessary accord between the world and human moral ends. 'In this way, philosophy necessarily falls into the incomprehensible and therefore religious affirmation of such an accord' (DI 252). As a result, reason collapses in favor of an irrational transcendence: 'The cosmological easily becomes an article of faith for apostolic Roman Catholicism. The romantic gives way to the Robespierrist cult of the supreme Being. The historical is degraded into the dogma of the infallibility of the Party or the Invisible Hand' (DI 252). The other option, aside from declaring that value and being are necessarily linked, is 'to affirm that we can joyously submit our ends to the necessity of the world without falling into cynicism, since virtue procures true happiness by itself' (DI 252). Meillassoux's terms for these two approaches are *reasonable belief* and *virtuous atheism*. In the first case, the split between value and being is denied by claiming that being itself is saturated with value. In the second, virtue becomes its own reward, and happily copes with whatever the world throws in its direction. These positions easily turn into two extreme solutions. The first case, which is the 'reasonable belief' that the world is already saturated with value, degenerates into '*[affirming] untruthfully that the world is just, in such manner that this illusion produces the fervor necessary to render the world actually just*' (DI 253). The second approach, or 'virtuous atheism', easily turns into a position reminiscent of Nietzsche, '[affirming] that the accord between the world and any particular value is a matter of illusion, but at the same time [making] *that illusion itself into a value*' (DI 253–4), a value that we would follow only 'because of the vital intensity generated by such a disciplined belief' (DI 254). The problem is that both of these positions share a contempt for *the true*. In the first case values collapse into a pre-existent necessity of being, while in the second they lose all connection with being. 'The contemporary ill repute of truth ... can be linked to the domination of these two desperate attempts at symbolization' (DI 254).

This contempt for the true, Meillassoux says, disappears in his own *factial* model of symbolization. His ontology demonstrates the truth of contingency, and thus of advent *ex nihilo*. The Good may be imaginary, but none the less it is something imaginary *at which thinking beings aim*. 'It is a Good ... perfectly inexistent in the world that precedes the rise of humanity, and which manifestly exceeds the capacities of matter, in whose midst it has *none the less* emerged in the form of an obstinate hope' (DI 254). The illusory character of value is no longer simply an artistic creation to be celebrated or a tragic defect to be mourned. For 'the illusion no longer leads [thinking beings] to despair or to faith, but to the lucid hope that the world in the future will be able to reproduce the measureless novelty borne by their thought' (DI 255). This is neither the best nor the worst of all possible worlds, but one that has the potential to be either of these. 'Value is inserted into a reality no longer identified with a determinate and perennial substance, but rather with the possibility of lawless change' (DI 255). At last we are able to aspire to the Good once more, since 'Being is now the realm in which something *can take place*' (DI 255).

Human Supremacy

We now encounter a contradiction between two systems of ethics: a current ethics as we await the fourth World, and the ethics that would exist once that World arrives. After all, '*the realization of this waiting would abolish its very constituents*' (DI 256). In the present moment, we can have a fervor for justice, a fervor produced by its symbolization. 'Values return to life because they are wagered on the being to come; hope refounds the unity of the human collective, giving it a common project' (DI 256). Our fidelity is 'initially aimed at those who are closest among the deceased' (DI 256), but is soon transferred to the community as a whole, both 'the living and the dead' (DI 256). But once this is achieved there is nothing left that is worth awaiting, and this means that the relation between being and value would lose its creative tension, so that 'once again there [would be] a suppression of the Symbol' (DI 256). The senselessness of such a world would leave us with 'no other choice than to turn towards religion' (DI 257). But in fact justice has value beyond any symbolization of it, meaning that to imagine the fourth World ultimately forces us to face the question of what legitimates the desire for justice. 'Thus it is a question of showing how the factual can *ontologically* establish the *value* of the human: the essential human dignity, by which every act of justice always draws its legitimacy' (DI 257). The ethics ruled by the Symbol is not the deepest form of ethics. What ultimately founds ethics is the supremacy of human beings.

We cannot found ethics on a transcendent God, quite apart from Meillassoux's own personal distaste for transcendence. For if we did so, we would subordinate truth and justice 'to the actual irrationality and immorality of the revealed God, and would thereby subordinate the universal to its exact contrary' (DI 258). That is one possible danger for ethics. The other is to fall into mere tautology, as in 'the Kantian moral law, which is valid simply because it is valid' (DI 257). Our task is '[to counter] the cynical and religious devaluations of the human by establishing *the essential ultimate status of the human*' (DI 258). This cannot be simply the *de facto* superiority of humans as the smartest and technologically strongest species on earth, but must be 'the *necessary superiority* ... of the thinking being over all other beings, while refusing the necessary existence of such a being, which runs counter to our ontology' (DI 258). The solution to this problem, Meillassoux holds, lies in the fact that human thought is both actual *and* contingent. 'Stated differently ... the human is *the factial but ultimate effect of advent*' (DI 258). Thought is vastly different from all that came before it in the cosmos, and since thought is already capable of absolute knowledge, no further entity can be imagined that would be an equally vast leap beyond thought itself; only justice would qualify for that honor, and justice is justice only for thinking beings. 'The necessity referred to here means that it cannot be circumvented, not that its existence is eternal' (DI 259).

To say that every human deserves justice is no longer a tautology, but stems from the fact that the value of humans cannot have any cause, '*since every cause is inferior to humans*' (DI 259). In Meillassoux's system the effect is always greater than the cause.

And so it is with humans, who draw their value 'from the *thought* of the eternal of which it is the mortal stakeholder – not from the eternal itself, which only amounts to the neutrality of becoming' (DI 259). It might be objected that placing humans at the center of the picture is a typically banal modernist gesture that has now out-lived its usefulness. Against this assumption, Meillassoux makes the striking claim that human pre-eminence '*has [never] been seri-ously maintained*' by any other thinker (DI 259). On one side, the value of the human has been founded in human contemplation of the Good, or human resemblance to God. On the other side, humans are valued merely as the juggernaut victors of a Darwinian death match between millions of living species. Against both of these options, Meillassoux holds that 'humans acquire value because they know the eternal' (DI 260). And yet the eternal in its own right has no value, since it is merely 'the blind, stupid, and anonymous contingency of each thing' (DI 260). What is always of value is only human *knowledge* of the eternal: 'humans have value not because of *what* they know but *because* they know' (DI 260). And the content of this knowledge is a mixture of 'the theoretical and absolute knowledge of ontological truths, and the worried and attentive knowledge of our mortality' (DI 260). Meillassoux asserts that classical humanism is too fixated on knowledge of our finitude or mortality as a *negative* sort of knowledge, when in fact 'our capacity to think our own death refers to our power of envis-aging the real nature of contingency as a possibility of each thing: of all disappearance as of all appearance' (DI 260). In other words, 'the negative knowledge of our mortality . . . refers to the positive knowledge of our possible rebirth' (DI 260). The limit is not there to be mourned, but to be surpassed. 'With humans, *the ultimate has in fact taken place*' (DI 261).

Faced with the universal, which every human is capable of grasping, all individual heroism falls to the side. 'We must orient all power towards the universal; we must know how to jettison the ballast of destiny so as not to make of our virtues the sign of being chosen' (DI 261). None the less, humans remain superior to the blind becoming of the world, and there is no third, transcen-dent term that outstrips both. If there were, then 'becoming and its whole retinue of disasters and cruelties, marked by the stamp of transcendence, would thus acquire a mysterious value that would supposedly be superior to the morality comprehensible by humans, although identical in its manifestation with the barbarism of pure contingency' (DI 262). And this leads Meillassoux to oppose firmly any *Promethean* vision of the human, which would simply transfer to humans all the negative features of God as pure power. 'It is an idolization of power in humans: not power in God, but in humans become God' (DI 262). Feuerbach and Marx were wrong to say that humans transpose their own essence into God, for what they really put there is 'the degradation of their own essence' (DI 262). Or as Meillassoux puts it in a classic harangue against the mainstream concept of God:

> Humans, instead of revering their own baseness in God, now venerate it in themselves. For in all religion the worst violence (murderous cataclysms, grievous mortal illnesses inflicted upon children, lives absurdly cut down by 'fate') are ordinarily *reserved* for God ... But if humans are made God, then why should they deprive themselves of the same sorts of actions? All the crimes of God become accessible to humans, and the deified human can always justify them with the same subtlety as that of the theologian deciphering the superior goodness of the Lord in natural catastrophes. (DI 262–3)

In the twentieth century, so filled with criminal horrors, humans lowered themselves to the level of the omnipotent God. But only through the refusal of such hideous power, in the name of justice, do humans show their superiority to nature (DI 263).

Messianism

Given the pure contingency of the possible World of justice, the question might be raised as to why we should worry about it at all, or put any effort into bringing it about. The World of justice will come or not come regardless of our actions, and for this reason careless hedonism or the aggressive pursuit of injustice for selfish reasons would seem no less defensible than a pious sense of justice toward the living and the dead. The result would be the figure of the 'factial fatalist' (DI 263), who would passively await the advent of the rebirth of humans without any work towards bringing it about. But as Meillassoux sees it, 'the fatalist really just manifests the arbitrary desire of his own vital perpetuation: an individual and capricious desire for rebirth that envisages this rebirth as an end and not as a condition of the end' (DI 264). Yet the desire for personal rebirth is only preliminary to the desire for the World of justice. And more than this, 'it is also necessary to maintain that the World of justice is itself possible only on the condition that it should be desired in action in the present World' (DI 264, emphasis removed). To await the World of justice passively is to make it something alien to thought, and this makes it impossible. And 'the whole point is that if rebirth were to occur in such a way that no act of justice had awaited it, it would contain nothing of the universal: we would be dealing only with a blind recommencement imposed anonymously on humanity' (DI 264). The point is that a simple, anonymous return of life would not be a *novel* advent; what makes it novel is only *the fact that it has been awaited*. Indeed, the World of justice must be 'actively awaited by acts of justice that display the fervor linked to a belief in the radical requirement of universality, and in the discovery of the non-absurdity of such a requirement' (DI 264). In short, 'the final World can commence only on the condition that it be a recommencement' (DI 264, emphasis removed). Stated differently, 'the fact that the fourth World corresponds *de facto* to a hope that existed anterior to its advent forms part of its *essence*' (DI 264). An act of justice is a manner of awaiting the advent of the World of justice itself. Meillassoux sums this up in an analogy drawn from the poetry of Mallarmé: 'One can thus compare the free act to a throw of the dice. A throw of the dice never guarantees chance, but is that alone which makes chance possible' (DI 264, emphasis removed).

The idea is unusual, since it holds that we can *condition* rebirth without being able to *cause* it. Yet it is 'immediately implied by the status of the ultimate World, which mixes the ontological novelty of the fourth World with the ethical character of the World of justice' (DI 264). We have been speaking interchangeably of the fourth World and the World of justice, but we can now see that there are two separate strands involved here that need to be considered individually. Not only is the ultimate World *causally independent* of our actions, it is also *non-causally dependent*, related intimately to our thought without being caused by it. To demonstrate this, Meillassoux reminds us that his theory of rebirth is rather different from Nietzsche's Eternal Return of the Same. The fourth World of Meillassoux will be something truly novel, not just a blind repetition of life by actors who are ignorant that they are even repeating. The missing element in Nietzsche's model of repetition is memory, which for

Meillassoux makes up the very essence of the fourth World. Lives in that World

> are lives charged with the singular *past* of their preceding existences, surmounting the incompleteness and the dehumanizing misery sustained by each of them in the third World, and capable as such of being the field of new inventions of thought, since they recommence without returning to their point of departure. (DI 265)

The fourth World *must* be charged with memory: 'to be charged with a past is not for the World of justice a factual property but an essential one, since a World of justice that occurred without such a passage would not be a World of justice' (DI 266). If unjust deaths were simply to disappear from the cosmos without our having desired this beforehand, 'we would thus be in an improved *third World*, indeed in a *perfect* one. But it would not be a world that would *surpass* the World of thought' (DI 266). We ourselves would still be *external* to such a world, despite being lucky protégés of its goodness rather than tearful victims as in the world of today. 'This would be a World of the demigods: beings who are spontaneously happy, having lived nothing other than this happiness and having never done anything for their condition to be such as it is' (DI 266). They would effectively be nothing more than 'successful fatalists' (DI 266). Sounding somewhat Hegelian, Meillassoux adds that 'an accomplishment should *respond* to an ethics in such a way that subjectivity and objectivity should not simply be in external relation, that this exteriority should be happy or unhappy' (DI 266). Although our demand for justice cannot bring justice into being, an undemanded justice would be nothing but luck.

In response to those who insist that there is really no difference between a perfect World of thought and the completed World of justice, Meillassoux develops the difference further. The novelty of the new World needs to be a novelty concerning thought itself, 'not just concerning its environment or its vital envelope' (DI 267), and hence the identical happy content of the two worlds is of no philosophical significance. The difference between the two would have to be a difference affecting thought, and thus would not be inherent in the Worlds themselves, but in 'the *relation* of thought to such Worlds' (DI 267). From this Meillassoux opens a fascinating new path: 'this relation, proper to the sole order of justice, is none other than that of *beauty*' (DI 267, emphasis modified). This is not difficult to explain, since 'if the fourth order arises, it will correspond *de facto* to our universal aspirations. It will therefore be beautiful, in the sense in which Kant speaks of natural beauty as the non-necessary *encounter* of phenomenal mechanisms and our rational ends' (DI 267). Even though we act 'as if' the world was created in accord with our rational demands, this can never be demonstrated. And thus, 'according to Kant, it is precisely the *contingency* of such an accord that occasions the feeling of surprise and rapture when the beauty of a landscape or sunset is revealed' (DI 267). It hardly needs to be explained how this Kantian idea plays directly into Meillassoux's hands, for in everyday life, 'we often collide with the neutrality of a world directed by laws and forces indifferent to our ends' (DI 267–8). By contrast, with the advent of a fourth World *'the beautiful is revealed . . . as the emergence without reason of an accord between reason and the real*, a real which would have been established *beforehand . . .* in its essential absurdity' (DI 268). Beauty would arise through the Symbol as an accord between humans and 'a finally hospitable world that they would be destined to inhabit' (DI 268). By contrast, 'a World of the blessed . . . [would] be *deprived of such a possibility of representation*' (DI 268). Beauty needs to be founded on a previous scission, which any World of the blessed would lack.

However, the difference between the Meillassouxian and the Kantian theories of beauty remains significant. The 'as if' of the Kantian beautiful refers to an unknowable sphere of things-in-themselves.

> Even if we have no conceptual knowledge to support the assertion, and even if phenomenal appearance seems entirely reducible to the anonymity of mechanism, the unknowability of reality-in-itself permits us to 'think' that it is actually directed by a divine finality. Beauty would be the sensible trace of the providence of this finality. (DI 268)

Obviously, no such option is available to the Meillassouxian philosopher: 'for we *know* for our part that no end directs the accord between our aspiration and the world' (DI 268). There is no divine will guaranteeing the accord between human aspiration and reality as it is. Instead, 'beauty will result from the fact that just people in the third World have actually hoped for this World, thereby enabling the possibility that it could arise *as if this hope*

were the source of it' (DI 269). The 'as if' of beauty is no longer
'as if the divine will had made it happen' but 'as if *human hope*
had made it happen'. A present but hypothetical divine power
is replaced by a past but actual hope. In a lovely turn of phrase,
Meillassoux describes hope as 'a gift of the just made across
time' (DI 269). Otherwise, the fourth World would simply be 'a
kingdom of demigods indifferent to the heritage of durations' (DI
269). In this way, we ourselves are involved in the coming of the
fourth World, even though blind becoming is not affected by our
desire that the dice land with a particular side pointing upward.
And 'it is henceforth impossible to hate or regret the present
World, which opens up *the very possibility of a history*' (DI 270).
And this history of miseries, atrocities, and crushing early deaths
is crucial for the emergence of the fourth World. Our hope is not
for 'the Edenic emergence of a garden of innocents, but the recommencing of an earth weighed down with the memory of humans'
(DI 270).

This brings us to another interesting question: what would life
be like if the fourth World were actually attained? Meillassoux
cannot dismiss this question as idle speculation about the unlikely,
since he does not find it 'unlikely' at all. The problem is that the
ethics of the future 'appears to be, literally, an ethics of despair
. . . [since factial ethics] is rendered impossible by the very realization of its object' (DI 270). But recall that even though the Symbol
would already be realized in this case, the Symbol is only the
condition of the universal rather than its foundation. For 'the universal reposes on the value of the human, and this remains unaffected by the fact of its eventual rebirth' (DI 270). Once justice is
attained, the desire for it will be replaced by 'a benevolence that is
inherent in a condition emancipated from early destruction', since
irredeemable deaths would have been eliminated from the world.
As a result, 'the universal would cease to designate the requirement
of conditions necessary for the blossoming of every life, and would
refer instead to the invention of possible links between humans
devoted to thought' (DI 270). Even in a world of attained justice,
there is still room for new benevolent links.

It remains to be seen how the religious desire for resurrection is
different from Meillassoux's *immanent* desire for it. As he puts it,
'what is religious is every incapacity to take the human for the end
of action, an incapacity that ends in the submission of humans to
the blind power of becoming, identified with a destinal mystery

resulting in the incomprehensibility of transcendence' (DI 271). Religious desire aims at the advent itself rather than at *that which arises* in the advent. In other words, it is aimed at the productive power of being to create novelty, rather than at justice. But 'desiring the manifestation of the power of being, and thereby desiring the inhuman, amounts once more to a religious subordination of the end to its origin, or the human to the power that causes him to be born or reborn' (DI 271). More generally, Meillassoux says, 'all "morality" that does not support the perspective of the realization of its object is a religious morality. For what the religious spirit desires is that there should be something *entirely other*: something inconceivable, or absolutely inhuman' (DI 271). Anyone who feels despair over the possibility of the last advent is 'in fact despairing over the fact that nothing inhuman can arise any longer in the ultimate world' (DI 272).

From here we move to one of the strangest ideas of Meillassoux's book, one with a markedly Christological flavor. We have seen from the difference between religious and immanent hope that two different attitudes would be possible even in the midst of the fourth World. But it needs to be shown what links 'the hope placed in being (the advent) and the hope placed in humans (its highest moral possibility)' (DI 272). The link, Meillassoux tells us, must be a 'gesture'. And that gesture must be the abandonment of power. This is impossible in the religious vision of the world, because 'the sudden advent of rebirth escapes the possibility of such abandonment' (DI 272, emphasis removed), given that the advent lies beyond the possibility of all action. And in this spirit, 'the idolatry of being' amounts to 'an amorality of power ... inherent in the awaiting of an advent for which no gesture is possible' (DI 273). The only way to ensure that the universal is immanent rather than religious is through a gesture of the abandonment of power, and this 'amounts to a requirement that the advent of the universal should be *incarnated*' (DI 273, emphasis modified). Here, in a twenty-first century work of French philosophy that is ostensibly materialist in spirit, we are led by a rational argument to a concept of *incarnation*.

There must be a '*human mediator* between the advent and the specific realities that appear in it' (DI 273, emphasis modified). The mediator will not only have the power of producing rebirth, but must also '[accomplish] the unique gesture of abandoning the power of this advent, once the justice is accomplished for which the advent was (only) the condition' (DI 273, emphasis removed). Meillassoux will now be on thin ice with his materialist comrades when he offers the following list of five determinations that must be attributed to the human mediator:

1. Goodness.
2. Omniscience.
3. Omnipotence.
4. The power to abolish his or her own Omniscience or Omnipotence.
5. That the mediator actually *does* abolish his or her own power once the rebirth occurs.

Meillassoux knows full well what this list will sound like to the reader: 'The "Christlike" aspect worn by the universal does not make it a "rational religion", but ... an ethics that finally excludes the temptations of transcendence' (DI 274). By abolishing his or her own power, the mediator embraces the contingency of that power in abandoning it to become the equal of everyone else.

From messianism we move to the theme of *infans,* or the child. 'The child is the one who teaches us that its power is not the manifestation of a superior providence, but of contingency alone, of the absurdity burrowed so deeply into itself that it becomes meaningful' (DI 274). The child teaches us all that power is unimportant, and also teaches 'the impossibility of despising ourselves with respect to which makes us human' (DI 274). In this way the devotion to being and to humans is brought into relation, since in hoping for rebirth we also hope for an end to arbitrary power through a deliberate gesture that abandons it. There is a vague but definite link with the theme of the 'child' in Nietzsche's *Thus Spoke Zarathustra:*[3]

> to be worthy of such an occurrence is to be worthy of *infans*: of its possible gesture of liberty in which are conjoined the supreme abandonment of power and the call of all humans to the unequalled value of their own humanity. (DI 274)

This is followed by a clear allusion to the philosophy of Badiou: 'we can define the hope of the universal as the anticipation of fidelity to the unique gesture' (DI 274, emphasis removed).

Believing in the God Who Does Not Exist

A new French philosopher, born in the late 1960s, emerges from a deeply materialist and leftist background. In principle it would seem easy to predict his attitude toward the topic of God: his atheism should be safely assumed. But that is not quite what we find in *The Divine Inexistence*. Instead, we find critical remarks toward atheism of the following sort: 'The principle of atheism is a *ratification of the religious partition of existence*' (DI 274). And this: 'Atheism is a strategy of the besieged' (DI 275). And finally, 'atheism consists essentially in ratifying the religious partition between immanence and transcendence: *for atheism consists in being satisfied with the unsatisfying territory that religion cedes to it*' (DI 275). For Meillassoux, this is the result whenever we accept a split of existence between two mutually opposed zones, one of them earthly and the other unearthly. 'One begins by admitting that the territory of immanence is just as religion describes it, then one declares that this territory is the only one that exists, and finally one invents every possible way of rendering it livable *despite* that fact' (DI 275).

Having wrongly accepted the truth of this predicament, the atheist has two options: renunciation and revolt. 'In renunciation, the atheist explicitly recognizes the misery of the condition of immanence' (DI 275). It is an attitude of mourning, a gloomy intellectual asceticism with stoical overtones. As for revolt, it 'consists in heroically assuming the immanence such as religion describes it, in order to profit from the intense jubilation belonging to all defiance' (DI 275). If you are not yet familiar with this type, Meillassoux describes it with withering sarcasm: 'It is always a question of giving provocative and paradoxical praise to . . . the "gallant" and "ironic" joy of our finitude, a superior amusement procured by incessant struggles, a jubilation over our body which is said to be sensitive precisely because it is mortal, etc.' (DI 275). Meillassoux observes that the priest need not fear either of these types, precisely because both of them *regret being right*. 'In the case of renunciation, the regret is explicit; in the case of revolt, it is masked but still obvious. For revolt is a classically "demoniacal" attitude, which is to say that it is always religious' (DI 275). Both attitudes accept the religious denunciation of their hopeless limitations, and merely try to change the minus sign to a plus sign, while leaving the basic religious division of existence unchallenged. Like the priest, both affirm 'the tragic character of immanence' (DI 276), while merely denying the alternative that the priest provides. And with a final bit of sarcasm, Meillassoux adds that

> this attitude culminates in the pleasure of declaring neither hate nor contempt for religion, but total indifference to it: an indifference that will be developed, repeated, and multiplied by atheists always in search of believers in order to flaunt their total absence of interest in matters of the beyond. (DI 276)

He frankly describes this attitude as 'reactive', and declares that the priest will never find it threatening.

Meillassoux argues that philosophy should reverse this scenario and make *the priest* regret being right (or right in his own eyes, anyway). Factiality allows us to do this by showing that 'all that is objectively desirable in the religious can be *repatriated in immanence*' (DI 276) while freeing us from the horrible, amoral God worshipped by the priests.

> This submission to a God capable of sending the cruellest scourges into the world, which are none the less supposed to be viewed as a manifestation of his love for humans, this pure aberration of religion purely and simply *disappears* in the philosophical divine. (DI 276)

Thus, there is no longer any need for 'the endless contortions of the exegetes' (DI 277), who find every possible means to rationalize the actions or permissions of God, whose transcendence is supposed to be 'essentially full of love, although it is indifferent or even horrifying in its manifestation' (DI 277). Meillassoux defends the God of the philosophers rather than the God of the priests, and this means that God is no longer allied with blind, amoral chaos, but with the rebirth of humans in a World of justice, as incarnated in the child.

We now reach the beautifully written conclusion of Meillassoux's book, in which the major themes of the manuscript are nicely tied together. It begins with the familiar theme of how to unify Jewish religion and Greek reason, though we have seen that the answer Meillassoux provides is highly unorthodox. We seek the unity of philosophy and religion but without a mediating term, since none exists. The need for this unification holds good for both East and West, which 'have received these two heterogeneous "truths" – *and no others*' (DI 277). The only choice is whether to have a religious unity of the two or a philosophical unity. But factiality allows us to unify them in a new way:

> Jewish messianism no longer thwarts the eternity of mathematical truths, since the latter cease to designate the real eternity (which is thus without a future) of this world order and refers on the contrary to the eternal contingency of this world (which is thus full of promise). (DI 277–8)

The search for justice inherent in Jewish messianism goes hand in hand with the immanence of Greek reason (DI 278).

Religion is no longer one camp in a war against atheism, but '*names the battlefield* where the two camps confront one another' (DI 278). We have seen that even the atheist accepts the negative model of immanence proposed by religion, meaning that there is a sense in which atheism is not even a meaningful option. Instead, there is an important choice to be made: 'either the revealed God of religion or the God of the philosophers' (DI 278). The atheist merely barricades himself against transcendence, while philosophers alone are able to hunt it down in its lair and slay it. As Meillassoux describes it in a wonderful passage, 'the atheist stands outside the field of battle, and confuses the philosopher and the priest just as one confuses two combatants in a hand-to-hand struggle viewed from afar' (DI 278). And just as wonderfully: 'for the atheist, God is a matter for the priest; for the philosopher, God is too serious a matter for the priests' (DI 279). Sophists and other anti-philosophers always give way for the priests, since with the limitations they place on meaning 'they inaugurate an *inexpungable* field of nonsense that tacitly legitimates the revelation of a transcendence exceeding all *logos*' (DI 279). Meillassoux concludes with a stab at the assumptions of scientism:

> all anti-philosophy, all positivism, all scientism, and all logicism thus have a mystical, religious essence … In declaring that rationality is illegitimate outside the scientific framework, these theories condemn reason to an inability to account for the facticity of the laws in the midst of which science always already unfolds, or to respond to the essential questions of existence. (DI 279)

Instead, even outside the scientific framework there is an 'intelligibility of being qua being' (DI 279). And we have seen repeatedly that this intelligibility entails the contingency of being, while the historical systems of philosophy all assume 'that a necessary existence is possible' (DI 280), and we know that for Meillassoux this is a completely meaningless notion.

That to which humans have always aspired 'is to give birth to God just as matter gives birth to life and life to thought. We are the possible ancestors of God rather than his creatures' (DI 280). And in even edgier terms, 'we bear God in our wombs, and our essential disquietude is nothing other than the convulsions of a child yet to come' (DI 280). God would be the final birth of humans, since no advent is possible beyond this one. And for this reason, 'the project of beings with reason thus consists in *enduring together*, from generation to generation, by the establishment of a link between the living and the dead, in the midst of a world whose knowledge is able to maintain our waiting' (DI 281). Our link with God is with the *inexistent* God: 'this link, which makes each of us the possible forerunner of God, I call the divine' (DI 281). And furthermore, our link with future humans and the justice to come is embodied in *infans*, the child, which Meillassoux now pushes in an even more *literal* direction than before: 'the desire for a child does not break the link between lovers, but transfixes desire to the point of instituting an amorous rupture, by this other being, in a spirit of expectation' (DI 281). The theme of love mixes with that of death: 'we wish once more to "drink with the dead", without a revealed God returning to spoil the party and trouble our intimacy with tombstones' (DI 281). But unlike the heaven of religions, this ideal scenario need not come to pass.

Meillassoux's model of the divine 'carries both atheism and religion to their ultimate consequences in order to unveil their truth: God does not exist, *and* it is necessary to believe in God' (DI 282). If God existed, we could not believe in his advent, and we would be stuck with the amoral God who allows miserable things to occur. Belief now means hope for the future immanent God rather than faith in a current but hidden one. But we should also remember that 'atheism diminishes humans and humiliates their projects by deposing what it believes to be a simple myth' (DI 283). We have seen that what it gives us instead is a Promethean model of humans who are debased as badly as the amoral God of religion himself. For this reason, all the present-day efforts at demystification are 'a mocking enterprise . . . that only allows our species a few mediocre projects compared with what we are capable of envisaging. It is a sarcasm of humans toward humans, and thus a hatred of oneself' (DI 283). Religion is no better, but simply 'the undercurrent of a world that is not infinitely desired: a world not seized in its infinite power of advent, and loved for the eternal promise of which its madness is the guarantor' (DI 284).

To believe in the existence of God is wrong, and amounts to not believing in God at all, since such belief 'is to make of him a God who is not only love, but also and especially omnipotence' (DI 284). In a daring inversion of normal religious doctrine, Meillassoux holds that to believe in God's existence is a form of blasphemy and idolatry. As for blasphemy: 'To say that God exists is the worst of blasphemies, for this amounts to saying that God reigns over the world in a sort of *grand politics*, without ever having been weak enough to modify his designs to prevent the atrocities that have taken place on earth' (DI 284), seeing even 'a certain divine goodness in allowing a child to be devoured by dogs' (DI 284). As for idolatry, religion is duplicitous and 'believes simultaneously in God as the amorous promise of the rebirth of the dead, and in the existence of God through the servile and malicious desire for an omnipotent master' (DI 286). Against such blasphemy and idolatry, 'the words "the divine inexistence", clear and pure as moonlight, guarantee hope so long as a just person remains in existence' (DI 285).

We now come to the final pages of the book, where Meillassoux gives us a fourfold schema of possible attitudes towards God. First, we can take the classical atheist position and *not believe in God because he does not exist*. But this has already been rejected as a route to anguish and despair, as a morose acceptance of what religion tells us about the immanent sphere. Second, we can *believe in God because he exists*, which is obviously the classical theist position, rejected by Meillassoux for its devotion to an amoral God who sends plagues and dogs to destroy innocent children. The third option is also rejected, though it is stranger and subtler than the first two: *not believing in God because he exists*. 'It is the Luciferian position of rebellion against the Creator which expresses the need to hold someone responsible for the evils of this world' (DI 287). This position would rather *hate* God than concede that he does not exist. Although not mentioned by Meillassoux, Captain Ahab of *Moby-Dick* also comes to mind.[4]

This leaves us with only the fourth option, Meillassoux's own, which has never yet been tried: *believing in God because he does not exist*. We end this survey of *The Divine Inexistence* with the final three sentences of the manuscript: 'It has now been done. The four possible links of humans to God are henceforth known. One must choose' (DI 287).

Notes

1. Henri Bergson, *Time and Free Will*.
2. Quentin Meillassoux, personal communication, 3 September 2010.
3. Friedrich Nietzsche, 'On the Three Metamorphoses', *Thus Spoke Zarathustra*.
4. Herman Melville, *Moby-Dick*.

5

Reflections on Meillassoux's Non-Euclidean Philosophy

The philosophy of Quentin Meillassoux departs to a considerable degree from common sense. While theories of a reality outside the mind are often dull and stuffy (bad realism) or aggressive and dogmatic (bad materialism), Meillassoux's way of thinking is so imaginative that even admiring readers will have a hard time enlisting in it. He compares himself with Lobachevsky, and the metaphor of 'Non-Euclidean Philosophy' seems perfectly accurate in describing Speculative Materialism. After initial resistance, non-Euclidean geometry gained acceptance as a glittering mathematical exercise, though only with Einstein was it accepted as the proper description of physical space. Perhaps Meillassoux's coming works will achieve an Einsteinian moment in his own lifetime; perhaps only some distant future admirer will show his insights to be unavoidable; or perhaps the reading public will remain puzzled and choose a very different path. For there is certainly a degree of contingency in the history of philosophy, even if we decide not to concede it in the case of physical laws.

There are many features of Meillassoux's thought that command admiration. His lucid and economical style refutes the mediocre cliché that French philosophy consists entirely of precious obscurantists. His talent for reversing the accepted readings of past philosophers is so uncanny that students at the École Normale Supérieure viewed him as a nearly unparalleled tutor when preparing for the *Agrégation*. He has a dramatic flair that enables him to imagine lengthy speeches by critics years before these critics even appear. His power of argument in defense of some of the most bizarre theses of the twenty-first century is at times almost incredible. So too is his originality in attacking the principle of sufficient reason, since even the handful of forerunners who approach him in this respect make skeptical rather than productive use of these attacks. His assault on probabilistic reasoning is both formidable and strange. His critique of 'correlationism', in my view, will be remembered as the death blow to the mainstream continental philosophy that ran from 1900 (Husserl's *Logical Investigations*) to 2005 (the year before *After Finitude* was published). And finally, one can only admire his audacity in leading an ostensibly materialist philosophy to the realm of a Christ-like mediator and a virtual God, both of whom may or may not appear.

This chapter will reflect on the merits of Meillassoux's key concepts, after which the reader will find a fascinating interview with Meillassoux and some lengthy excerpts from *The Divine Inexistence*, never published before in any language. The organizing principle of this chapter is to build on what I have called the six pillars of *After Finitude*, though they are my own selection and not proclaimed as such in that book itself. Each of these topics branches out into further interesting themes, all of them establishing Meillassoux as one of the most intriguing figures in present-day philosophy.

First there is his critique of correlationism, which resembles the proverbial head of Janus. One face condemns the correlate of thought and world in the name of a reality independent of thought. Meanwhile, the other face condemns naïve realism in favor of the ingenious argument of the correlate. Given that Meillassoux's entire philosophy ironically hinges on his profound *respect* for the correlationist position, we should examine the possible difficulties faced by this position.

Second, there is the related point that Meillassoux believes in the existence of a position called 'Strong Correlationism' that does not cross the line into Absolute Idealism. For this reason he sees no merit in my claim in the interview (QM 213) that he closely resembles the German Idealists in the same manner as Badiou and Žižek. By contrast, it seems to me that Strong Correlationism is an impossible position, and if impossible then it does not survive long enough to be reversed into Meillassoux's Speculative Materialism.

Third, there is the very heart of Meillassoux's philosophy: factiality, or the absolute contingency of existence. While his proof is ingenious, the experience of trying to explain it to undergraduate students shows the difficulty of making it convincing to the average intelligent reader. Even for some readers who admire Meillassoux's verve, his proofs sometimes have the flavor of St

Anselm's ontological argument, in which the agility of the mind outruns genuine belief.

Fourth, there is the fact that Meillassoux is more interested in time than in space, as seen in his summary refusal to expand ancestrality and diachronicity to include cases of spatial distance from human observers. A vase falling unwitnessed in a country house is no challenge to correlationism, he says, since an unob-served event that is synchronous with humans is merely a lacuna, and this means that in principle it could be filled at any time we please. And this leads directly to the otherwise inexplicable fact that a philosophy built on radical contingency would make room for natural *laws*. The contingency defended by Meillassoux seems to entail only that laws could change without notice *from one moment to the next*. Within a given moment, he seems untroubled by the fact that there should be binding connections among things. He also focuses on the non-necessity of *causal* connections over time, and says nothing about the necessity of *compositional* con-nections in any given instant. It is unclear whether Meillassoux believes that in one instant a chunk of gold could be made of gold atoms, in the next of neon atoms, later of dirt, then of miniature armies, then of large-scale armies, then of a pack of feral dogs, and finally of all the odd-numbered buildings on the rue Danton in Paris, with all of these cases still being equally gold. Given the utter cosmic chaos entailed by his position, there is no reason to think he would say otherwise. But it remains striking that he focuses so exclusively on the connection between one moment of time and another, and rarely or never on the connections existing *within* any moment.

Fifth, there is Meillassoux's wonderful claim that contingency need not lead to instability. This is the very point on which he appeals to Lobachevsky as his model. This same point serves as the engine of *The Divine Inexistence*, since the transfinite elimination of probability at the level of Worlds is what allows Meillassoux to reject any worries about plausibility, and to imagine a World of justice in which the dead are reborn as the serious principle of ethics and politics today. Instead of weighing probable out-comes within a pre-given framework, he surfs along the contours of virtuality and finds four key moments: matter, life, thought, justice. None of these advents is any less probable than the others; indeed, none of them can meaningfully be described as probable or improbable at all.

Sixth, there is the claim with which *After Finitude* began: primary qualities are those that can be mathematized. Despite Meillassoux's admission in the interview that he has not yet published the full proof of this claim (QM 216), some aspects of the topic can already be discussed. The mathematizability of primary qualities is deeply intertwined with the project of a philosophy of immanence, which Meillassoux joins Bergson and Deleuze in endorsing. Although one can imagine plenty of immanentist philosophers who would not aspire to mathematize qualities, the reverse does not hold: any theory of the mathematizability of primary qualities must be an immanent philosophy, and any philosophy *opposed* to immanence will surely not allow primary qualities to be mathematized.

Finally, I will close with some general reflections on the challenge posed to us by Meillassoux's philosophy as of 2011. It is my belief that this philosophy stands at or near the center of the crucial decisions that will decide the next fifty years of our field, at least in the continental tradition. On two other occasions[1] I have used a 'hyperbolic' method for assessing the merits of philosophers. The method consists in no longer nitpicking the supposed mistakes of a philosopher, which tend to be relatively trivial. Instead, the hyperbolic method imagines the complete triumph of a philosopher, focusing on virtues rather than vices. We then ask ourselves: what would still be missing from philosophy if this particular thinker were to triumph completely? Why would I not cease my individual efforts and simply embrace this thinker as the final hero of all philosophical effort? Although this method could be humiliating when applied to works of specialist scholarship (which make no claim to a comprehensive vision of the world), it seems to be the proper method for dealing with systematic philosophers like Meillassoux. At the end of the day, any detailed complaints one might make about this or that aspect of his writings are less interesting than what he has already accomplished: the bold construction of a new system of speculative thought. Meillassoux deserves a hyperbolic reading.

Realism

As of 2011, Meillassoux remains most famous for his critique of 'correlationism', a term he coined himself. It is hard to defend realism these days against its natural opposite, idealism, for the paradoxical reason that so few philosophers admit to being idealists. As Meillassoux tells us in the interview in this book, the shortage of confessed idealists was precisely his reason for coining a new word:

> I had to avoid the term 'idealism', since it is loaded with ambiguity, and since there are numerous correlationists who refuse to be recognized as idealists ... But beyond the indeterminacy of the term ['idealism'], quite a game of denial takes place surrounding this name: it is claimed that Kant is not an idealist, since he produced a 'refutation of idealism'; that Husserl refutes the idealism of Platonic essences or Fregean significations, since he relates these to acts of subjectivity ... Thus I wanted a 'clean slate' freed from this system of evasions in order to localize a decision that none of these traditions can deny: the uncircumventible correlation between a subjective pole and an objective pole, both understood in the broadest sense of the term. (QM 212–13)

The struggle against correlationism soon became the guiding principle of the movement known as Speculative Realism, whose adherents agree on so little else. When reactions to this struggle are negative, it is usually because they overlook what is stated in the interview passage just quoted. Meillassoux does not claim that Kant, Husserl, and others are outright *idealists*, but simply that they take the correlate between human and world as the irremovable center of all rigorous philosophy. This correlate is obviously at the core of Kant's so-called Copernican Revolution. It is true that Kant was unwilling to abandon the things-in-themselves, despite rapid critiques by successors whose works he lived to read. The *Ding an sich* exists beyond human access; that is the whole point of this notion. But while positing something beyond human thought is enough to escape idealism, it is not enough to escape *correlationism*. The role of the thing-in-itself in Kant's philosophy is merely to haunt human awareness as an inaccessible something that *causes* the phenomenal realm (inconsistently so, since we know causation only as a category of the human understanding). In no way does the Critical Philosophy allow us to speak of the relations among things-in-themselves beyond all possible access, and indeed we cannot even be sure that they are multiple in number. Although Kant openly rejected the idealism that would eliminate the *Ding an sich*, he remains the textbook example of a correlationist. Thought and world, together and only together, stand at the center of his philosophy. This portion of the Kantian legacy is never decisively challenged by phenomenology, the movement that forms the very backbone of what is still called continental philosophy. To say that the thinking subject is always already outside itself, whether it be in intentional acts, practical dealings, lived embodiment, or a web of signifiers, does not refute the charge of correlationism: instead, it *proves* it. Everyone is quick to deny that a remote *cogito* aloof from the world has any meaning, and at the same time the autonomous world of inanimate entities is treated as unphilosophical, and exiled to natural science. The permanent correlation between human and world becomes the sole topic of philosophy. The initiation fee for all continental (and much analytic) philosophy has been that one must swear an oath never to speak naïvely of thought or world in isolation, but only in their mutual interplay. The best name for this default assumption, neither realist nor idealist, is in fact *correlationism*. And even if Meillassoux is right that pointing to resistance in one's opponents is not a rigorous argument against them, there is much educational value in considering what such resistance tells us. It would be an understatement to say that the critique of correlationism has struck a nerve; the basic dogma of continental philosophy is now under assault, and rightly so, in my view.

Kant is the figure at the storm center of debate over correlationism, and thus it is worth reflecting on his status. We begin with a few words from the unjustly forgotten Spanish philosopher José Ortega y Gasset. Though Ortega fancied himself an anti-Kantian, he began his career with ten years of ardor for the Kantian School, beginning with his student years under Hermann Cohen in Marburg. Reflecting on those years, Ortega writes as follows:

When the young men who between 1907 and 1911 learned their manual of philosophical arms in the fortress of Kantianism reached their twenty-sixth year – an age usually decisive in the career of a thinker – they were no longer neo-Kantians. We had not, however, completely wasted our time. We had studied Kant in depth, which is no small thing. More often than one would believe, even philosophers of a certain standing go through life dragging an insufficient knowledge of Kant behind them like a ball and chain. There is no making up for this lack because with Kant European thought swings a hundred and eighty degrees and takes its stand against the past in the form of a daring paradox. It is difficult for anyone well along in life to fill this lacuna in his education. In order to penetrate Kantian philosophy one needs the good will of those early years when good will is all one has.[2]

But Ortega was even more indebted to Kant than he realized. The central phrase of his career ('I am myself and my circumstances') and its central concept (life in the biographical – not biological – sense as the radical reality) are sterling examples of the correlationist standpoint. Ortega repeatedly attacks both naïve realism and modern idealism as excessive positions, to be remedied by a perpetual interplay of self and circumstance. While this leads him to abundant philosophical and historical insights, its ontological basis can be found already in Kant. There are revolutions, and then there are revolutions. The magnitude of philosophers can be judged by the magnitude of whatever previous revolution they succeed in inverting. Any philosophy that openly or tacitly endorses Kant's basic duopoly of thought and world, no matter how fresh and insightful, simply cannot be of the same magnitude as the philosophy of Kant. For all the genius of Heidegger (his assault on presence-at-hand is the high-water mark of twentieth-century philosophy), his perpetual interplay of *Sein* and *Dasein* remains within the Kantian horizon. The obvious greatness of Kant is worth reaffirming here, in view of repeated groundless assertions that the Speculative Realism movement 'bashes Kant' or holds that 'Kant is evil.' (In the latter case we are confused with Ayn Rand.) None the less, two questions still need to be posed. The first is whether Kant's basic outlook is still worth maintaining, and the second is this: if Kant is wrong, then *in what way* did he go wrong? On the first question Meillassoux and I would agree that correlationism has run its course, as an idea once but no longer liberating. But on the second question, we could hardly disagree more. That is the topic of this section.

We have seen that in Meillassoux's eyes, the correlational circle is a *powerful* argument. As he puts it in the interview:

I try to give to correlationism its most rigorous form – to isolate the fundamental argument in it. Ultimately, this argument amounts to a demonstration that every realist is condemned to a pragmatic contradiction: he claims to be able to think that which is independent of thought, but from the very fact of his thinking it he makes of it a correlate of his thought. (QM 213)

Apparently, there is no escaping it. To say 'a dog beyond thought' is a performative contradiction, since we are obviously now thinking of that dog, and thereby turning it into the *thought* of a dog. For Meillassoux this is no better than saying 'the book of which I am not speaking', even as I speak of it. To be a rigorous philosopher, he holds, one must run the correlationist gauntlet. The inability to think something while also not thinking it becomes the central problem of philosophy, which Meillassoux resolves by saying that of course *we are* thinking of it. This is the same basic claim found in German Idealism, but supposedly freed of the idealist's hypostasis of thought, as will be discussed in the next section.

It is also strikingly similar to the argument long known as 'Meno's Paradox', which asserts that we cannot search for something if we already have it and cannot search for it if we do not have it. As we read in Plato:

> *Meno*: But how will you look for something when you don't in the least know what it is? How on earth are you going to set up something you don't know as the object of your search? To put it another way, even if you come right up against it, how will you know that what you have found is the thing you didn't know?
>
> *Socrates*: I know what you mean. Do you realize that what you are bringing up is the trick argument that a man cannot try to discover either what he knows or what he does not know? He would not seek what he knows, for since he knows there is no need of the inquiry, nor what he does not know, for in that case he does not even know what he is to look for.[3]

This passage sets the stage for the theory of recollection, introduced in the famous discussion with the slave boy. Against the opposing views that (a) we can know nothing or (b) we already know everything that can be known, Socrates defends the famous third way: *philosophia*, a love of wisdom that neither knows nor fails to know its object. We do not have the wisdom we seek, but neither are we penned in amidst the limited confines of a pre-existent knowledge. We do have some direct access to reality itself, without this reality being confined to the access we have to it. This is the founding moment of genuine philosophy. My only regret is that the theory of recollection is the wrong way to proceed, since it places the things themselves back into the mind in the guise of something merely forgotten, thereby *conceding* Meno's point in indirect fashion. Instead of trying to put the things themselves into the mind in concealed form, we should realize that they do not need to be in the mind, since we are able to get them from the outside. By contrast, correlationism follows the path of Meno, claiming that we cannot know something unless we already know it. The father of *immanence* in philosophy is neither Spinoza nor Bergson nor Deleuze, but Meno himself, and thus philosophical immanence is a harmful project rather than a liberation.

Meillassoux is unpersuaded by this objection. In response to my question about Meno's Paradox, he answers in the interview as follows:

> It seems to me that the path you propose of a partial knowledge (in Socratic fashion) also fails: for this 'partial' character of knowledge, or this wisdom loved from afar, can only be in relation to a subject that is supposed to evaluate it as such. (QM 215–16)

In short, there is no way of thinking something without making it the correlate of my thought. We cannot love wisdom itself, since by being loved it is already a correlate of my thinking; there is only love of wisdom *for us*. For this reason Meillassoux views correlationism as the only rigorous starting point for philosophy, and it must be escaped on the basis of its own features rather than simply denied, as he puts it later in the same response:

> My thesis, in its harshest form, is that there is only one path by which to escape correlationism: the one that turns against it the weapon that even now has allowed it an undisputed reign over philosophy (continental philosophy, at least). This ultimate weapon, which allows it to challenge naïve realism no less than subjectivist metaphysics, is not the correlational circle alone, but rather the facticity of the correlate. (QM 216)

But even many who would not accept Meillassoux's route to factiality already accept his basic point about the correlate of thought and world. For them, there is no thinking of the real world without thinking of it, and in this way everything is circumscribed within the correlate.

We have already considered several different positions along what I called Meillassoux's Spectrum. As a reminder, here is the

Spectrum once more, simplified this time by collapsing Strong and Very Strong Correlationism into one:

- Dogmatic/Naïve Realism
- Weak Correlationism
- - - - - - - - - - - - - - - - - - -
- Strong Correlationism
- Absolute Idealism.

For our present purposes, the key dividing line runs between Weak and Strong Correlationism. What Weak Correlationism shares with Dogmatic/Naïve Realism is the view that it makes sense to speak of things outside thought. What Strong Correlationism shares with Absolute Idealism is the opposite view: namely, that it is a 'performative contradiction' to speak of things outside thought.

Let us now look at the two extremes on the list. Both Dogmatic/Naïve Realism and Absolute Idealism hold that absolute knowledge is possible. But for the former it is an absolute knowledge of things lying outside us, while in the latter there is no outside to reach, and thus absolute knowledge is a purely internal affair. Now, each of these positions is softened by the correlationist partner in its group. Whereas Dogmatic/Naïve Realism holds that things-in-themselves exist and can be known, Weak Correlationism says that they exist but cannot be known. And whereas Absolute Idealism holds that things-in-themselves are meaningless and therefore cannot exist, Strong Correlationism admits that they are meaningless but asserts that they none the less might exist anyway.

At the same time, Weak and Strong Correlationism are both called 'Correlationism' for good reason. For although the former is more strictly Kantian than the latter, the two inherit *both key aspects* of Kant's Copernican Revolution: (a) the human–world relation stands at the center of philosophy, since we cannot think something without thinking it, and (b) all knowledge is finite, unable to grasp reality in its own right. The two kinds of Correlationism differ only as to whether we can *think* the in-itself without reducing it to a correlate of thought (Weak) or whether this is a contradiction in terms (Strong).

And here is an interesting point of comparison between Meillassoux's ontology and my own. Meillassoux's position can be seen as a radicalization of *Strong* Correlationism, whereas my own Object-Oriented Philosophy can be read as a radicalization of *Weak* Correlationism:

- Dogmatic/Naïve Realism
- Weak Correlationism [reverses into Object-Oriented Philosophy]

- - - - - - - - - - - - - - - - - -

- Strong Correlationism [reverses into Speculative Materialism]
- Absolute Idealism

Let us consider what Meillassoux does and does not share with his neighbors on the Spectrum (a 'spectral dilemma' in a different sense from the one he intended). As we saw in Chapter 1, Meillassoux rejects Absolute Idealism because it has no reason to hypostatize the thought–world correlate; there *could* be something outside the correlate, no matter how unthinkable this may seem. At the same time, he rejects both Dogmatic/Naïve Realism and Weak Correlationism because he thinks they are wrong to hold that we can think the in-itself outside thought, as if escaping the correlational circle by pistol shot. And finally he does not remain with Strong Correlationism, but radicalizes this position by showing that its own presuppositions contain the principle of a type of absolute: the absolute contingency of everything that exists. This leads him to an unexpected proof that things-in-themselves must exist, since for contingency to exist there must be something that is contingent. In short, he rejects Absolute Idealism for being too absolute and Strong Correlationism for not being absolute enough. He thereby ends up *both* with the things-in-themselves rejected by the former *and* with the absolute knowledge rejected by the latter.

Let us now consider briefly the key spectral features of the Object-Oriented position. This philosophy rejects Dogmatic/Naïve Realism due to the impossibility of coincidence between a thing and the knowledge of that thing; in this respect, it accepts the Kantian critique. This issue will be covered in the sections on 'Immanence and Absence' and 'Mathematized Qualities' below, but the basic idea is that knowledge of a house *is not itself a house*, and therefore any immanent model of philosophy is impossible. Contra Bergson, the world cannot possibly be made of images, since any image of a thing is merely a translation of it. This philosophy rejects both Strong Correlationism and Absolute Idealism because it does not find compelling that we cannot think of something without thinking it. And finally, it does not remain with Weak Correlationism any more than Meillassoux remains with the Strong. Instead, it radicalizes the Weak position by showing that finitude is not merely a special feature of human knowledge, but a general feature of relation in all its forms, including the collision of inanimate clods of dirt. This leads to an unexpected proof that we *can* speak about the things-in-themselves, since there are perfectly good indirect ways of alluding to things that do not collapse into a 'negative theology' of the absent. In short, Object-Oriented Philosophy rejects Dogmatic/Naïve Realism for being too sanguine about the power of knowledge, but also rejects Weak Correlationism for being too pessimistic about knowledge. It thereby ends up *both* with the finitude rejected by the former *and* with the knowledge of real things rejected by the latter.

In this way, Meillassoux's Speculative Materialism and my own Object-Oriented Philosophy can be viewed as mirror images of each other. What bothers Meillassoux most about correlationism is its belief in the limitations of human knowledge; hence his title *After Finitude*. What bothers the Object-Oriented thinker most is the idea that finitude haunts human knowledge alone, and in so far as this is the basic principle of Kant's Critical Philosophy I could have written a book called *After Critique*. When Meillassoux thinks Kant is wrong, he turns to Fichte and Hegel, who restore the absolute. When I think Kant is wrong, I turn to Whitehead and Latour, who restore the flat ontology that treats humans no differently from candles, armies, and stars. While our different approaches to correlationism may seem only slightly different at first, the difference in results is staggering. Simply consider *The Divine Inexistence*, which portrays a world of special human priority marked by our ability to know the absolute. By contrast, any object-oriented work would display the opposite features: a world without human priority and without absolute knowledge. In this way we can even comprehend the initial misunderstandings between these two philosophies. Meillassoux has sometimes suggested that Object-Oriented Philosophy anthropomorphizes inanimate matter, which is not strictly true; I have sometimes viewed Speculative Materialism as a variant of German Idealism, which is also not strictly true.

But so far, I have merely described the difference between these two positions without arguing for why one is preferable. In this book we have already seen Meillassoux contrast them in one way, and I will do it in my own. There was a time in my earlier years when I also found the argument of the correlational circle to be an exceptionally powerful starting point for philosophy. The reason for my abandoning it was through a specific reading of Heidegger's famous tool-analysis. Not everyone draws realist conclusions from this analysis, but I have done so in my own published works. Since it is impossible for there to be a realist interpretation of the tool-analysis on Meillassouxian principles, to show how I read it in a realist manner will go a long way toward explaining the root of the difference between Object-Oriented Realism and Speculative Materialism.

It would be fair to describe Husserl's philosophy as one in which all that exists is either present to consciousness or at least potentially so. Heidegger's famous rejoinder is that for the most part we do not deal with things as entities populating the phenomenal sphere, but as what he calls *equipment*.[4] Normally, things are simply relied upon or taken for granted. The hammer is noticed only when it fails; we become conscious of the earth only during seismic tremors or when injuring ourselves while barefoot, and so forth. We thereby find a dualism between ready-to-hand items that are unconsciously taken for granted (*Zuhandenheit*) and present-at-hand phenomena that appear in consciousness (*Vorhandenheit*). One typical reading of this analysis sees it as a simple distinction between *theoria* and *praxis*: all conscious theoretical knowledge must emerge from a tacit background of unnoticed everyday practices. But there is a serious problem with this view. In Heideggerian terms it is true that phenomena in consciousness fail to do justice to the full depth of things, to their inscrutable withdrawal from all presence. Yet it is *also* the case that the practical handling of entities fails to do them justice as well. The geological survey of a mountain and the climbing of that mountain have a very different structure, but what both have in common is their failure to exhaust that mountain in its very being. The geologist must always leave many of its features unnoticed, while the climber also fails to grasp aspects of the mountain that are relevant for birds, ants, snow leopards, or yeti. In short, human theory and human praxis are both translations or distortions of the subterranean reality of mountain-being, which is no more exhausted by sentient action than by sentient thought.

And even beyond this, we have to consider that not only sentience fails to grasp the things in their depth. A raindrop does not make contact with the full reality of the mountain, and neither does a snowflake, a gust of wind, or a helicopter crashing into its face. All of these objects encounter the mountain-object only in some translated, distorted, oversimplified form, despite their apparent lack of 'consciousness'. The withdrawal of one object from another is not produced by a magical entity called the mind, but is the very nature of relationality, even among mindless hammers and atoms.

As a result, the tool-analysis leads to a strikingly *realist* outcome. Things are never identical with the human knowledge, handling, touching, tasting, or hatred of them. All of these activities could possibly be linked under the term 'intentionality', but whereas the intentionality of Brentano and Husserl is a matter of *immanent* objectivity, we are now concerned with a transcendent kind of object. It is true that the hammer takes on a specific configuration both for the construction worker and for the scientific specialist on hammers (assuming the latter person exists). But what is most relevant here is the *transcendent* hammer that startles us with surprises, shattering in our hands or rotting and rusting more quickly than expected. The present-at-hand hammer cannot explain these sudden surprises, and hence by subtraction we arrive at the notion of a withdrawn, subterranean tool that enters into relation with me and with other animate and inanimate entities as well.

It is easy to imagine two possible responses by Meillassoux to this analysis. The first is that he would play the card of the correlational circle. It is true that the hammer shatters unexpectedly, but this shattering is still only a shattering *for me*. Even if we do not wait for such an incident, and simply deduce beforehand that there must be a thing-in-itself deeper than the present-at-hand hammer, then even this deeper hammer is only *deeper for me*. The correlational circle is inescapable, and can only be radicalized by working through its facticity, as Meillassoux himself does. His second response would say that even if we *can* deduce that there must be something lying outside our relation to us, as a principle explaining future change, this makes sense only if we assume the truth of the principle of sufficient reason. For if we join Meillassoux in allowing for the advent without reason of broken hammers amidst functional hammers, in *ex nihilo* fashion, then any need for a cryptic reservoir of hammer-being immediately disappears. We can thus return to a philosophy of immanence without worrying about ghostly, non-relational utensils hidden in the shadows of the cosmos.

In other words, we imagine that Meillassoux would respond to Object-Oriented Philosophy with *a twofold theory of gaps*. First, the Object-Oriented thinker asserts the possibility of gaining some sense of the hammer lying beyond our access to it. Meillassoux answers that this 'sense of the hammer' is merely a 'sense of the hammer *for us*', and thus there is a gap between the hammer we encounter and whatever hammer might exist in itself apart from our knowledge of it. Second, the Object-Oriented thinker says that the apparent hammer has a *reason* for appearing, and that this reason is a withdrawn hammer that generates the appearance (in partnership with the perceiver) while never directly appearing in its own right. Here Meillassoux answers that new accessible hammers can simply arise *ex nihilo* without having a source in some hidden hammer-thing.

These two themes are not just intimately related; they are actually one and the same. The first is the absolute gap found in Strong Correlationism between knowledge and being. (Meillassoux does eventually offer his own proof that things-in-themselves must exist, but for now we are dealing only with his rejection of realism as a starting point.) In this case, the gap is created by denying that any initial link exists between thought and what lies outside thought, since the correlational circle renders impossible any contact between the for-us and the in-itself. The second theme is the absolute gap found in Speculative Materialism between appearances and the deeper layers that generate them. Here, the gap arises by denying that one of the two sides of the gap exists; for Meillassoux, *there are* no deeper layers hiding beneath appearance. In short, both points stem from Meillassoux's denial of a connection between one realm and another. He denies the principle of sufficient reason, which lies at the very core of Object-Oriented Philosophy. It is already safe to say that disagreement over the principle of sufficient reason is the key difference between the two philosophies. I will deal with this topic in the section entitled 'A Raid on Sufficient Reason' below.

The Real and the Thinkable

In Chapter 1 we saw how Meillassoux's Speculative Materialism arises as a radicalized version of what he calls Strong

Correlationism. If Strong Correlationism is impossible, then so is the philosophy of Meillassoux. We can easily see this by looking at the other three basic positions on the Spectrum. Obviously, Meillassoux can do nothing of interest with Dogmatic/Naïve Realism, which simply *asserts* the existence and the knowability of a reality independent of the mind. This position has not taken the trouble to run the gauntlet of the correlational circle. It is a pre-Kantian philosophy that fails to address the paradox that if I think the independent existence of my hands, then I am *thinking* them, and therefore they are simply *hands for thought*. Just as obviously, Meillassoux cannot do much with Weak Correlationism, since despite its Kantian awareness that appearances are appearances only for us, it still harbors a lingering remainder of the dogmatic position, with a *Ding an sich* that can be directly thought even if not directly known. This is not a sufficiently consistent form of correlationism to satisfy Meillassoux, who insists that to *think* something outside thought is just as problematic as to *know* something outside thought.

The true rival for Strong Correlationism is, of course, Absolute Idealism. Both positions agree that it is meaningless to think anything existing outside thought. The Absolute Idealist then draws what appears to be the only logical conclusion: since things-in-themselves are meaningless, they cannot exist. The thought–world correlate is thereby hypostatized, and existence is forbidden to anything lying beyond it. But Meillassoux responds that the fact of something being meaningless *for us* does not entail that it *cannot exist* in its own right. We only know what exists for thought, not what exists in and of itself; no one has ever taken a voyage outside the correlational circle to see what the outside might contain. Therefore, it is not impossible that there might be things in themselves. In this way, Strong Correlationism triumphs over Absolute Idealism. But Meillassoux does not remain here for long, since he holds that Strong Correlationism already contains the seeds of its own radicalization, and cannot endure as a halfway house of philosophy. We have already seen how he attempts to turn the flank of this position. The only thing that prevents Strong Correlationism from melting into Absolute Idealism is the principle that there *might* be something outside the correlate, however meaningless this sounds. And this 'might' is effective only in so far as it is as an *absolute* possibility, not just as a possibility *for us*; otherwise, Absolute Idealism would win the struggle. In other words, what is most important is not the thought–world correlate, but rather the *facticity* of this correlate. It did not *need* to exist, contra the views of Absolute Idealism. The correlate is purely contingent, and might never have come about. We thus enter Meillassoux's novel realm of the *factial*, and the rest of his philosophy follows with logical precision from this basis. No necessary being can exist; nothing is necessary but contingency itself; there can be no principle of sufficient reason, since this would lead to a necessary being, which has been shown to be impossible; there cannot be a contradictory being, since it would have no Other and thus would be a necessary being; things must exist independently of thought, or else there would be no contingent beings. All these basic features of Meillassoux's ontology hinge on his supposed demonstration that there is such a thing as Strong Correlationism that avoids melting into Absolute Idealism.

Yet it is far from clear that Strong Correlationism is even possible. We can understand why someone would be a Dogmatic/Naïve Realist; all they need to do is ignore the correlational circle. We can also understand why someone would be an Absolute Idealist; all they need to do is insist on the non-existence of anything outside the circle. We can even understand the source of Weak Correlationism: the ambivalent insight that human knowledge is trapped in the circle, but that there must be something outside the circle none the less. It is somewhat harder to accept Strong Correlationism, which is neither fish, nor fowl, nor fish and fowl at once. This hybrid position rides as a fellow traveler of Absolute Idealism *almost* to the end of the road. It joins the Idealist in calling it naïve and meaningless to think anything outside thought. But it then declares: 'Despite the senseless character of such a possibility, things might exist outside thought anyway.' If this is impossible then there will be no facticity of the correlate, and Meillassoux can only become an Absolute Idealist, given his passionate commitment to the supposed strength of the correlationist argument.

We find an extraordinary audacity, unnoticed by reviewers so far, in Meillassoux's distinction between Strong Correlationism and Absolute Idealism. First it is said that philosophy is confined within the closed circle of thought, so that any thought of things-in-themselves is simply a *thought* of them. But then this closed circle is said to have a *possible* Other: one that seems meaningless from the inside, but which might exist anyway, since there is no proof that the meaningful exhausts the real. The difficulty

here is obvious. Note that Meillassoux does not merely confront
the Absolute Idealist with a Zen *koan* pointing to an absurd and
ill-defined remainder that thought cannot recuperate. Unlike the
great Zen masters of legend, Meillassoux is not merely shouting
'Wu!', or cryptically placing a penny on his finger, or barking like
a dog when asked about the Buddha-nature, or punching Hegel in
the jaw when meeting him on the road. Instead, there is an actual
semantic content to his claim that Absolute Idealism is wrong.
And yet, the confessed meaninglessness of that content bears an
uncanny resemblance to 'the sound of one hand clapping' or the
problem of 'the gateless gate'. Meillassoux is effectively saying: 'I
don't even understand what "things-in-themselves" *means*. Yet
they might exist, and thus the Absolute Idealist is wrong.' But if we
take seriously the claim that things outside thought are a strictly
meaningless notion, then we have to be willing to substitute other
meaningless notions into the sentence just given:

1. 'I don't even understand what "things-in-themselves" *means*.
   Yet they may exist, and thus the Absolute Idealist is wrong.'
2. 'I don't even understand what "non-white white" *means*. Yet it
   may exist, and thus the Absolute Idealist is wrong.'
3. 'I don't even understand what "Buddha-less Buddha" *means*.
   Yet it may exist, and thus the Absolute Idealist is wrong.'
4. 'I don't even understand what "Wu!" *means*. Yet it may exist,
   and thus the Absolute Idealist is wrong.'
5. 'I don't even understand what "square circle" *means*. Yet it
   may exist, and thus the Absolute Idealist is wrong.'

Now obviously, Meillassoux cannot establish his philosophy by
means of 'radicalizing' Statements 2, 3, 4, or 5, whatever that
would mean. It is not simply *any meaningless statement at all*
that eventually does the work of dethroning Absolute Idealism,
but a *specific* form of meaninglessness: namely, the fact that to
think a thing outside thought has no meaning. With one gesture
Meillassoux initially denies existence to the thing-in-itself because
it makes no sense, but with a second gesture he admits that he
knows full well what it means, and uses *that very meaning* to
undercut the Absolute Idealist's closed circle of thought. This is
especially unusual given his unyielding commitment to the law of
non-contradiction.
 Once the Strong Correlationist position is established and

dethroned, Meillassoux does try to prove the existence of things existing independently of thought, as we have seen. But this occurs only through the long detour of the correlational circle, and we will find in the section on 'Immanence and Absence' that the argument is nearly bankrupted by the toll it pays along the way. The withered thing-in-itself that remains after this long journey is one of the least robust forms of *an sich* I can imagine, and this is the basis of my continuing to group Meillassoux, despite his objections, with the German Idealists he so admires. As we know from the interview, this admiration extends even to their immediate forerunners:

> [The most underrated thinkers in the history of philosophy are] Reinhold, Jacobi, Maimon: the German thinkers who formed the junction between Kant and Fichte. With these philosophers, we draw close to the edge of what would soon become the volcano of German Idealism. It is a volcano that would not have been able to erupt without them, even though Schelling and Hegel esteemed them lightly. (QM 221)

New Laws Without Warning

One of the obvious pillars of Meillassoux's philosophy is the contingency of the laws of nature. Contingency entails that one thing is not caused by another, but arises by itself for no reason at all. His defense of contingency is due partly to his horror that the principle of sufficient reason cannot enter an infinite regress of causes, and hence must come to rest in some necessary being, which is impossible (since things are defined by their predicates, and there is no 'prodigious predicate' that could make a thing necessarily exist). It is also due partly to his vivid sense that effects must exceed their causes. The hyper-contingency and hyper-chaos of Meillassoux's system should thus point to a universe in which nothing is connected with anything else.

But as already described in Chapter 2, Meillassoux does not push this claim all the way to the end. Plenty of chaos reigns in his system at the level of laws of nature, which can change at any moment for no reason whatsoever. Here, probability does not apply. We cannot index a finite number of cases of Universes so as to measure the likelihood of *our* universe of laws existing rather than another. The apparent stability of our own world does not prove the existence of a concealed reason that secretly guides the universe towards our own present array of natural laws. But the question raised in Chapter 2 is why Meillassoux needs any concept of *laws* at all. For the most part, intra-worldly events for Meillassoux are governed by laws. These are said to be contingent, but only in the sense that they might change at any moment: not in the sense that *for as long as they are established* they might be violated every now and then. Advent in Meillassoux's universe always comes from the top, through the sudden change of laws for no reason, not from local rogue incidents in which specific billiard balls would violate the general rule by weeping or exploding when struck. Worlds change by advent *ex nihilo* without reason; the intra-worldly is governed by laws. Even an aleatory approach to nature cannot make the intra-worldly realm contingent, since the statistical laws of quantum mechanics are still statistical *laws*. And while it is true that Meillassoux also uses 'advent' in *The Divine Inexistence* to refer to such special intra-worldly occurrences as the appearance of new animal species or revolutionary artworks, he never extends the use of 'advent' to refer to *all* intra-worldly incidents no matter how mediocre. A wall is always built between the exceptional and the banal, between the status of laws themselves and that of incidents governed by those laws.

In other words, Meillassoux gives us a frankly dualistic ontology when it comes to contingency. Advent is not for everyone and everything; it is an elite sort of event that happens without reason once in a while, not constantly in every tiniest happening in the cosmos. The rabble of everyday incidents is governed by law, and any contingency that emerges from these incidents must be ordained in the Palace of Worlds, not *within* a given World. Despite its ominous name suggesting ubiquity, hyper-chaos functions as an intermittent trickle-down economy, not as a provincial, grassroots uprising. As I will say in the concluding section 'A Raid on Sufficient Reason', the real problem with this model is that it allows for only two kinds of connection between things: complete causal connection (law), and no connection at all (contingency). But the real trick is to explain the fact that things are *both* connected and disconnected. The proper name for this ambivalent connectivity is 'the principle of sufficient reason'. Once this principle is abandoned, as in Meillassoux's philosophy, we are left with nothing but gaps and direct connections, with no possibility of the incomplete transmission of influence between things. The problem of how things can touch without touching, the central problem of Object-Oriented Philosophy, could only be nonsense for Meillassoux; for him, they are either already touching or never touch at all. It is yet another performance of Meno's Paradox, for which having without having is impossible.

There is a long historical context for Meillassoux's position on this problem, as well as for my own. Although causal influence is an important theme of Ancient Greek philosophy, it is never viewed as especially problematic. Even in Plato, for whom the gap between the intelligible and sensible worlds is so immense, it is never doubted that one world can influence the other. In Plotinus, there are certainly discrete leaps between the levels of emanation, yet this emanation occurs without obstruction, as can the reverse movement of the lover, musician, and philosopher who (with varying degrees of success) move backwards towards the One. Aristotle gives a magnificent account of causation, but again with no sign of perplexity that causal influence should ever occur. It is only with the Ash'arite theologians in Iraq that we witness the birth of what is now known as *occasionalism*. Here, the causal gap between realities is very real: so real that only Allah can cast a stone or burn a ball of cotton. The apparent natural causes for these events are merely occasions for divine intervention; even the creation of the world must occur again in every instant.[5] In the fourteenth century we meet the French skeptic Nicholas of Autrecourt, 'the medieval Hume', who may or may not have taken his ideas about the lack of necessary connection from al-Ghazali. In the sixteenth century there is Francisco Suárez, who attacked the occasionalists (without knowing their names), but whose own model of substantial forms requires that things interact via accidents rather than directly.

But it is once again in France, with no less a figure than Descartes, that the problem of causal gaps takes on full-blown form in European thought. Given the total difference in kind between cognition and extension, God is needed to link mind and body. With Cordemoy and Malebranche, body–body interactions again become a problem. From this point onward, gaps become perhaps the *dominant* theme of European metaphysics. Whether in Spinoza's parallel attributes, Leibniz's windowless monads, or Berkeley's disconnected appearances generated by God, direct causal contact between at least some kinds of realities becomes impossible. And while this era of high-rolling metaphysics might seem quaint and amusing to the professional technicians of 2011, a variant of the occasionalist gap can still be found at the core of mainstream philosophy. For if God is no longer allowed a monopoly on real causal interactions, the human mind assumes the same monopoly. In Hume it is custom or habit alone that links the things, while in Kant the categories of the understanding fulfill this function. If in occasionalism properly speaking we have independent substances with no way to connect them, in the Hume/Kant era we have the connections while knowing little to nothing about the underlying substances. In the first case things are totally disconnected, and only God can touch them. In the second case things are always already connected, and it is their possible existence outside this connection that is under dispute. In any case, the gap or lack thereof between things and things, or things and appearances, has become a durable part of the philosophical landscape of the West. Managing the interplay of these two extremes is now a crucial aspect of every philosophy, whether openly or not.

We should ask where Meillassoux fits into this landscape of ontological gaps. In spring 2007, I published an early review of the French version of *Après la finitude*, in which my concluding section was entitled 'Hyper-Occasionalism'. There, comparing Meillassoux's position with those of the classical occasionalists and the Hume/Kant axis, I wrote as follows:

> Meillassoux's philosophy can be read as a more extreme form of occasionalism than either of these schools. In his system there is no God able to do what inherent causal power cannot accomplish, since he excludes all necessary beings. Nor does he merely say, with Hume, that we 'cannot know' whether causal powers exist – after all, Meillassoux states absolutely that there is no reason, no cause for anything to happen. His occasionalism is not merely a de-linking of distinct entities viewed from the standpoint of human knowledge, but an explicit decree about the ancestral things themselves. He leaves us with a cosmos of utterly isolated entities, none capable of exerting determinative forces against the others.[6]

Although I would not back away from the spirit of this passage today, I would qualify it by saying that Meillassoux is only *half* a hyper-occasionalist. This description is perfectly suitable when referring to his treatment of the possible alteration without reason of laws of nature. But it does not work at all when describing the action of laws themselves in linking intra-worldly beings; nor is Meillassoux's epistemology notable for an occasionalist spirit, since he sees no difficulty, in principle, for rational subjects simply to know things absolutely as they are. Like every philosopher who deals with the problem of gaps, Meillassoux finds it impossible to allow a universe of disconnected points of reality utterly unlinked with one another. But whereas such philosophies in the past always allowed either God or the mind to provide the missing link, in Meillassoux's case it is *laws* and *knowledge* that serve the role of direct connection, though these laws need not be durable and the knowledge need not arise if humans remain ignorant. But for Meillassoux, no less than for occasionalists, Humeans, and Kantians, connections are either direct or they do not exist at all. None of these positions considers the possible alternative: that connections between things do exist, but in *indirect* form. But this is the true meaning of the principle of sufficient reason.

Immanence and Absence

As early as Chapter 1, we saw that Meillassoux is far more interested in time than in space. The ancestral world before humans, and its 'diachronic' expansion which includes events following human extinction along with those preceding our appearance, is seen as posing a challenge to correlationism. The same does not hold for the synchronic realm of space, no matter how distant a place we have in mind. Spatial absence is treated as a mere lacuna ('I can always choose to go to the country house to watch the vase and reabsorb it within the correlate'), as are very ancient events that do not pre-exist the correlate of thought and world. The point of this is that Meillassoux cannot see any threat to the correlate in the present instant, because for him the present is always entirely immanent, with nothing withheld in any sort of cryptic reserve. The mere spatial distance of the Andromeda Galaxy does not conceal it from the correlate, since in principle *one could* travel there and bring the entities of that galaxy directly before our view. The fact that these entities are not before us right now is of no ontological significance; it is merely a lacuna in perception, no different from the unseen faces of a mailbox or pylon in the descriptions of a Husserl.

There are several things to be said about this. We already saw that this exclusive focus on the *temporal* challenge to correlationism gives too much attention to efficient causation and the sequence of events it triggers across time. But if we ask instead about what Aristotle calls material and formal causation, in this case we are speaking of a 'synchronic' issue confined in a given instant. Rather than speaking of causation in the usual sense, we are referring instead to the internal composition of things. And on this level the radical contingency of everything, while not strictly impossible, is more difficult to imagine. I have already given the examples of gold being made of silver atoms, of miniature horses, or even of skyscrapers larger than the gold itself. In Meillassoux's hyper-chaotic universe there is perhaps no reason to assume that strange compositional laws of this sort cannot emerge and develop, but what is noteworthy is that the issue is one that he never chooses to discuss. This fact is worrisome for those suspicious of the idealist overtones of his system (no less than the systems of Badiou and Žižek), because it suggests continuing allegiance to a vision of the world as merely a depthless counterpoint to human thought. If we consider instead a contemporary thinker of levels and layers such as Manuel DeLanda,[7] we can easily feel the difference. One of DeLanda's major themes is how smaller assemblages or societies build up into larger ones, thereby giving rise to new emergent entities. This many-layered aspect of realism is perhaps not ruled out in Meillassoux's ontology, but like other inanimate interactions it plays a very small role in his philosophical drama. He speaks of advent, not of emergence, because novelty for him is something that arises from one moment to the next, whereas for DeLanda novelty arises at each level as we proceed from protons, to atoms, to molecules, to chunks of gold, to jewelry fashioned from these chunks, to museums filled with the jewelry, to international museum associations. For DeLanda, there are many novelties in any instant; for Meillassoux, they happen only between one moment and the next.

But perhaps this lack of a mereology or theory of composition in his thinking is merely an error of omission; indeed, perhaps he could provide such a theory on demand immediately after reading this book. Yet there is a more serious difficulty with his preference for time over space: namely, his assumption that only remoteness from accessibility enables us to make an initial challenge to the thought–world correlate. The current status of the center of the earth remains invisible to humans and their most advanced machines. Yet in principle we *could* invent a mighty drill and a heat-proof camera capable of illuminating the core of our planet, whereas we cannot do the same for things existing prior to the emergence of thought. The latter are no mere lacunae, and hence they cannot easily be recuperated into the thought–world correlate. But the tendency to go to ancestral depths of the past in order to call the correlate into question suggests that Meillassoux's concept of *the present* is too correlational from the start.

This can be seen in his concept of the in-itself, which I have already said is insufficiently robust. When Meillassoux gives his proof for the existence of things-in-themselves, what he has proven is simply that there are things that continue to exist even if all intelligent life is exterminated. The reason this is insufficiently robust is as follows: continuing to exist following the death of humans is only *one* aspect of the independence of things from us. The other aspect is that they must be independent of us *right now*, when we are not yet eliminated from the cosmos. This is the more serious problem concerning things-in-themselves, but Meillassoux's commitment to *immanence* renders him unable to take the problem seriously, or indeed even to notice it.

The problem concerning the things before us right now is whether we are really able to have adequate knowledge of them. For instance, consider the moon. It is easy enough to hold that the moon will continue its orbit long after the rising seas and spreading deserts destroy us all. But until that happens, we humans remain on the earth's crust, making scientific observations about the moon, writing poems about it, or simply staring at it with glazed and sentimental eyes. And no matter how exhaustive our knowledge of the moon may be, that knowledge *is not itself the moon*. Our knowledge does not reflect sunlight; it does not affect the tides; it does not orbit the earth; travelers do not visit our knowledge in spacecraft to plant national flags; comets do not strike our knowledge and leave craters. Here I do not jest. If our knowledge of the moon were truly an accurate copy of the moon, then it would *replicate* the moon, making it perfectly dispensable. Not only would the moon exist following the extermination of humans, but also humans could happily endure *the extermination of the moon*, sleeping soundly in the awareness that it had already been duplicated in countless minds.

Whenever I raise this objection to the model of absolute knowledge, the complaint is always heard that the argument is ludicrous. After all, who since Berkeley really thinks that the moon manifested in knowledge is the same as the moon itself? Yet this sarcasm misses the point. For it is not a question of whether philosophers are truly insane enough to think that their knowledge of the moon is interchangeable with the moon itself. Obviously, few would defend such an absurdity. But the question is this: if partisans of absolute knowledge recognize an asymmetry between the moon and its appearance in thought, why do they persist in thinking that exhaustive knowledge of anything is possible? The moon as it appears to us is a more or less adequate model, composed of a vastly simplified range of features: a glowing white circle moving through the sky, accompanied by all the known lunar facts that we attach to the friendly circular shape known to everyone from childhood onward. But *none of this information adds up to a moon*, and neither would the exhaustive reams of information available to almighty God. Thus, there is 'something more' to the moon. And to think that this 'something more' is nothing but an ill-defined *physical matter* in which the form found in knowledge is stamped and gains autonomous power – this is merely a primitive version of classical ontology that need not be refuted here. The 'something more' of the moon is not just matter, but a unifying principle never exhausted by all attempts to approach it from the outside.

For this reason, to challenge the thought–world correlate we need not ask about the ancestral moon before any thinking creature arose. For even the 'synchronic' moon in the moment you read this sentence continues to orbit and sleep and attract in a way that our knowledge of the moon cannot fathom and certainly cannot replace. For this reason I cannot understand the appeal of 'immanence' in philosophy, unless as an overreaction to the long reign of hidden religious entities that crushed the imaginative spirit beneath its heels. But the danger is that this spirit of immanence will return the favor by crushing the moon beneath its own heels, reducing it to a polished surface accessible to a human knower. This very disagreement leads to the following exchange in the interview:

GH: *On a related point, you call your position 'Speculative Materialism', yet you do not believe in an objective world of material lying outside all thought . . . How would you answer the charge that this materialism is no materialism at all?*

> QM: I believe that my previous response has shown the unjust charac-
> ter of this critique. I do not 'believe' in an objective world indepen-
> dent of thought because I maintain that it is possible to *demonstrate*,
> in a precise sense, that such a world external to thought does indeed
> exist, and necessarily so. I 'know' that there is such a world – and
> that is what makes me a materialist, not a believer. (QM 217)

Meillassoux's response is understandable, since he has in fact
taken the trouble to demonstrate that the world *would continue to
exist even if humans were exterminated*. Even so, I would repeat
the charge that he does not accept 'an objective world of material
lying outside all thought' (his negative response to the word 'belief'
is not germane to the present dispute). The moon for Meillassoux
will continue to orbit after our collective human demise. Yet this
does not mean that Meillassoux's philosophy grants the moon
its proper degree of depth, which requires withdrawal behind its
accessibility to thought, a withdrawal that undercuts any immanent or absolute form of knowledge. The latter simply never does
justice to the moon itself. For this reason, Speculative Materialism
is certainly a materialism, given that materialist philosophies
have never been shy about reducing entities to a limited number
of tangible properties. But if it also claims to be realism (and
Meillassoux has been using this term less frequently of late), then
this is dubious. Speculative Materialism is too quick to make the
moon fully convertible with knowledge of the moon.[8]

Non-Totalizable Worlds

Another of the most intriguing ideas in Meillassoux's philosophy
stems from his use of transfinite mathematics. More specifically,
we have seen that he uses the insights of Cantor to exempt the
laws of nature from all probability or improbability. The mea-
surement of probability requires a Whole of indexed cases, even
if they are infinite in number. In other words, we have to know
how many possibilities there are before we can calculate the probability that any one of them might occur. If not for this portion
of Meillassoux's argument, *The Divine Inexistence* would be an
impossible book. The brazen hope for the rebirth of humans laid
low by miserable deaths, and the possible emergence of a virtual
God who does not yet exist, would obviously be laughable if pre-
mised on the laws of everyday probability. In response to such

laughter, Meillassoux reminds us that the contingency of laws of nature cannot be described as either probable or improbable. Perhaps even more persuasively, he recalls Pascal's remark that the rebirth of the dead would hardly be more incredible than the fact that the living were born at all.

Here I will not critique the logic of Meillassoux's claim. While I initially found it the least convincing claim of *After Finitude*, it is also among the most fascinating, and fascinating plants deserve to grow for a season before being exposed to the frost of critique. What I will do instead is speculate on whether this aspect of his philosophy might survive in philosophies very different from Meillassoux's own. One of the ironies of building a system of philosophy is that the thinker always aims at certain detailed *results*, even though these results are never accepted except by the most slavish of disciples. Only rarely does discussion of Spinoza insist on the correctness of his detailed ethical prescriptions; instead, Spinoza inspires allegiance at the most basic level of his ontology. Fans of Leibniz almost never literally believe that we live in the best of all possible worlds; this conclusion was extremely important for Leibniz himself, but is dismissed with a wave of the hand by most of those who adore his writings, including me. The same goes for Nietzsche, who sincerely trembled when thinking the eternal recurrence of the same, though I have never met a Nietzschean who trembles before the recurrence as well, or even believes in it in the slightest. Nietzsche is loved by his fans for his verve and style, for his vision of the will to power, for his spirit of affirmation despite the tragedy of existence. But his central doctrine, the eternal recurrence, is accepted by no one.

Philosophers aim at conclusions, yet their effect on history is often more pronounced through their *route* toward those conclusions. Even if we imagine the most illustrious possible career for Quentin Meillassoux, it is likely that this phenomenon will befall him as well. Perhaps his admiring readers two centuries from now will never dream of accepting his sudden advent of justice *ex nihilo*; maybe they will see it only as an intriguing historical *curio* in much the same way that we now view Leibniz's optimistic theodicy. None the less, it is quite conceivable that Meillassoux's use of the transfinite realm to eliminate probability will survive as a method even after his own deductions from it have vanished amidst the disbelief of his intellectual heirs.

His method is certainly appealing. Normally, we confine our

reflections to the interior of a specific natural world. We size up the chances of one thing or another coming to pass, and fix our attention on the most likely positive options that might be available. Even if it is *possible* to wake up tomorrow as a king, or to share our next breakfast with the Messiah, only children, fanatics, and the mentally ill ever expect such things to happen. But by removing all talk of probability with respect to the basic structure of reality, Meillassoux acquires the right to speak as a child or a madman would while still keeping a straight face. Instead of focusing on the most likely possibilities within a given World, we travel along the contours of the world itself, mapping its possible folds. We articulate reality into the most *interesting* or most *important* segments rather than the most 'likely' ones. And in this way we end up with matter, life, thought, and justice as the four major spheres of Meillassoux's world. But for him, as for every philosopher, his future influence may owe less to this specific conclusion than to his model of advent itself. Once philosophical speculation is untethered from the laws of probability, what use might future thinkers make of Meillassoux's topology of being? If they do not accept matter, life, thought, and justice as the major folds in the mountain range of the world, then what alternative landscapes might they suggest?

Mathematized Qualities

Here we can be brief, since this topic was already addressed in passing. For Meillassoux, the distinction between primary and secondary qualities is perfectly valid, and primary qualities are those that can be mathematized. But this suggests the same isomorphy between thought and being that was rejected in the section on 'Immanence and Absence', since by definition the mathematical is the knowable, and we have seen the problem that arises from equating knowledge with being. In the interview, I asked Meillassoux the following question: 'If you say that the primary reality of what exists is that which can be known about it, isn't this just a form of idealism?' (QM 216). In response, he emphasized that while mathematics may be a form of construction, this does not disqualify its constructions from being independent of thought. For he rejects the analogy of *architectural* construction as something planned and created by humans, and embraces the alternative model of *archaeological* construction:

But let's suppose that by 'construction' I refer instead to the mechanisms by which an archaeologist has set up a dig site in order to excavate some ruins without damaging them. In this case the 'constructions' (a complex of winches, sounding lines, scaffolding, spades, brushes, etc.) are not destined to *produce* an object, as in the case of architecture. On the contrary, they are made with a view to *not* interfering with the object at which they aim: that is to say, excavating the ruins without damaging them, in unearthing them 'as is', and not as modified or even destroyed by the impact of the excavation tools. Thus, mathematics and experimental sciences can certainly be human 'constructions': but this does not prove that they are such in the sense of architectural construction rather than archaeological 'discovery' (in the manner in which one speaks of 'the discovery of ruins or of a treasure'). (QM 216–17)

The passage is remarkably vivid. But here, as in the section on 'Immanence and Absence', it addresses only one side of the problem. For it is not enough to show that mathematics is able to address things that exist without humans having made them, and which will endure even after all humans are extinguished. Instead, it also must be shown that the mathematical, the knowable, is truly capable of grasping the qualities of the things themselves.

For reasons discussed in the case of the moon in the section on 'Immanence and Absence', I deny that this is possible. Against Meillassoux's claim, I hold that the primary qualities of things can only be those which *are not* mathematizable, not strictly knowable. But rather than placing us in a worthless limbo where things-in-themselves exist but at an unapproachable distance from humans, this brings us to a place that is neither the knowledge found in gods nor the ignorance found in serpents and bison. Instead it is the love of wisdom, the *philosophia* that lies between the bison and the gods. We know without knowing, and think without thinking, by *alluding* to a thing rather than reducing it to a model contained within thought.

A Raid on Sufficient Reason

It is admirable to nitpick rough drafts and half-formed thoughts, just as it is healthy to file our fingernails. But on those rare occasions when a new speculative philosophy arises in the world, trivial fault-finding is worthy of our dismay. Although niggling critique strikes a pose of intellectual rigor, in forbidding the new any leeway to be wrong it ratifies the staleness of the old. A new philosophy is a rare opportunity; its author should be boxed with gloves, not assaulted with knives. This is the principle of hyperbolic reading. The power of trivial critique to demoralize its target comes from its stalling of forward progress: 'You shall not leave the schoolhouse before acquiring remedies for your thirteen weaknesses.' But once this is done a fourteenth is discovered, and so on into old age. The antidote should be obvious: we allow the new philosophy *maximum forward progress*, concede all or most of its claims, and then ask whether we are now satisfied. If so, then we have found our philosophy in the work of another and can accept it with minor modifications. If not, then we profit from the new philosopher by sensing the corners of our minds where light has still not been shed.

Imagine, then, the absolute triumph of the philosophy of Quentin Meillassoux by the year 2050. Correlationist philosophy is now a smoking ruin, pitied on those rare occasions when it is not an object of public mockery. The non-totalizability of worlds has become a basic truth of philosophy, familiar to every student by the age of twenty. Meillassoux's heirs argue only over the specific list of the stages of advent ('Is the leap from plants to animals, or fish to amphibians, as great a shift as that between matter and life?'), not over the theme of advent itself. His proof of non-contradiction and rejection of sufficient reason are accepted as commonplaces, celebrated even by his dwindling number of opponents. With his eighty-third birthday just months away, the Great Sage of the Sorbonne receives student visitors with typical kindness, greatly pleased with the fortunate events of the past half-century. Against all odds, even the concept of the virtual God has taken root in the public mind. The former atheists of the Left have long since enlisted under the banner of messianic justice, while the faded name of Nicolas Sarkozy is now a badge of national shame. Indeed, even Christian theology has been shaken to its foundations by Meillassoux's philosophy, and only the most archaic of priests continue to assert that God already exists. A survey done by *Le Monde* in a feature on Meillassoux reveals that 80 percent of European academics now *literally* hope for the rebirth of humans who have died atrocious deaths. Not since Kant has the intellectual climate of the world been so markedly changed by the work of a single thinker. While this scenario might not seem 'likely', it is Meillassoux more than anyone else who has taught us to ignore the likely and unlikely when dealing with the broadest outlines of any World.

Among the remaining minor rivals in 2050 is Object-Oriented Philosophy. Though widely viewed as an anti-Meillassouxian school, its adherents (including its eighty-two-year-old founder) have already been won over to most of the French philosopher's claims. His elaboration of *The Divine Existence* in a series of powerful sequels has led to insights that are simply too powerful to resist. Nearly everyone has been swept away by the dominant spirit of the age. However, a point of doubt still remains. The Object-Oriented school has never been fully abandoned despite its increasingly marginal status, and its elderly president is asked to give a simple explanation as to why. A muckraking journalist asks the following question: 'Why persist in opposing Speculative Materialism when you yourself are now convinced that it is mostly right?' The philosopher answers roughly as follows:

'It's pretty amazing what he's done. I remember when his books first appeared, early in the century. There was obviously a lot of promise in these works, though it was hard to imagine some of the points ever becoming mainstream. Absolute contingency and a virtual God? The rebirth of the dead? But here we are, and I'm on record as admitting that it's all become pretty hard to disprove. Philosophy is a lot more interesting now than it was in 2005, and he deserves much of the credit for it. Even so, you're right to say that I'm not entirely satisfied. What always bothered me was the treatment of the principle of sufficient reason. His whole system was a kind of *raid* on sufficient reason, like the Vikings rowing up the Seine to attack Notre Dame in the fog, but this time succeeding. No one defended the cathedral, but someone should have, and even could have.

'Now that you ask, I can think of at least two things about sufficient reason that he never liked. There was the point that if everything that exists has a reason, then the reason must have a reason, and so on indefinitely. This turns into an infinite regress unless the chain stops in a necessary entity that is its own reason for existing, *causa sui*. But that's impossible, since it would mean that some entity has an essence that implies that it *must* exist. As Meillassoux used to put it, this means that the thing would have a "prodigious predicate" that makes its non-existence impossible, just like God in St Anselm's proof would not be what it is (the greatest thing that can be conceived) if it were nonexistent. And if a necessary entity is impossible, then metaphysics is impossible, since he tried to show that every metaphysics has been based on some sort of necessary entity. I at least have to agree that no predicate or quality directly implies the existence of the thing to which it belongs.

'That was one of the things he disliked about sufficient reason. Another was that he was convinced that the effect is always in excess of its cause. As he always claimed, to say that a thing has a sufficient reason for what it is implies that it's *reducible* to the series of causes that led to it. Metaphysics requires some concept of a necessary being, and Leibniz went even further and said that *all* beings and events are necessary: Caesar crossing the Rubicon could not have been otherwise, and neither could you be smoking opium right now rather than cloves, my friend. Your clove cigarette at 8:52 a.m. is a metaphysical necessity, and we can hardly blame Meillassoux for feeling horrified by the thought.

'The problem is, I never thought any of this was fair to sufficient reason. Let's start with the first point. Who says there can't be an infinite regress of reasons? Don't get me wrong; I can see the problem with a finite regress ending in a necessary being. If everything has a reason outside itself for what it is, then it makes no sense to think there can be one hypocritical exception to this rule. How can there be one superpotent entity caused by nothing but its own essence? It's an *ad hoc* solution just to avoid the infinite regress. But when you think about it, Meillassoux's approach is really nothing but the opposite *ad hoc* solution. Instead of avoiding the regress by stopping it arbitrarily in a final underlying being, he avoids it by saying that nothing comes from anything at all, so the regress never even begins. Advent *ex nihilo* of the laws of nature. A thing only is what it is, with no causal background. And as I've always said, he has no choice but to make the same claim not just about causes over the course of time, but also about causes in a single moment of time, which is also known as the problem of part and whole. Meillassoux might as well say that nothing can be made of pieces, because the pieces would have to be made of pieces, and so on until we would reach some ultimate tiny pieces, which are impossible just as the necessary God is impossible. And therefore, nothing can be made of anything else. Not only is there no historical depth to anything that exists, there isn't even a depth of composition.

'But my question has always been this ... I can understand why Meillassoux doesn't want a finite regress ending in a necessary being, since this would allow an arbitrary exception in which everything can be traced backwards *except* for one necessary being. What I never understood is what's supposedly wrong with an infinite regress. There's no *logical* contradiction here, after all; it's just hard to *visualize* an infinite regress. And since when does Meillassoux disqualify things that are *logically possible* simply because they aren't easy for the human mind to *imagine*? Remember, this is the same person who told us to ignore the apparent stability of the world because it's only proven by the senses, and that instead we ought to trust reason when it tells us that everything is contingent, even though the laws of nature appear to be stable.

'Fair enough, Meillassoux is right to say that a finite regress is impossible, because it terminates in an entity that is cause of itself, and that's impossible. But there's still a legitimate dispute between the infinite regress and Meillassoux's "no regress" model where nothing is the result of anything else. Back in 2011, I wrote about the problem Meillassoux would have when talking about, say, the moon. Supposedly the moon is sitting there before us, exhaustively knowable because its primary qualities can be mathematized. My point was, and still is, that *no amount of knowledge of the moon ever turns into a moon*. Meillassoux thinks the moon encountered by knowledge is perfectly sufficient as it is; it arose from nothing, and in that sense depends on nothing but itself for being as it is. It's true that Anselm's God is necessary while Meillassoux's moon might never have existed. But this difference hides a more important similarity between the two cases: namely, both are endpoints in the cosmos, arising from nothing else. *Once the immanent moon exists*, its status is no different from that of the necessary God: both forbid any regress, since both are caused by or composed of nothing outside themselves.

'Meillassoux thinks the metaphysical God is the very embodiment of sufficient reason, when in fact it embodies the *denial* of such reason. To be caused by nothing or caused by oneself amounts to the same thing; the only real alternative is to be caused by or composed *of something else*. Another way of putting it is that God and the moon have the same ambiguous status. In one sense they are completely cut off from all other entities, since both are causally independent. But in another sense they are completely connected *with the mind*, since there is no difficulty in knowing them. It doesn't really matter if God and the moon exist after we all succeed in killing ourselves. The point is that *if we were still alive*, our knowledge would drink God and the moon to the dregs, with nothing held in reserve. Anselm's God may not be immanent in the world in the same sense as Meillassoux's mathematizable moon, but this God is perfectly immanent *to knowledge*; we can know God's crucial predicates perfectly well through reason, which is precisely how we prove his existence. As I said, both God and the moon have no connection with other things but are perfectly connected with thought, when what we really need is the opposite: entities that *are* connected with other things while being *disconnected* from thought. Instead of an immanent philosophy opposed to sufficient reason, we need a non-immanent philosophy *devoted* to sufficient reason. Fear of an infinite regress is no grounds for flattening God and the moon onto a surface where being and thought are as fully convertible as Yen and Yuan.

'Let's move on to the other problem I have with this onslaught against sufficient reason, which is not unrelated to the one we were just talking about. Meillassoux has always seemed to think that if something has a sufficient reason, then it is *reducible* to that reason: contained in what came prior to its advent, like a "pale pink specter" existing earlier than full-blown red. It's little wonder he doesn't like this idea, but it's not the right way to look at sufficient reason. A thing and its reason are never the same. The cosmos is made up of multiple entities, each transmitting influence to others only in part. If we say (already oversimplifying) that the sufficient reason for a pony is its two parent horses, the fact remains that the pony exceeds the causal influence of those horses, while they in turn have countless important and unimportant features that play no role whatever in the generation of their off-spring. When one thing leads to another, the first is never entirely preserved, but is translated into something new. We do not need a *pony ex nihilo* in order for novelty to occur in the world, because the naturally generated pony is already something over and above its forerunners, and that's remarkable enough.

'This is my worry about Meillassoux's philosophy: his all-or-nothing approach to relation. Either it's nonexistent, or it's total. Either things happen without the least influence from anything else, or they exist in total dependence on each other – and the latter case is not just described polemically in his writings, since it's exactly what he means by *laws*: intra-worldly connections that remain necessary until a groundless change in law occurs. We can't try to touch something if we're not already touching it, and we can't try to touch it if we're already touching it. But *philosophia* was supposed to mean exactly the opposite: touching wisdom without touching it. And beyond the human realm, objects must touch without touching: a "love of causation" to match the human love of wisdom. You say it sounds weird? Not half as weird as the God who does not yet exist.'

Notes

1. The method of 'hyperbolic reading' was first introduced in 2008 in the article 'DeLanda's Ontology', and employed again the next year for the case of Bruno Latour in the book *Prince of Networks*.
2. José Ortega y Gasset, 'Preface for Germans', in *Phenomenology and Art*, p. 41.
3. Plato, *Meno*, 80d3–e6, trans. W. K. C. Guthrie, in Plato, *Collected Dialogues*, p. 363.
4. In my debut book, *Tool-Being*, I followed Heidegger's analysis at considerable length. Indeed, my entire philosophical position can be viewed as an attempt to radicalize the features of Heidegger's withdrawn tool-beings.
5. See Majid Fakhry, *Islamic Occasionalism*. An even more thorough account is available in German by Dominik Perler and Ulrich Rudolph, under the title *Occasionalismus*.
6. Graham Harman, 'Quentin Meillassoux: A New French Philosopher', pp. 115–16.
7. Manuel DeLanda, *A New Philosophy of Society*.
8. In *After Finitude* (AF 12), Meillassoux says that the Cartesian position toward physics (and he takes the side of Descartes on most issues) must be distinguished from the Pythagorean position that the mathematical is reality itself. The Cartesian position is supposedly different in so far as it is the *referent* of equations which has existence independent of humans, not the equations themselves. This sounds plausible enough in Descartes's case, given the explicit role in his philosophy of physical substance. But assuming that Meillassoux means to take an anti-Pythagorean line in this passage (which he probably does), it remains unclear what *his* residual 'referent' would be beyond the mathematical other than the 'dead matter' that we have already found lacking.

6

Interview with Quentin Meillassoux (August 2010)

Translated from the French by Graham Harman

The following interview was conducted by email, in a single round of questions and answers. In January 2010 I sent Meillassoux several dozen questions in English. He selected a number of these questions and in August of that year sent his responses in French, which I then translated. This history explains why in three of the questions (two about German Idealism and one about materialism) I seem to raise an objection repeatedly that he already answers in the first of his responses. My response to his responses can be found in Chapter 4 above.

The interview sheds new light on Meillassoux's intellectual background, his intellectual relations with his father (Claude Meillassoux), wife (Gwenaëlle Aubry), and mentor (Alain Badiou), and the origin of some of the key concepts of his philosophy. Throughout, we are reminded of Meillassoux's remarkable talent for answering objections, a skill that is even more formidable in person.

> Graham Harman: *You have been described, by no less an authority than Peter Hallward, as the most rapidly prominent French philosopher in the Anglophone world since Jacques Derrida in the 1960s. Was it surprising to become known so quickly?*
> Quentin Meillassoux: I was indeed surprised by the reception of *After Finitude* in the Anglo-Saxon countries. This was a significant contrast with the relative indifference in France. Given the rather elevated level of abstraction of the work, I had hoped for two or three reviews in French academic journals, nothing more than that. Instead, I had an impressive number of favorable reactions and criticisms outside France – including, in part, those of contemporary artists or Left activists. But there was more or less nothing in the learned journals of my own country. This was amusing, and

made me realize that the reception of a book decisively escapes any foreseeable logic.

GH: *Your father, Claude Meillassoux, was an anthropologist of international renown in his field. What sort of intellectual influence did he have on you?*

QM: My father was quite a remarkable Marxist, inventive and individualistic (distant from every party, very anti-Stalinist, very anti-Maoist) and someone who saw in Marxism a method rather than a body of doctrine. He was very suspicious towards philosophy, which he viewed only from afar, and which he saw as a rather abstract jargon cut off from social reality. What he transmitted to me was the requirement of clarity, the taste for interesting ideas, and the capacity to follow them all the way to the end, with an attitude of indifference towards any group affiliation or pre-existing intellectual current. From him I also take my impulse towards solitary investigation, not bound to the spirit of the age.

GH: *How did you become interested in philosophy? Who were the authors who led you to the subject?*

QM: I enrolled at the École Normale Supérieure in 1988 under the 'Philosophy' option. But during my first year at the ENS I registered for Logic and History. I also considered enrolling at the Institut des Études Politiques (Sciences Po). Despite my already pronounced taste for philosophy, I was still dominated by my father's suspicion of it, and regarded this art of the concept as being at best a propaedeutic to more 'serious' or 'concrete' disciplines. At bottom, I was always wrapped up in a sort of 'Marxist *Bildungsroman*': one begins with philosophy (which everyone knows is always idealist . . .) and then ascends to history, science, and politics. But it didn't work out that way. I spent my whole first year reading Hegel's *Phenomenology of Spirit* and *Science of Logic* instead of doing quantificational logic. And I failed miserably in the history exams, for which I didn't even bother to study, since I was bored by any apprenticeship to positive facts alone. Finally I had to admit it: I was definitely good only in philosophy.

GH: *One imagines that your encounter with Alain Badiou must have been decisive, and readers of this book will be fascinated by that topic. Was he teaching at the ENS when you enrolled? What made him such an important model for you?*

QM: Badiou was not at the ENS when I enrolled, but at Paris VIII (the University of Vincennes in Saint-Denis). Only later did he arrive at the ENS. I discovered him through a reading of *Being and Event*, a copy of which I also sent to my father. They met just once, I believe, at the home of a mutual friend: the anthropologist Gérald Gaillard, who did something quite remarkable. Since he very much admired both Badiou and my father, he simply tape-recorded their dinner conversation! Upon the death of my father, Gaillard sent me a copy of the recording, and I was astonished to learn of their long conversation.

To summarize briefly, *Being and Event* was in my possession from 1988 onward. But since I was occupied with my own studies, I only opened it for the first time in 1991 – during the year of my *agrégation*, while looking for something else to read besides Plotinus, Kant, and Bergson, who were the three required authors on that year's 'annual program'. And from that moment I was quite simply captivated by *Being and Event*. Once I passed the *agrégation*, in 1992, I finally had time to read the book in its entirety, and immediately understood that it was a major work. It reconciled me with mathematics, by making me understand some things that I never imagined I would one day be able to grasp. And it contained that blend of rigor, knowledge, and absolute strangeness found in every great book.

That said, in 1992 I had already sketched the major outlines of my own philosophical ideas on contingency. But none the less, Badiou provided me with the mathematical soil needed for their development, along with essential intellectual support for my desire to reactivate philosophy in its most speculative aspect.

GH: *Your wife (Gwenaëlle Aubry) is also a remarkably talented person: a prolific novelist and scholar of ancient philosophy. Did you meet her at about this time as well? What I am really curious about is whether you had any arguments related to philosophy. And if so, what was the topic of your disagreement?*

QM: Gwenaëlle and I met in 1994. At the time she was working on Plotinus, and then decided to write a thesis on the notion of potency in Aristotle and its transformation into omnipotence in medieval Christian theology. Of course, we talk together a great deal about each other's works, and we are also each other's first readers. I feel much admiration for her work as a novelist, and for a long time I have been fascinated by her philosophical research. Indeed, Gwenaëlle has unearthed a historical process that I already suspected in very imprecise fashion in *L'Inexistence divine*, but which in her work appears in all its force: Christian theology, or at least an essential portion of it, is based on the idea that it is blasphemous to say that God is good. For to say this would amount to saying that God is subordinated to an order of value that he is powerless to overturn (and above all *unjustified* in overturning). The essence of the Christian God, which makes him the opposite of Aristotle's God, is the power freely to create or de-create the standards of good or evil, not being devoted to some eternal good independent of his own power. This thesis, which I am reformulating here with a brutality for which I alone am responsible, is an essential element of my own reflections on the divine.

GH: *You have just referred in passing to your thesis,* L'Inexistence divine: *a somewhat legendary work that has not yet appeared in print. At the center of this book is the strange but fascinating concept of a virtual God who does not yet exist but might exist in the future. At what stage did this idea first come to you, and in what connection?*

QM: From the very start, this idea accompanied the thesis of radical contingency (which I now call 'super-contingency'). Neither of these two ideas determined the other; they arrived together as a systematic configuration of 'theory' and its 'practice'.

Here's how I look at it. If I take supercontingency seriously (or super-chaos, an expression that I now prefer to hyper-chaos), then I ought to divide the possible into potentialities (which are submitted to the natural laws of our universe) and virtualities (which are not submitted to those laws).[1] If potentialities can be probabilized, in my view virtualities cannot, by reason of the transfinite character of the number of possibles. Thus it is pointless to ask what the chances are of one virtuality arising rather than another, or to think that a particular virtuality has an infinitely small chance of arising in view of the immense number of other possibilities. On the other hand, I can do two things with respect to the virtual that are able to transform my subjective relationship with the experience of this world. First of all, I can grant prominence to the most radical novelties of the past: the emergence of life understood as a set of qualitative contents by contrast with an inorganic matter that feels neither sensation nor perception; then the emergence of rational thought by contrast with a life that cannot attain the concept of the infinite or eternal truth (of the mathematical or speculative type). This having been done, I can ask what the next advent would be that is capable of just as much novelty in comparison with thought as thought compared with life, or life with matter. For if we grant that thought can attain the absolute (that is to say, contingency considered as necessary), then nothing can transcend thought except for the re-emergence of thought in accordance with the reign of a rigorously egalitarian justice among thinking individuals. We are in the framework of an 'analogy of incommensurabilities': if time is still capable of a novelty just as radical in comparison with thought as thought with life, or life with matter, this novelty can only be the emergence of egalitarian Justice for the living and the dead.

Consequently, religious messianism or revolutionary radicalism can be rethought within the framework of an attempt at radical equality for the living and the dead alike – an advent that is contingent but none the less eternally possible, totally improbabilizable, and outside the grasp of our action and even of our Universe in so far as it is subject to its own laws. This 'eternal possible' frees me from suffering over the appalling misfortune of those who have experienced atrocious deaths, allows me to escape being paralyzed by an impossible mourning for the atrocities of the twentieth century, and also permits me to invest my energy in an egalitarian politics that has become conscious of its limits. Indeed, politics is delivered from all charges of messianism, since eschatological awaiting is entirely recuperated by individual subjectivity. This partition of tasks (individual messianism, political finitude) allows us to avoid the totalitarian temptation of collective action. We can efficiently expel the eschatological desire from politics only by allowing this desire to be unfolded openly in another sphere of existence (such as private life or philosophy).

GH: *Why are you still working on* L'inexistence divine *even now? Is it really so unsatisfactory to you in its current state? You do realize that thousands of readers are awaiting it eagerly, don't you?*

QM: I am aware of this, and of course I feel sorry about it. But my thesis of 1997 was definitely too imperfect, and in the mean time numerous complications have arisen for all of its developments, and these require a patient re-elaboration. The excerpts you have chosen from this thesis [see Appendix] will perhaps allow the reader to form an idea of the original project, but also to gain an idea of its insufficiency at that stage.

GH: *Your most famous concept is perhaps 'correlationism', a powerful critical term. What led you to invent this concept?*

QM: With the invention of this term, I wished to 'identify' a ubiquitous adversary in contemporary philosophy, one that takes extremely diverse forms. I had to avoid the term 'idealism', since it is loaded with ambiguity, and since there are numerous correlationists who refuse to be recognized as idealists. And in fact, 'idealism' designates to an equal degree the Platonic realism of ideas, speculative idealism (whether in the subjective form of Berkeley or the absolute form of Hegel), and the transcendental idealism of Kant or Husserl. But beyond the indeterminacy of the term, quite a game of denial takes place surrounding this name: it is claimed that Kant is not an idealist, since he produced a 'refutation of idealism'; that Husserl refutes the idealism of Platonic essences or Fregean significations, since he relates these to acts of subjectivity; it is also recalled that Sartre, even while refusing metaphysical realism in the name of the phenomenological requirement, called himself a 'materialist', etc. Thus I wanted a 'clean slate' freed from this system of evasions in order to localize a decision that none of these traditions can deny: the uncircumventible correlation between a subjective pole and an objective pole, both understood in the broadest sense of the term. In this way I could show how it is possible to break with this decision and with the various currents that took it to be irrefutable.

GH: *But despite this critique of correlationism, you do not adopt a traditional realist position. Instead, you agree with Fichte and the other German Idealists that we cannot think things-in-themselves without thinking them, and thereby turning them into correlates of thought. So in a sense, you think the correlationist has a very important point to make. You have also said (in your lecture at Goldsmiths in 2007, and elsewhere) that you think this is the only possible route to a rationalism in philosophy. Is this a fair description of your current position?*

QM: No, not at all. Here there is a misunderstanding. I try to give to correlationism its most rigorous form – to isolate the fundamental argument in it. Ultimately, this argument amounts to a demonstration that every realist is condemned to a pragmatic contradiction: he claims to be able to think that which is independent of thought, but from the very fact of his thinking it he makes of it a correlate of his thought. This argument is very powerful indeed, and it can lead either to a correlationism in the strict sense ('I don't know what there is outside of what is given to thought') or to a subjectivist metaphysics ('I affirm that being in itself is the hypostatized correlation'). Henceforth I will use the term 'Era of the Correlate' for this conjunction of correlationism and metaphysical subjectivism that defines what is essential in modern philosophy since Berkeley. My concern in *After Finitude* is to give a rigorous *refutation* of this standpoint (and certainly not to accept it) and thus a refutation of the argument that I call the 'correlational circle' (namely, that there is a vicious pragmatic circle contained in any realist position). To refute it is thus to affirm that we can very well have access to a reality radically independent of the fact that we think, and in this way we can escape the reproach of the pragmatic contradiction.

I make this demonstration in two steps: (1) the contingency of the correlation, which correlationism needs in order to refute absolutist subjectivism, cannot itself be thought as a correlate of thought. Thus there is necessarily contingency, whether I think it or not; (2) contingency can be thought only as the contingency *of something that exists* (this is the first Figure of the factial: a demonstration that there ought to be something rather than nothing). Hence, there are necessarily contingent things, whether I exist to think them or not. It is an eternal necessity that there be contingent things, whereas thought (like every being) is contingent with respect to them. We can disappear as a species, as can all other life on earth; there will always be contingent beings whether we exist or not. We thus obtain the first postulate of all materialism (but in a form that is demonstrated rather than just posited). But we also establish the second postulate (which is rationalist and not skeptical) of all materialism: thought can think being that is independent of thought.

GH: *My main worry about this position, as you know, is that it sounds too much like Meno's Paradox in Plato. In other words, the German Idealist position essentially runs like this: 'You can't think the unthought if you're thinking it, and you can't think the unthought if you're not thinking it; therefore you must confine yourself to what is thought.' But this sounds to me a lot like Meno's claim that you can't search for something if you already have it and can't search for it if you don't have it, and therefore you must focus on what you already have. What about Socrates's response, which is that both having and not having are possible simultaneously? Isn't this the very meaning of* philosophia *as love of wisdom? And isn't the German Idealist position, which survives today in Badiou, Žižek, and even in your own position, in danger of trying to turn philosophy into a wisdom about thought rather than a love of wisdom of that which lies* outside *thought?*

QM: In the previous response I have already dealt with the idea that I remain within the standpoint of German Idealism; all of my effort consists in responding *by* thought *to* thought, and thus to attain a realism that would not be naïve, since it is able to traverse the correlationist objection in its strongest form. Thus I am opposed to two points of view:

a. That of Žižek, and perhaps also that of Badiou, which would consist at bottom in making of materialism a 'misfired correlationism'. Ever since Derrida in particular, materialism seems to have taken the form of a 'sickened correlationism'; it refuses both the return to a naïve pre-critical stage of thought *and* any investigation of what prevents the 'circle of the subject' from harmoniously closing in on itself. Whether it be the Freudian unconscious, Marxist ideology, Derridean dissemination, the undecidability of the event, the Lacanian Real considered as the impossible, etc., these are all supposed to detect the trace of an impossible coincidence of the subject with itself, and thus of an extra-correlational residue in which one could localize a 'materialist moment' of thought. But in fact, such misfires are only further correlations among others: it is always *for* a subject that there is an undecidable event or a failure of signification. Unless we fall back on naïve realism, we cannot treat these misfires as 'effects' of a cause that could definitely be established as external to the subject or even to consciousness. In any case, a correlationist would have no difficulty in retorting that this genre of materialism is either a disingenuous idealism or a dogmatic realism of the 'old style'. When a chair is wobbly, the 'wobbly' exists only in relation to the chair, not independently of it. When one clogs up the Subject, one does not go outside it; instead, one merely constructs a transcendental or speculative Wobbly Subject – a subject that is assured *a priori*, and according to a properly absolute Knowing, for which things always turn out badly in its world of representations.

b. But I am also opposed to every form of realism that claims to challenge correlationism without striking at the root of the difficulty. This is the only reason that I take the role of the correlationist or borrow his 'voice': when I am dealing with a realism that to my mind has not responded correctly to the vicious pragmatic circle mentioned previously. In this case I try to show why the path I have taken seems necessary to me, despite its difficulty: every other path seems defective in each case, incapable of a true refutation of correlationism. It seems to me that the path you propose of a partial knowledge (in Socratic fashion) also fails; for this 'partial' character of knowledge, or this wisdom loved from afar, can only be in relation to a subject that is supposed to evaluate it as such ... My thesis, in its harshest form, is that there is only one path by which to escape correlationism: the one that turns against it the weapon that even now has allowed it an undisputed reign over philosophy (continental philosophy, at least). This ultimate weapon, which allows it to challenge naïve realism no less than subjectivist metaphysics, is not the correlational circle alone, but rather the facticity of the correlate.

GH: *On a related point, you begin* After Finitude *by insisting on the old distinction between primary and secondary qualities. Yet for you, the primary qualities are the ones that can be mathematized. How can this be the case? The mathematical is what can be known. If you say that the primary reality of what exists is that which can be known about it, isn't this just a form of idealism?*

QM: My concern is to demonstrate that the specificity of mathematical language stems from its capacity to describe that which is independent of all thought. There is every reason to find this thesis paradoxical, given that I have not yet published a demonstration of it, but it does contain the purpose of my enterprise. At first glance the very idea seems absurd, since mathematics is an intellectual 'construction', that of a formal language – just like the experimental mechanisms of the natural sciences, which do not exist outside science and scientists. I cannot respond in detail here to this sort of challenge. I would say only that it is necessary to distrust the constant use of the term 'construction'. If I employ this word in connection with the work of an architect, what I mean is that the building thereby constructed would not have existed without the architect's plan or the labour of the workers. But let's suppose that by 'construction' I refer instead to the mechanisms by which an archaeologist has set up a dig site in order to excavate some ruins without damaging them. In this case the 'constructions' (a complex of winches, sounding lines, scaffolding, spades, brushes, etc.) are not destined to *produce* an object, as in the case of architecture. On the contrary, they are made with a view to *not* interfering with the object at which they aim: that is to say, excavating the ruins without damaging them, in unearthing them 'as is', and not as modified or even destroyed by the impact of the excavation tools. Thus, mathematics and experimental sciences can certainly be human 'constructions', but this does not prove that they are such in the sense of architectural construction rather than archaeological 'discovery' (in the manner in which one speaks of 'the discovery of ruins or of a treasure').

GH: *On yet another related point, you call your position 'Speculative Materialism', yet you do not believe in an objective world of material lying outside all thought. In this sense, you are a 'materialist' only in the sense that Žižek claims to be a materialist. Iain Hamilton Grant has been very critical of this claim in Žižek's case, and I would joint Grant in expressing that worry. How would you answer the charge that this materialism is no materialism at all?*

QM: I believe that my previous response has shown the unjust character of this critique. I do not 'believe' in an objective world independent of thought because I maintain that it is possible to *demonstrate*, in a precise sense, that such a world external to thought does indeed exist, and necessarily so. I 'know' that there is such a world – and that is what makes me a materialist, not a believer.

GH: *Perhaps this would be a good time to ask you about your attitude toward Hegel. I've heard a few readers claim that you dislike Hegel, but I have never had this sense. And in fact you once told me in conversation that Hegel is your unaddressed hidden source, much like Nietzsche was for Foucault. Could you say a bit more about this?*

QM: It is quite astonishing to me that anyone could think that I dislike Hegel! Hegel, along with Marx, was my only true master: the one on whom I had to depend in order to achieve my own thinking. As mentioned earlier, I read Hegel fervently as a student, and can say without exaggeration that the love of dialectic 'consumed me from within' during my youth. I abandoned this mode of thinking once I understood the profound reason why there could never be *contradictions* in reality. There could be tensions, conflicts, and collisions, certainly; but contradictions, never. This understanding of the impossibility of contradiction immediately pushed me to the heart of the necessity that I call 'factial': for dialectics, if there is an absolute necessity it ought to harbor a contradiction that is simultaneously real and always already on the way to being outstripped. For me, the necessity of contingency entails that there cannot be contradiction, since a contradictory entity, being always already that which it is not, is destined to be revealed as ultimately necessary. To my mind, believing in real necessity (metaphysics) and defending it with the greatest degree of rigor, obliges one to become a dialectician, and thus to be condemned to the stating of contradictions. Hegel understood this better than anyone. He unveiled the core of all metaphysics as a pure and simple contradiction, and demonstrated that if one wishes to continue to defend the former absolute necessity, it would be necessary to rehabilitate the notion of contradiction, which is the irrational notion par excellence. And here we find the true greatness of the dialectic: it exhibits the contradictory character of all real necessity. And conversely, it indicates the price that must be paid by the absolute refusal of all ontological contradiction: the related refusal of any necessity of things, laws, or events.

GH: *On what issue do you and Badiou most diverge? He is obviously a great admirer of your work, but perhaps you have disagreements at times?*

QM: Badiou sent me a letter in which he clearly distinguished our major point of divergence: I believe in a necessity of contingency, while he upholds a contingency of necessity. Indeed, for him the experience of necessity occurs on the basis of an undecidable event that cannot be reduced to the situation in which it intervenes, and from which there follows the infinite series of inquiries in light of a truth. For me, one can extract the meaning of a really unconditional necessity on the basis of the more radical level of contingency. This is why I am interested, in Alain Badiou's thinking, by what I would call the 'archi-facticity' of his categories. On the near side of the undecidability of the event in which truth procedures take root, there are some more basic facts that condition his philosophy as a whole. Among others, these include: the very fact that there are events and thus thinking beings rather than simple repetitive nature; the fact that in humans there are four truth procedures rather than more or fewer (Badiou considers this possibility in *Logics of Worlds*, in the case of non-human thinking beings); the fact that it should be mathematics that constitutes ontology, rather than a discipline pertaining to another truth procedure, such as art. For my part, I claim to intervene at this radical level of 'archi-facticity' in order to extract a necessity that is itself anterior to that of the Badiouian event.

This disagreement on modalities intensifies the disagreement we have concerning the capacity of philosophy to produce truths. For Alain, it is impossible for philosophy to achieve a level of necessity that outstrips that of the truth procedures, or in any case that of mathematics as ontology. For me, philosophy is in a position to think the deepest level of facticity of the various positive disciplines – here we find the content of philosophy, the soil of its own proper truths, which remain in a foundational position with respect to these disciplines in however paradoxical a manner.

GH: *Another notable feature of your work is that phenomenology (Husserl, Heidegger, Levinas, Merleau-Ponty) has apparently had little influence on your own position. What is the problem with phenomenology?*

QM: On the contrary, I am a diligent reader of the great phenomenologists, and see in them a rigorous school whose vitality appears to me to be one of the last ramparts against the exclusive domination in the academic world of one sole type of philosophy (namely, analytic philosophy). I perfected my model of correlationism in close contact with phenomenology.

What I essentially reproach in this current of thought is the medley of tricks and denials by which phenomenologists shield themselves from the exorbitant consequences of their idealism. For example, Husserl, Heidegger, and Sartre never cease to distinguish themselves from an idealism of the Berkeleyan or solipsist type, yet they never draw out the essential problem inherent in all anti-realism: what would remain of reality if every conscious subject or every living thing were to disappear? Must we say that we absolutely don't know? That the question makes no sense? But in that case, what is it that the sciences of ancestral realities are talking about? Is it necessary to affirm that nothing can exist outside our representation of the world? But then how would we think the emergence of life in the world? Phenomenology has established a mechanism of intimidation and of elaborate sophistry that aims at making these kinds of questions appear naïve. But to my knowledge it has never squarely faced up to the problem, and in my view it has never treated these questions with the needed rigor and honesty. None the less, phenomenology remains for me a formidable *descriptive* enterprise of the complexities of the given: that is to say, of the world as it is presented to consciousness. We ought to protect the richness with which it restores our experience of the sensible, in particular against all the contemporary reductionisms that want to eliminate our historical being in favor of our inorganic naturality or materiality alone.

GH: *You told me several years ago that Bergson had also had a great influence on you. In what sense?*

QM: I am fascinated above all by question of emergence, creation, advent. This is one of the reasons why I have never been satisfied by anti-speculative philosophies: critique or transcendental phenomenology replaces questions of genesis with questions of condition or constitution, and for this very reason abandons as senseless or pointless the side of the real that harbors the most captivating problems. For me, Bergson represents a great enterprise of the liberation of philosophy in comparison with merely transcendental problems. With his intuition of *durée*, he proposes the most powerful thought on creation that has ever been produced. This is precisely why it is with him that I sought to understand this question: because my conception of advent is directly opposed to his conception of novelty. For Bergson, it is because the present and past are part of an unbreakable continuity that creation is incessant; for me, since the rupture is absolute and incessant between present and past, there can be pure supplementations in the course of temporality: advents of what did not even exist in potency before coming into existence (life in comparison with inorganic matter, thought in comparison with life). I have the same disagreement with Deleuze, who essentially interests me for the reason that he was the greatest Bergsonian of the twentieth century; much more than Nietzsche or Spinoza, it is Bergson (especially his conceptions of the virtual and intensity) who determines the decisive options of Deleuze. To be in dialogue with the author of *Matter and Memory* is also to be confronted *de facto* by his major disciple Deleuze, who for me is the last great French metaphysician, along with Badiou.

GH: *Although your book on the virtual God is not yet published, some critics are already attacking it in the same way that St Anselm's ontological proof has always been attacked. For example, 'Why doesn't Meillassoux speak about a virtual unicorn that does not yet exist but might exist in the future?' Or, as Adrian Johnston puts it in a forthcoming critical article on your work, 'a virtual flying spaghetti monster that does not yet exist but might exist in the future'.[2] What makes God so special out of all these virtual objects that might arise contingently without reason at any time in the future?*

QM: Everything is possible, as I have said. But it is senseless to believe in the rise of a virtual event (one that does not conform to the laws of our world) in the same fashion in which I await the rise of a potential event (one that does conform to the laws of our world). I can justifiably evaluate the probability that a comet will strike the earth and destroy every form of life: it is a potential event. On the other hand, a virtual event lies outside probability. And there we find its true strangeness: it is neither probable, nor improbable, nor impossible. If I have to determine my relationship with this type of possible, it would be in a very different fashion than in relation to a potentiality. The question becomes: of what absolutely remarkable event is virtual becoming capable, and how can this event modify my subjectivity once it is recognized as possible? And here it is not unicorns (or spaghetti monsters) that appear in the first rank. Instead, it is the end aimed at by all messianisms and all revolutionisms, though in a form that seems to me always defective. It is universal Justice, the equality of everyone, and even the equality of the living with the dead: Justice guaranteed as eternally possible by the absolute inexistence of God – that is to say, by the ultimate Non-sense of super-chaos. For if God does not exist, everything becomes fragile, even death. If God does not exist, things become capable of anything: whether of the absurd, or of reaching their highest state. Everything is irreversible, but nothing is definitive.

GH: *One would assume that you take some interest in the natural sciences as well. But how can you reconcile science with your belief in absolute contingency?*

QM: On the contrary, the insightfulness of contingency seems to me rather pertinent to every scientific mind, for every science ends by stumbling over the facticity of its postulates and its fundamental laws. Indeed, it is because the facticity of laws of nature is thought as uncircumventible by scientists that they ultimately ought to be validated by experience and not by *a priori* demonstration, the existence of laws and of ultimate constants of the Universe. It is because logicians and mathematicians have a sharp consciousness of the contingency of their axioms that they are capable of sensing new heterodox logics or interesting new axiomatics. It is because philosophy is aware of this increasingly obvious role of contingency in science that it ought to lay hold of it as a new principle: the sole absolutely necessary one.

GH: *If you had to name the most underrated thinker in the history of philosophy, who would it be?*

QM: Reinhold, Jacobi, Maimon: the German thinkers who formed the junction between Kant and Fichte. With these philosophers, we draw close to the edge of what would soon become the volcano of German Idealism. It is a volcano that would not have been able to erupt without them, even though Schelling and Hegel esteemed them lightly.

GH: *You have described yourself as politically of the Left. Last year I spoke with some of your students from the ENS, and they told me that you are generally a very calm lecturer, except on one occasion they recall when you were discussing politics. I believe this had to do with French President Nicolas Sarkozy's proposed educational reforms. They said you became passionate and animated, just like the professional revolutionary that you decided not to become. Are there other political issues that make you especially passionate or even angry?*

QM: I am very hostile to neo-liberalism, which has turned the contemporary world (and the work world in particular) into a nightmare of rare intensity, one with which the politics of Sarkozy is utterly impregnated. In the thirty years since this doctrine invaded the world, the great political issue remains knowing how and when we can finally be rid of such moral and intellectual madness, which the crisis of 2008 was apparently insufficient to bring down.

GH: *Aside from the question of the greatest book in the history of philosophy, we might also ask about a thinker's favorite book in the history of philosophy. For example, the young Heidegger's favorite philosophy book was Brentano's doctoral dissertation on the many senses of being in Aristotle. Nicholas of Cusa always favored the commentary by Proclus on Plato's* Parmenides. *Perhaps neither would have ranked these favorites among the greatest philosophy books ever written, but there was something personal in these books that drove the careers of these thinkers. Did the young Meillassoux have a favorite philosophy book that wasn't necessarily among the handful of greatest books ever written?*

QM: In the first years of my studies, the books that gave me the most violent feelings and the purest enthusiasms were all works by heterodox dialecticians. I was bewitched by three authors in particular: Feuerbach in *The Essence of Christianity*, Kojève in *Introduction to the Reading of Hegel*, and Guy Debord. I was a passionate reader of the Situationists (having co-founded in my youth a journal called *Delenda* that was entirely devoted to their standpoint and lasted for two issues). I endlessly read and re-read the three major works of Debord: *The Society of the Spectacle*, *Comments on* The Society of the Spectacle, and *Panegyric.*

GH: *Surprise is perhaps one of the greatest cognitive tools that humans have. What do you think would be the most surprising thing about Quentin Meillassoux as a thinker or person that your readers might never expect?*

QM: I think no one can imagine the number of works I have in progress, or their frequent incongruity with respect to what is commonly viewed as the center of my interests. They are works on Hegel,

Nietzsche, Mallarmé, Marcel Duchamp, Darwinism, Pyrrho ...
My 'hidden' works may be very different from my 'public' works,
and I hope one day to be freed from this 'double identity' – this gap
between what I do and what people think I do.

Note

1. Meillassoux later revoked the expression 'super-chaos' in his April
   2012 Berlin Lecture (BL 11, footnote 5), on the grounds that mixing
   the Latin 'super' and the Greek 'chaos' is a linguistic barbarism. Thus,
   'hyperchaos' remains his preferred term.
2. Adrian Johnston, 'Hume's Revenge: À *Dieu*, Meillassoux?', in Levi
   Bryant, Nick Srnicek, Graham Harman (eds), *The Speculative Turn*,
   p. 112.

Appendix: Excerpts from *L'Inexistence divine*

Translated from the French by Graham Harman

This long-awaited work was originally submitted as Quentin Meillassoux's doctoral thesis in 1997. The following excerpts are taken from the revised version of 2003, and amount to approximately one-sixth of the total manuscript at that stage. As Meillassoux says in the interview found in this book, he saw a number of problems with this version of the project and decided to start anew. *L'Inexistence divine* has since been reconceived as a more ambitious, multi-volume work that is now in preparation. Its major arguments were summarized in Chapter 3 above, with Meillassoux's kind permission. But he did add one reasonable proviso: commentary would be permitted only on those passages that could be reproduced in full as an appendix to this book, to allow readers to see for themselves the context in which each idea appears. In this way, the project of a book about Quentin Meillassoux unexpectedly became a translation project as well.

The titles of these excerpts are Meillassoux's own; each is a section from *L'Inexistence divine*. All excerpts appear in their proper order, though over 80 percent of the book is omitted here for reasons of space. The result, I hope, is a readable abridgment of Meillassoux's book that gives a taste of all its crucial themes. The most painful deletions involved cutting his inventive readings of past philosophers, especially his numerous remarks on Hegel and Heidegger. What I have chosen to translate instead are those passages in which Meillassoux's own system is developed.

Excerpt A: Advent *ex nihilo* is a Rational Concept

We hold that if immanentism is maintained in fully radical form, it implies a world with nothing outside that could limit its power of novelty. If nothing exists outside the world, then the world alone is the source of the advent [*surgissement*] or disappearance of anything. That which *is* belongs fully to the world because it belongs *only* to the world, and is contingent *to the core*. Thus, novelty should not be considered as the action of a transcendence that is 'always already there' and would therefore forbid anything truly new. If an infinitely perfect God were the source of advent, time would essentially be poor, since what followed this Origin could be no better than a diminishing of it. But if instead time is rich in creative advents, then these need not be limited in arbitrary fashion by empirical constants or by ideal worlds outside our own. These two options are two ultimately identical ways of restoring time to an essential and divine Steadfastness of the possible, in which everything would already be contained before it ever appeared. Reason teaches the contrary. For in no way is it illogical (i.e., contradictory) to think a becoming always capable of breaking with the laws that currently determine its possibilities, thereby establishing a novelty that was nowhere before coming into being – one that contains no originary Principle in germ, as if it were hidden away in the secret drawer of a demiurge before becoming manifest. This is the rational meaning of time, once we think the contingency of laws. If laws themselves are temporal, then the advent of what is ultimately obeys no law – no *arche* where it would already be present before its advent.

God did not create thought, and nothing in the world was thinking before the advent of thought; God did not create the suffering or pleasure found in vital activity, and nothing suffered or enjoyed in the world before the advent of life. This indicates in the most striking fashion that if we think advent in its truth, it is an advent *ex nihilo* and thus *without any reason at all*, and *for that very reason* it is without limit. In revealing the contingency of laws, reason itself teaches that becoming is ultimately without reason. It is this very paradox, which is constitutive of the rational, that must be developed in all its consequences. In particular, we will see that if anything governs what time can or cannot do, this can only be time's own capacity to make all determinate beings (whether laws or events) appear or disappear. For the sole necessity to which becoming is subordinated is its own eternal power of the advent or abolition of each thing.

If advent is immanent, then it is absurd; thus it is capable of anything. By advent *ex nihilo* we do not mean that being arose entirely from originary nothingness. What we mean, stated in classical terms, is that there is more in the effect than in the cause: that this 'more' therefore has no reason at all for its advent, and hence nothing (no law) can limit it. As a result, advent *ex nihilo* does not conceal an essentially religious notion, but forms instead the sole immanent concept of becoming. It expresses the fact that what arises suddenly in the world does so thanks not to a Supreme Being, but to the absence of any governing principle of becoming.

In a certain respect, philosophy amounts to an astonishment that God does not exist. It is an astonishment at the universe lying before us, following the collapse of good sense, which wants the originary real to be richer than what ensues from it. For the inexistence of God is what unveils the staggering power of novelty of *our own* world. This power alone (precisely because it has no peer) patiently destroys the framework of its own laws. In this way we see that the world is by no means the prisoner of whatever arises within it, because this advent concerns the *sum total* of what belongs to it. The worldly is destined for a transformation *without reserve* in which there remains no substrate of becoming, no determinate substance that remains unchanged amidst change. To think becoming thus means to think the eternal excess of a becoming-without-law beyond the laws of becoming. It is the eternal excess of time over and above its temporary constancy.

Excerpt B: Becoming and Quality

The concept of contingency that we have begun to construct allows us to specify the sense in which the capacity for becoming exceeds all constancy. Our return to the problem of induction aims to demonstrate that we can abandon the idea of a necessary constancy of laws without reaching the opposite notion of a *necessarily* disordered world. For the disqualification of probabilist reasoning, which serves as the basis for refusing any contingency of laws, suffices to show that the possible transformation of the constancy of this world does not necessarily require a disruption of these laws. In affirming that the world can really subject its laws to its own process of becoming, we propose a contingency superior to all necessity. *Precisely for this reason, this contingency is subject to no constraint*, and above all it is not subject to a frequential law that would supposedly render the non-effectuation of certain possibilities increasingly improbable. For to affirm that the transformation of laws *ought* to occur as long as it *can* occur is once more to subordinate the contingency of becoming to the necessity of the law that all possibilities must ultimately be actualized. In principle, an utterly chaotic world in which all laws are subject to the power of time might be phenomenally *indiscernible* from a world subject to laws that are actually necessary. For a world that is capable of everything ought *also* to be capable of not accomplishing those things of which it is capable. If the power of the advent of becoming is total, then it ought to be considered *as* power: that is to say, as the eternal capacity to produce or *not* to produce new laws.

To say that becoming is rational means that becoming can actually produce everything that is thinkable (i.e., non-contradictory). And that amounts to saying that belief in the stability of laws is essentially irrational, in so far as it does not grant the world the radical power of disorder resulting from a conception of the world that would be logical at last. But other than thinkability, nothing is supposed concerning the world in its present, past, or future state; the contingency of laws forbids us to say what disruption (if any) has occurred or will occur, or whether the world exempted from all necessity might remain indefinitely stable. Moreover, this thesis is of no importance whatever for the experimental sciences, given that it says nothing as to the determination of existent laws or their supposed endurance or breakdown.

Yet the true stakes of the discussion are found elsewhere. Abandoning the necessity of laws has no effect on the state of the world, and we have also begun to see that it dissolves a number of speculative impasses and the false mysteries to which they give rise, since they derive from a postulate that we now know to be unjustified. Of these false mysteries, the first to be dispelled is that of the necessity of natural laws, which could obviously only be 'explained' by some obscure pre-established harmony between our certainties and the order of nature. What was said about advent *ex nihilo* now allows us to touch on a second speculative impasse that results from the totalizing and necessitarian model of becoming: the apparently inexplicable 'mystery' of the appearance of life and thought from a material realm that supposedly excludes them from its potentialities.

We maintain that becoming is irreducible to an actualization of possible cases (perhaps recordable in a list) of a constant, determinate Universe. The essence of this Universe is disclosed in the advent of a Universe of possible cases that cannot be recorded in a list (in fact or in principle) in the form of a Universe of Universes of cases, because the Whole of these Universes cannot exist. The possible universes cannot be recorded in a list as possible cases of a Universe of Universes. The emergence of these universes is an advent literally *ex nihilo*, for it is irreducible to the actualization of some sort of potentiality that would be pre-existent in the supposedly perpetual Universe-Whole of what is able to happen. Now, from these considerations we obtain the theoretical weapons needed for the idea *of a true novelty*, given that the result of the advent of a Universe of hidden cases is no longer reducible to the simple manifestation-actualization of an eternally fixed reservoir of possibilities. If such a universe were to arise, it would manifest immediately as a set of cases irreducible to every other Universe, especially that or those Universes in which its advent would occur. We would be faced with a radical novelty that would be a becoming essentially capable not only of actualizing cases, but even of creating them from nothing. It would be a becoming in excess of all deterministic or aleatoric constancy, since it could never be totalized in a divine law of laws.

Advent *ex nihilo* thus presents itself as the concept par excellence of a world without God, and for that very reason it allows us to produce *an irreligious notion of the origin of pure novelty*. Suspicions against the idea of origin are always based on the same prejudice: the problem of origin or of the originary advent of novelty is linked with the religious theme of Creation. As such, it is viewed as meaningless or uninteresting for a thinking of immanence. Obviously, it is in connection with the origin of life or thought that the refusal to confront the logic of their emergence rationally takes on full scope. A strict opposition appears between philosophers who ignore such problems in magnificent fashion, and the apologists who capitalize on the difficulties of explaining them scientifically as a means of justifying their faith. In truth, this refusal once again displays a subordination of the concept to the sacred. For it transposes the religious ban on thinking about the origin into the sphere of rationality. The origin of novelty is supposed to be unthinkable for a purely human understanding; it is pure non-sense, because it is transcendent; it is a divine act. Such statements are the inaugural declaration of faith, whose victory over human minds is now so complete that even the most intransigent atheists seem to pay homage to it.

Thus, the present-day inability to think the origin results from the postulate that it can be thought only through the intervention of transcendence. And in fact, if we reject advent *ex nihilo* this *seems* to imply the obvious unthinkability of novel advent. The impasse here is that the advent of novelty is impossible by definition to reabsorb into what previously existed, unless we deny it true novelty. As long as reason is identified with thinking the constancy of laws, it remains impossible to think rationally about the advent of life in matter, because it cannot be understand how the lifeless can produce a qualitative multiplicity of affects and perceptions from a certain 'molecular geometry'. It will always remain without reason (essentially contingent) that certain affections, perceptions, or indeed thoughts should be *superadded* to certain material configurations. Perhaps it is not meaningless to think that certain molecular combinations that are compatible with observable constants might be regarded as so many 'potentialities' of matter (since here it is only a question of arranging some elements that actually exist in physically possible totalities). And perhaps one could imagine the combinations inherent in the organization of the living as 'possible cases' of a Universe-matter. But even so, we still cannot speak in these terms of the advent of affective, perceptive, or cognitive contents that accompany some of these configurations. For these affective contents of living and thinking beings were obviously not contained in the actually existing particles that presided at their formation, whether as elements or as some sort of 'potential force'. This essential excess of life and thought beyond matter implies a scission that ruptures all continuity, leaving the divine and the soul free rein to fill the resulting chasm. Nevertheless, such 'mysteries' collapse once the qualitative component of life is identified with the advent of a Universe of cases that were *in no way* contained in the universe previously. Such a Universe gives us the advent of a pure novelty whose possibly regular concordance with material complexes does not obliterate the radical excess found in the affective qualities of suffering or jubilation and the travails of life or consciousness. From this we recognize that the qualities inherent in the affective and perceptive world of life are immediate signs that becoming makes its novelties emerge *from nothing*. A pain or pleasure does not pre-exist its effectuation in the living, because life itself does not pre-exist the material components that accompany its advent. No affections (those weak ticklings of matter) exist before they seize an organism, and no perception or thought haunts a matter supposedly sensitive enough to be myopic and stupid enough to have confused thoughts.

All quality as quality is without why, since none of its content refers to anything other than the advent *ex nihilo* of its being. The absurdity of asking why red is red suffices to reveal the excess of becoming over every law: its capacity for creating new cases from nothing, cases for which no genealogy can be established in the world prior to its emergence. A red is without why because no material counterpart can ever tell us how this red is red. A red is without why because there was *nothing* of this red in the world prior to its advent that would provide us with a reason by relating it to a pre-red where it had always been contained. For matter is not haunted by any potentiality of red, any pale pink specter, before the advent of red among the sensitive powers of the living.

A world of contents and qualities, given immediately to us as a set of facts irreducible to all determinism and all causal genealogy – such a world can thus be identified with the sudden advent *ex nihilo* of a Universe of cases. Quality is a pure fact referring only to itself, and as such it displays the irrecuperable excess of a Universe of cases (namely, that of the living) on another (that of material configurations). It is given as a brute existence that essentially cannot be deduced, and which refers to its actuality alone. If quality suddenly arises, it does so *from nothing*, not from the potentiality of a Universe-Whole where it would have lain in ambush for all eternity. The remarkable thing is that *the brute facticity of quality is where the inexistence of the Whole is immediately given*. For the facticity of quality refers to its advent *ex nihilo*, which refers in turn to the absence of an originary Whole from which it could be inferred with complete necessity.

In this way we circumvent the impasse of traditional materialism, which identifies life as a potentiality of matter, as a necessary effect of certain configurations of matter. This would amount to the claim that the affects are a possible property of matter in the same manner as nuclear fission. Such a position tries to sound reasonable, but it always stumbles over its own extravagance in supposing that *matter lies dormant* – that if life is not manifest in it, then it is still somehow intimately present in it, and that the appearance of the living is nothing more than the awakening of matter. For to say that matter has vital content 'in potency' is to ascribe to matter a certain tendency toward affectivity, and this tendency can itself only be understood according to the model of the living. On the contrary, the simple fact of recognizing that matter does not sleep (that matter is not a cataleptic life, does not harbor any affectivity in its depths, that it is simply *lifeless*) imposes a pure discontinuity between matter and vital content.

In short, *if it is consistent*, the materialism that rejects advent *ex nihilo* due to its fantastical character is led to the equally fantastic (and indeed irrational) assertion that life is *already* found in one manner or another in the heart of matter. This is the founding thesis of *hylozoism*. For if life does not result from an absolute advent, it is necessary to conclude (assuming one is not a religious believer) that life and even thought are somehow already present in matter. As such, the rigid alternative that supported Diderot's belief in universal sentience continues to hold: either we renounce the materialist hypothesis and institute an irresolvable dualism between soul and body, or we maintain the essential unity and require 'that stones think'. The category of intensity will then be happily summoned to give an account of the different orders of the real. Yet we know that no such monism of intensive differences has ever solved anything. For we can certainly go ahead and affirm that there is only a difference of 'degree' between matter and organic life. Yet this difference is manifested in such a manner that it once more becomes incommensurable with all unity. No one has ever grasped what the continuity of mineral 'life' (the supposed 'minimal degree' of life) would be with life carried to the point of maximum intensity. Take, for example, the vital experience of artistic creation: despite what has been said of Rodin, there was nothing of intensified marble about him.

Hence these mysteries, which are inherent to hylozoism, are apparently only resolved by the notion of intensity, which was justly criticized by Bergson for serving only to mask qualitative discontinuity by means of mathematical continuity. And this is precisely the point, as we have shown, where only the mathematical discontinuity of Cantorian infinity is adequate to the rupture generated by the advent of qualities. Thus it is sufficiently demonstrated that hylozoism, the only possible model of life if sudden advent *ex nihilo* is rejected, leads immanence to an impasse.

Excerpt C: The Advent of the Living

We have seen that the experimental sciences are unable to give an account of the qualitative excess of life beyond its material counterpart, and clearly this is not their goal. They do not even aim at such an explanation, which is simply meaningless with respect to their procedures. We have none the less shown that the incapacity of experimental science to touch even remotely on this problem does not doom every rational approach to it, as long as we accept the disjunction between reason and real necessity.

We then saw how it was possible to dissolve certain enigmas that seemed to be insoluble. Yet the same approach can be applied to problems *internal to science itself*: not the problems connected with the appearance of the qualitative contents of the living, but those dealing with the material configurations to which they are linked. Indeed, the advent of material configurations that could support life or thought now seems *highly unlikely* in the light of known physical laws, whether we are speaking of the appearance of the first constituents of life, of the evolution of species, or of the emergence and evolution of the human brain. In all these cases, the aleatory model seems powerless to explain the novelty and improbability of the becoming of life. To account for this failure of chance to explain the emergence of new forms of life, the need once more arises for some sort of enigmatic principle of finality, since religiosity continues to look like the only alternative to algebraic rationality.

We should emphasize that we are confronted here by a difficulty *of fact* for experimental rationality rather than a difficulty of principle. Indeed, if science cannot resolve this problem of the qualitative advent of the living (for it cannot even pose it), in principle it can discover the frequential and/or deterministic laws at the origin of the material configurations that accompany vital and conscious contents. Thus, by recourse to its own procedures alone, science can resolve the second difficulty inherent in the aleatory model. It would thus be necessary that the advent of life *ex nihilo* would be exclusively qualitative, that it would concern nothing but the irreducible excess of affective and cognitive contents of human and animal life beyond their material counterpart. But the notion of contingency that we have theorized does not *require* that it happen this way. It could be that, like all radical novelty, the advent of life (the appearance of a hidden anatomical organization or cognitive activity) *is accompanied by the simultaneous advent of material configurations that rupture with the physical laws in the midst of which they emerge*. Indeed, nothing forbids us from thinking that the advent of the qualitative universe of vital contents *should be one and the same as the advent of the material counterpart by which these contents are inscribed in the material Universe* that precedes them. In that case, the appearance of the material organization of life would have *no reason to obey the frequential constants of matter*. The configurations of life would break the laws of chance, because they would not at all be the possible cases *of* matter, but rather the correlate *within* matter of the appearance *ex nihilo* of vital contents.

In short, we aim to show that, in this case as in previous ones (the constancy of laws and the sudden advent of contents), it is possible to *invert the value of the signs*. Our astonishment in the face of the enigma of the constancy of laws, or of the sudden advent of life, ceases to point toward a mystery exceeding reason. Instead, it unveils the full power of an immanence that can be thought as a non-Whole. Likewise, if the formation of organizations underlying life remained aberrations of the laws of physics (and admittedly this can never be firmly established), there would never be anything to this except the striking manifestation of a becoming able to break its own laws by creating certain Universes that exceed all constancy and all frequency. The aberration in probability represented by such phenomena would no longer refer to the incomprehensible aberration of transcendence. Instead, it would become *the parousia of immanence*, the full accomplishment of a time that could no longer be surpassed by anything: a time in excess of the determinist and aleatory time of algebraic reason, creating *simultaneously* the qualitative content and its material organization. This is a sign that the latter is not the 'necessary cause' of the former, but that what we have here is an advent linked both with a life-Universe not existing in the matter-Universe, and with the material organization that is *de facto* correlated with such a hidden life-Universe.

Stated briefly, under the hypothesis that configurations of life have an undefined resistance to deterministic and aleatory laws, we could advance the following (indirect) discourse, whose purpose would be to neutralize in advance any religious exploitation of the 'miracle of life':

The advent of the living in the midst of matter can be characterized by three basic givens:

1. *Qualitatively*, there arises a multiplicity of perceptions and affections. Unless we wish to defend the position that matter itself is endowed with sensation, we ought to admit the novelty of

advent *ex nihilo* – since *nothing* was alive before the advent of the living.

2. This multiplicity of sensations is linked with a *constancy* belonging to it. From an empiricist perspective, it will be said that the daily lessons of living creatures stem from such constants (the qualitative perception of fire followed by the sensation of burning, etc.).

3. This vital multiplicity *is added to* (and *inserted into*) the matter-Universe, retroactively modifying the latter by its advent in the midst of it. For the advent of life is not the necessary effect of a material configuration (such claims have never made sense). Instead, it is the contingent and conjoint creation of a Universe of qualities *and* material configurations that were both inexistent until then. It is in this sense (conjunction rather than causation) that the vital qualities possess a quantifiable material counterpart: a geometrical configuration that supports them and by which they can *also* be approached, but without being reducible to them.

This latter point enables us to understand that the absolute character of the advent of the living in the midst of matter should be perceptible not only qualitatively but also *quantitatively*: that is to say, from the point of view of the laws of matter themselves, due to the extreme improbability of the advent of material configurations that underlie the living. For if it is true that, once the material configuration of life arises, it seems to submit itself by heredity to determinist and probabilist constants compatible with the physical laws of matter, the original appearance of this configuration clearly breaks all such laws. This extraordinary improbability of the appearance of the material components of life presents a major difficulty for contemporary biology. Evolutionism faces the same limit as the aleatory model, since the hypothesis that the chance recombination of genetic material lies at the origin of the novelty of species has no reasonable probability whatever. The difficulty is all the greater in so far as it is no longer a question (as in the appearance of life) of an initial event, but rather of a succession of events that are equally incomprehensible in terms of chance.

Let us now see how the distinction between chance and contingency allows us to remove these impasses.

Under the hypothesis of such a distinction, the world is presented to us in two ways:

1. As an advent of constancy which, due to the inexistence of a mysterious and transcendent unifying principle, cannot be subordinated to a law of the advent of laws. For this very reason it breaks with the previous laws (the frequential ones, in particular). This is precisely why we are able to notice some appearances that break all existing laws, seeming to display the action of a transcendence even while manifesting the total absence of it. If the appearance of life is able to break all probability of the laws of matter, this is because it is not a possible case of those laws. Likewise, if species have been able to arise while breaking all probability of heredity and genetic accident, it is because these new species are not monstrous cases of ancient species. The new laws do not need to be subordinated to a probabilistic law in order to appear, because they are not possible cases of ancient laws in the midst of which they emerge.

2. As a set of factual constants that the various natural sciences attempt to describe. But when the sciences are faced with the appearance of such constancy, they cannot hope in the same way to extract a law of the advent of laws. Thus they are faced with a phenomenon that exceeds any attempt to put them in equations or to estimate their 'probability'. For this very reason, the contingency of laws is manifested in their original caesuras, and that is what legitimates the essentially *descriptive* method of the empirical sciences. It is precisely in these descriptions of constancy that the epistemological notions of determinism and probabilism are legitimate. Therefore there is no need, if a phenomenon escapes every law, to appeal to transcendence on the pretext that the phenomenon exceeds scientific discourse. For on the contrary, what is revealed in such cases is the contingency of laws themselves – that is to say, the necessary impossibility of unifying the world in a principal Whole that the chaos of the world could never exceed. The current alternative between chance and finality is therefore outdated: the fact that a phenomenon is improbabilizable refers to the non-aleatory contingency of becoming: to the unwavering immanence of our world rather than to Providence.

* * *

In replacing the alternative of chance and finality with that of chance and contingency (the aleatory advent of an event in the midst of a law; the contingent advent of a law without there being a law for the advent of laws) we acquire the means of opposing the defenders of finalism. Such people profit logically from the scientistic (but not rational) belief in the necessity of laws to affirm that the extreme improbability of the appearance of life or the evolution of species is proof of transcendent intervention. As we have seen, these 'miracles' exhibit the opposite truth. The world is limited by nothing, and for this very reason it is identified with an advent without any law of laws, irreducible to probabilist reasoning.

To identify rationalism with the eternity of natural, deterministic, or frequential laws is to render thought powerless before originary phenomena, and ultimately to resign oneself to acknowledging a transcendent foundation. Reason teaches the exact contrary: laws have no reason to be constant, and nothing entails that they will not contain new constants in the future. Such cases of advent (which we will discuss in greater detail in the closing section) can be divided into three *orders* that mark the essential ruptures of becoming: *matter, life, and thought*. Each of these three appears as a Universe that cannot be *qualitatively* reduced to anything that preceded it. (No sensation can be reduced to a material configuration, and no concept of universal extension or mathematical concept of the infinite can be reduced to a finite mass of sensations.) As for the *quantitative* aspect, they can arise suddenly in a manner that is highly improbable in view of the preceding constants: the material supports of life, of new species, and of the human brain, all of them configurations possibly rupturing with the frequential constants of physics or genetics.

Excerpt D: Immanent Immortality

We have sketched the essential traits of an ontology that adopts once more the philosophical requirement of the anhypothetical principle, and shown how this eternal principle founds an immanent theory of truth. This ontology is the condition of philosophy, or rather its end: namely, the constitution of an immanent ethics based on such an ontology. We know that the eternal truth of contingency is the foundation of an immanent theory of being qua being. But what is an immanent ethics? An immanent theory presents comprehensible truths as the sole possible truths, excluding the religious idea of a *totally other* truth, of a revealed truth transcending the power of thought. In the same manner we can say that an immanent ethics is an ethics that *posits this life as the only desirable life*. It would thus be an ethics that (unlike religion) would not promise some *other* life than ours (a life founded on another truth) *but an ethics that manifests on the contrary such a desire for this life that it wishes this life to be immortal.*

Immortality is the philosophical desire for life, the desire that this human life and no other should again and always be lived. Philosophy wants a life without a beyond, and *that* is why philosophical ethics *must* be an ethics of immortality: *that is to say, an ethics of life with no elsewhere.* It will obviously be objected that this life is not immortal, and that in fact the desire for immortality is the religious desire for another life. But we maintain that philosophical ethics consists solely in *demonstrating* that *this life* possesses in itself the dimension of immortality, while religious ethics consists in affirming by an irrational act of faith *the existence of a totally other existence* that is unthinkable in this world and that would limit our present existence from the outside. Our present life is thus declared to be transient, as destined to open onto an existence incommensurable with our own. But in claiming to *demonstrate* that humans can hope for the immortality of their *own* lives, the philosopher affirms on the contrary (and for this very reason) that the hope of another life is illusory. Immortality is definitely the central concept of an ethics of immanence, an ethics of human life without a beyond precisely *because* it is immortal. And it is precisely because Spinoza and Nietzsche were the masters of irreligiosity that they were also the thinkers of immortality, though of an immortality *such that I am only capable of expecting the renewal without end of what is here in this world.*

Now, how can we demonstrate that this life itself possesses the dimension of immortality? The demonstration (and herein lies its great strangeness) is *without difficulty* given what has been established. The factial[1] is an ontology that allows us to think immortality directly as one possibility *among others*, but as a *real* possibility (since it is non-contradictory) of advent *ex nihilo*. There is hardly anything more to be said about the reality of this possibility. The factial, in demonstrating the effective contingency of the laws of this world, has no difficulty in *basing the hope of philosophical immortality on a radically irreligious ontology.*

What we call *divine ethics* (we will justify the term later) *rests on the real possibility of immortality, a possibility guaranteed by factial ontology.*

Let us consider this proposition more closely. What it expresses in general fashion is that since everything logically possible is really possible, then since *the rebirth of bodies* is not illogical it must also be possible. And not only is rebirth possible; it cannot even be deemed either probable or improbable. For if rebirth suddenly occurs, it ought to occur suddenly in the very fashion in which a new Universe of cases suddenly appears in the midst of the non-Whole. *Rebirth can thus be assimilated to the improbabilizable advent of a new constancy* in the same manner in which life suddenly arises from matter, or thought from life. It is an event that would be no more astonishing than these latter advents that *have* in fact *taken place.*

It is necessary to draw a distinction between the advent of what I call a *World* and the advent of the *intra-Worldly.* I call 'Worlds', or 'orders', the three categories of advent known as matter, life, and thought. I call 'intra-Worldly advents' those that are capable of occurring in the midst of a determinate World: for example, the advent of new species in the midst of the World of life, or advents of creative invention in the midst of the World of thought. And finally, I reserve the term 'world' with a lower-case 'w' to designate the non-Whole of what is. Worlds arise suddenly from the world, and if these have a right to a majestic capital letter for the first time, it is because there is more in a World than in the world, since there is more in what ensues than there is in the origin (more in the 'effect' than in the 'cause').

Why make this distinction? What is its basis? The distinction between World and intra-World aims to show that rebirth entails the advent of a World different from the World of thought, and not an advent internal to the creative activities of humans. Following the three Worlds of matter, life, and thought, *the rebirth of humans ought to be distinguished as a fourth World.* The point to be established is thus as follows: *if* a World were to arise beyond the three preceding ones, this World could *only* be that of the rebirth of humans. We will call this 'fourth order' the *World of justice*, a World where humans acquire immortality, the sole life worthy of their condition. World of matter, World of life, World of thought, World of justice: four orders, of which three have already appeared, with the fourth *able* to take place and *existing already as an object of hope, of the desire of every human qua rational being.* The World of justice ought to be viewed as the object of desire traversed by reason, or as the place where life is transfixed by the thought of the eternal.

Let us justify these propositions. I propose that *the kingdom of ends* (which was discussed by Kant as a just community of humans) *ought to be rethought as the anticipation by humans of the possible advent of a novelty ulterior to themselves*. This ought to be understood in the strong sense as a novelty that has the same relation to humans as humans have to life or life to matter. For we know that humans have access to the eternal truth of the world. *Thus nothing more can appear beyond humans considered as thinking beings*: there can be no further being incommensurable with our humanity, but only additional contingent variations of life or matter. By 'humans', of course, we mean rational beings capable of grasping the absolute truth of contingency, and not simply the bipedal species in which such a reality now happens to be encountered. This rational entity is the one that cannot be surpassed in the way that life is surpassed by humans. Here we are in a logic of incommensurables. Only a thought reaching a higher truth than that of contingency could re-enact the rupture inaugurated by thought with respect to animality. Only an all-powerful God, whose impossibility has already been sufficiently considered, could outstrip the beings of the third World just as these outstrip the second World. Every other creature (however intelligent and 'advanced' one imagines) would not change the World. They would only give us access to the imaginary modification of our humanity, without offering any higher truth about the eternal being of everything.

The human as a thinking being is thus presented as *the insurpassable effect* of advent *ex nihilo*. The problem, then, is as follows. In what could a World following the human consist? What advent could produce something other than a variant of former Worlds (some new law of matter, new living species, or new creation of thought) since no being can be incommensurable with humans in the same manner as humans are with life or life with matter? The response follows naturally from the question: namely, *the sole possible novelty surpassing humans just as humans surpass life would be the recommencement of the human*. That is why the fourth World ought to be called the World of justice: for it is only the World of the rebirth of humans *that makes universal justice possible, by erasing even the injustice of shattered lives*.

What is a World in comparison with an intra-Worldly advent? *The advent of an element that is constitutive for humans*. Humans are in fact defined by their access to truth, understood as the eternal contingency of that which is. As a consequence, there is of course no human without a World of thought, since thought is only this relation of the contingent being to contingency as such. But there could also be no humans without a World of life, for life is the sensible relation of contingent beings to other contingent beings: to the *particular* thing that can be perceived as such only by affect. And yet there can be no thought of contingency without a relation to particular things, to that which *is* contingent, since contingency is only the contingency of what is. Finally, there are no humans without matter: without non-living being. For life itself ought to be given as a contingent possibility that arises *ex nihilo*, and thus to be incarnated in a mortal existence for which matter always represents both the menacing other (which the living can always become once more) and the originary constituent on whose basis life can appear as a pure emergence. The three Worlds thus represent the three constitutive orders of the human. Whatever might be the laws of matter, of forms of life, or of intellectual or artistic inventions – whatever the various intra-Worldly advents might be – the three Worlds remain the definitional invariants of the human as a being of reason.

But humans are also defined by their relation to a fourth World, and this relation is that of hope as desire crossed by thought: the desire of humans torn between their present contingency and the knowledge of the eternal by which they reach the idea of justice. For this knowledge gives us access to the strict *equality* between all humans qua human. The eternal truths to which our condition grants access are in fact *indifferent to differences*, to the innumerable and necessary differences between individual thinkers. The differences are necessary because humans, as simple existents, are contingent and particular beings indefinitely differentiable from other humans. Yet these differences are undifferentiated by the impersonal reason that marks all bearers of truth. This is why humans, as long as they think, *are affected* by injustice whenever it strikes them, since nothing permits us to found an inegalitarian difference of humans from themselves. And of all these injustices the most extreme is still death: absurd death, early death, death inflicted by those unconcerned with equality. Hence those who exercise their humanity, those who think the impassable character of a condition shared equally by all beings of reason, *can only hope for the recommencement of our lives in such a way that justice would surpass the factual death that has struck down our fellow humans.* It is not a question here of some exorbitant conception of justice, but only of giving a precise exposition of it in its excessiveness, since justice is *only* such an extravagance towards the present world by which the human condition is specified. Justice can survive only as an idea of existent and irreparable wrongs, and we owe the dead nothing less. When the requirement of justice actually transfixes us, it *also* summons our refusal of injustice for the dead, for recent or ancient deaths, for known and unknown deaths. For the universal is universal only when it makes no exceptions.

The World of justice turns out to be a World in the proper sense: an advent that crosses the boundary of the third World as the third did the preceding one, because it contains *the sole* conceivable radical novelty following the human: the recommencement of the human in just form. And this World is a World in the sense of a definitional element of humans qua humans, as those who think *hope* by refusing the injustice done to their fellow humans, whether they are still alive now or not.

The core of factial ethics thus consists in the immanent binding of philosophical astonishment and messianic hope, understood as the hope for justice for the dead and the living. The bond is immanent, for while philosophical astonishment generates the hope of a World to come, it does not refer to any otherworldly realm but solely to the consciousness of the power of advent *ex nihilo*.

We well understand the specificity of this relation: the world is shown to be astonishing in the sense that it refers to no other world, because *for this reason alone* it is shown to be capable of making more (humans) arise from less (matter). On the contrary, if God existed, then creation would be poor and also quite astonishing, since it could not make less (humans) arise from more (God). Thus the hope of rebirth is bound to the astonishing awareness of the inexistence of God; *divine inexistence fulfills, for the first time, a condition of hope for the resurrection of the dead.*

This awaiting is not faith, since the event that serves as its object of hope is explicitly determined as a possibility that can be produced *or not* produced. No necessity, no probability, can guarantee its advent. But no impossibility and no improbability can discourage us from anticipating that it might happen. Beyond all calculation and all foresight, we are confronted with the very essence of the universalist hope. Like all hopes, it is a tormented joy: a life of the spirit in which our happy knowledge that justice is rendered possible is mixed with a voluntarily maintained disquietude, guaranteeing us against a religious relation to the desired advent, and linked to the symmetrical consciousness of a possible non-advent of the next World. It is a troubled certainty about possibility that protects us from the dogmatism of necessity, and which all subjects share once they associate the newly restored hope with their human condition.

Our shock at the existence of the world, and at our own existence within the world, ceases to be anguish or a contemplation turned back on itself. The philosophical astonishment that we feel before an existence deprived of any 'why' ceases to be identified with the shrill and desperate consciousness of a godless human condition that leads us to no specific *act* other than perhaps suicide. Instead, it henceforth becomes the source of both our most extreme and most immanent hope. The shock felt before what has already in fact arisen becomes by the same stroke the comprehension of that which can *really* be a world delivered to itself. Only those who know how to live this astonishment also know how to hope. For only those who comprehend the utterly staggering character of their own existence know that even resurrection would be less astonishing. Pascal already said what needed to be said on this point: the surprising fact of humans' rebirth would never be as surprising as the fact that they had been born at all. If rebirth were to occur, it would arise suddenly in such unspectacular fashion that it would be no more astonishing to be alive again than it would be that we are alive today.

Excerpt E: Symbolization

At the outset we should make a distinction, essential for the further pursuit of our goals, between the *foundation* in the strict sense of the universal and what we will call its *symbolization*.

The real possibility of the fourth World removes the hopeless absurdity (found in the case of every ideal) that results from its ontological impossibility. But this possibility would be unable to found the *value* of the original requirement of justice, a problem we will examine later. It is not *because* justice is possible as a world-to-come that the requirement of justice has value. The fourth World, conceived as a recommencement, is the necessary condition for the universal requirement of justice to have any meaning: for it surpasses unjust and early death, by which this requirement would otherwise be irremediably flouted. But the *possibility* of justice (its non-aberrant character as a radical, universal requirement valid for the dead and the living alike) is still not its *foundation* or its proper legitimation. The fact that justice is possible does not tell us *why* it is necessary to be just. Here we have something comparable to the relation established by Kant between the moral law and the postulates of God and immortality. These postulates prevent the moral law being felt as an aberrant requirement of reason, yet they provide no foundation for its value. In short, to demonstrate that the universal is possible does not found it as a properly ethical requirement.

The problem of the foundation of the universal will be dealt with later, in connection with a *problem* whose full comprehension first requires that we linger over the procedure that establishes the real possibility of the fourth World. Let us recall that with this demonstration we have escaped the habitual impasses of idealism. The requirement of justice is no longer reduced to an abstract principle deprived of all ontological basis. Nor does the possibility of justice rely on any transcendent reality. The fact of living for justice, of living an unselfish relation to other humans, means living according to the truth of the ultimate ontological possibility of the world: namely, our rebirth. The factial permits us to resume, in a hidden world, the lost relation between being and value; the absurdity of early death ceases to undermine our aspiration to universal justice, since it becomes the guarantor and no longer the obstacle of a possible justice for the dead and the living alike. This breaking of the despair *of* the absurd *by* the absurd achieves in a new form what I will henceforth call *symbolization*: *an immanent rational link between being and the universal.*

Symbolization thus represents the rational guarantee of a possible realization of the universal, which none the less does not provide us with its principle of legitimation. We will now show in more detail in what this operation consists; to my mind, it is one of the basic and original features of the present enterprise. In this way we will locate within the symbolized universal an inconsistency that imperils its very thinkability. We will soon evoke this inconsistency under the name of 'ethical scission'. It needs both to establish the principle of the universal (of founding it and not simply symbolizing it) and to provide it with an essential new determination: that of an *incarnation* of the rebirth that is imagined.

Excerpt F: Philosophy and Symbol

As already stated, what I mean by 'symbolization' consists not in the founding of values, but in understanding the *relation of values with the truth of this world* – with determining what the requirement of justice as such *teaches* us about the world. It is a matter of discovering an agreement between the discourse of values and the discourse of truth, or between world and justice, whatever form this agreement might take. Every philosophical enterprise starts from a postulate that may well be impossible to demonstrate, and which may even be false or ideological. That is to say, value *is not* a simple human invention but *the discovery of a truth* concerning the world, or extra-human reality, and this truth ought to be shown by reason alone *without the intervention of a transcendent revelation*. Philosophy begins with a wager on the still unjustified certainty that value is not a mere socially useful artifice, but rests on an ontological truth. It is by aiming at an accord between the requirement of justice and the impersonality of being that the philosopher can produce a system of values. The elements of such systems, the values it defends, are often quite similar. But their arrangement and general signification, the *basic coloring* taken on by the values in a specific accord between justice and being, vary in each case according to how these values are inscribed in the world. *How does a non-human real justify the requirement of justice?* How does the world outside humans relate ontologically with human requirements? This is the primordial axis of philosophical questioning.

The goal of every philosophy must be the immanent inscription of values in being. It is by mediating this inscription that the philosopher intervenes in values, and that courage, goodness, or justice can be recommended to an equal degree by numerous different philosophies according to a different systematization in each case. Stated in Kantian terms, the problem of philosophy is to confront the despair that results from the indifference of the world to my moral ends, and not to bypass that despair with the religious affirmation of a transcendent accord between world and justice. Philosophers oppose both the tepidity of lucid despair and the obscurantism of faith. They seek to establish that moral requirements are not simple conventions unrelated to reality, but are themselves the receptacles of truths about being. Faced with the overwhelming opposition between atheist resignation and religious ardor, the philosopher aims at what one calls *fervor* (*ardeur*): that is to say, the jubilation that results from rational knowledge of the ontological accord between the immeasurable requirement of justice and the absurdity of a world without God.

The inscription of values in the world opposes philosophy to sophistry in primordial fashion. The sophist is the one for whom value is nothing more than a profitable social convention. In the eyes of the sophist value is not based on any reality, is not linked to any objectivity, and reveals nothing about the truth of this world – a truth that remains entirely inaccessible to every exercise of thought. Value is sheer invention, a simple artifice created by humans whose sole aim is that everyone should live well. When viewed from such a perspective, it is pointless to submit to values and their possible expression in laws except in so far as I judge them advantageous either for me or for whatever elite group I favor. In this way the sophist is opposed not only to the philosopher, but also to the transcendent inscription of value in being that typifies the religious conception of value.

In light of all this, the philosophical inscription of values in the world consists in refusing the merely human character of norms of conduct; values *also* ought to teach us something *about the world*. This signifies in turn that the world itself should further the requirements of humans in one way or another. After all, humans cannot be satisfied with obeying an arbitrary tradition or an advantageous artifice but, in their search for the Good, must find the truth of their condition in the world, even in the deepest truth of the world itself. Philosophy is always born from this requirement of the immanent and comprehensible inscription of values in the world. This is what distinguishes philosophy both from the absurd and hopeless world of the sophist who sees value as nothing but convention, and from the transcendent world of the religious person who inscribes value in the world through the irrational means of a revelation, a tradition, an authority. Thus, the great epochs of philosophy are the ones initially dominated by the nightmarish duel between the traditionalism of religion and the vulgar cynicism of sophistry. Against the spirit of such epochs, any philosopher worthy of the name aims at an immanent inscription of values. This entails a new fervor for justice that must show how this requirement is not an illusion, a convention, or a submission to God and his earthly authorities. Seen from this perspective, the problem of the philosopher is not knowing the meaning of justice, but knowing what good it is to be just. It is a problem confronted not by those who are ignorant of what justice means, but by those who know quite well what it means, but who still see no reason to risk anything for it that would run counter to their own interests. They are those who see no reason to risk their lives for it, let alone waste them. This justice is opposed not to the ignorant, but to the hopeless.

The term 'Symbol' can be used for the immanent inscription of value in being. This term is selected for etymological reasons: the Greek verb *sym-ballein* refers to the action of joining together two pieces of material. We know that this term referred to a custom of Greek travelers called the 'hospitality tablet'. This tablet was a small piece of bone (shaped as in the game of knucklebones or jacks) that was broken in two, with each person preserving a piece. When a Greek traveler was hosted by a friend whom he would be unable to see again for many years, they were assured of recognizing each other or each other's children by *joining* (*symballein*) the two separate pieces along a unique line of breakage. In this sense, the symbol is what permits us to renew links of hospitality. And this is truly the task of philosophy. Even the hopeless do not feel themselves to be in a world that is unaware of their desire for justice, and the philosopher renews hospitality between humans and the world in *demonstrating* that moral aspirations are not absurd illusions or vulgar ideologies, but that they rest instead on the non-reflective, intuitive perception of the world in its ultimate truth.

The Symbol can thus be defined as an ontological link between being and value.

We can maintain that philosophy all the way to the present has managed to define three principal types of Symbols: the *cosmological* Symbol, the *naturalist* Symbol, and the *historical* Symbol. Let us briefly indicate their principal characteristics, proceeding roughly as if 'by hatchet-strokes'. Here again my aim is only to attain another relatively specific form: that of factial symbolization, which is the first to propose *a non-metaphysical Symbol*.

The cosmological Symbol is the first properly philosophical act in our history. It was sought by Socrates, inaugurated by Plato, and accomplished by Aristotle. Philosophy is born from the initial separation of the discourses of value and being. Astronomy, with its mathematical discourse on the motion of the planets, ceases to explain a phenomenon with the exemplary narratives of myth.

Ionian physics does the same when it speaks of *Physis*, replacing narratives with concepts. But during the time when this new regime of discursivity is being deployed, the discourse of values still preserves the structure of myth, as if by inertia. An unthought scission is produced between the science of phenomena and the representation of moral norms. And thus it is possible for a cultivated Greek to explain courage by narrating the exploits of Achilles even after ceasing to believe in such discourses as concerns the movement of the planets or the nature of becoming. Myth continues to serve as the legitimating source of values, though myth itself is in the midst of being delegitimized through its incapacity to discourse about the world. The sophist incarnates the separation between the two discourses and the loss it entails. Value ceases to be an innocent belief. All the marks of transcendence (myth, authority, tradition) are removed. Justice, courage, piety, and wisdom are assessed in terms of utility. They are no longer of value except in so far as they assure us the advantages of collective life. But in that case, what is the point of following these virtues when they become personally injurious to me? The sophistical conception of value is in fact the very abolition of the notion of value, for a value that has worth only according to an external norm (utility) is no longer a value. Instead, it becomes nothing more than a tool of my own interest. And if interest becomes the ultimate criterion of my actions, this signifies that I have ceased to believe in the idea of value.

In this context of rupture, Socrates shows us the first philosophical requirement. The pre-Socratics already attempted to explain the world rationally. But philosophy proper consists in *reunifying* the discourses of value and being that were unified in the religious sphere: a unity broken for the first time by science, as the rational explanation of what is. Philosophy begins when the break between knowing and value *has taken place*. It is meaningful only once we have a scientific rupture of the religious link between reality and norms, and it claims to attempt a reunification of humans with the world while also accepting the legitimacy of such a break. For the philosophical reunification should not be a new mythic being that would consist in restoring the new discourse of being to the former zone of values. On the contrary, philosophical reunification ought to discover a means of conceptualizing the discourse of values. This does not mean to return to the unity of religious discourse, but rather to liberate whatever is still dominated by the religious.

And yet philosophy also opposes any separation between humans and world, which would lead to a sophistical conception of life as a pure conflict of opposed interests ruled by the artificial norm of law. The search for philosophical unity is thus opposed to both the traditionalist reaction of the religious who view every adversary as a sophist, and the skepticism of the sophists who view every adversary as a priest. The first has a limited and authoritarian vision of value, which has value simply because it is there; the second sees in value only the conventional manifestation of a relationship of forces that one must learn to utilize and convert into cash for the advantage of itself and its chosen group. The priest sees those who reason about values as skeptics, while the sophist sees those who declare that the Good has absolute worth (beyond all particularism) as priests. Thus the philosopher is grasped between the pincers of formidable enemies who detest one another as well, and who remain blind to their own specificity. This is the philosopher's fate. Even today, the great philosophers are treated as sophists by the priests, and as priests by the sophists. This is a good sign that the thinker of immanence is on the right path, since the disquieting strangeness of the immanentist remains equally formidable to both parties.

Socrates, with his insistence on a non-religious accord between the Good and being, is the first to rouse the eminently philosophical project of symbolization. Or at least he does so in a *negative* sense, by seeking to demonstrate that those who remain faithful to values out of tradition can no longer *understand* their values. When Socrates asks the meaning of courage, piety, or wisdom, his interlocutors respond with a discourse that no longer explains anything – a discourse of examples, made up of specific anecdotes and edifying stories. But Socrates wants a conceptual discourse of value, a definition of the concept of wisdom, not a narrative based on the example of a specific wise man. The aporetic character of Socratic dialectic aims to render impossible the strange inertia in which the Athenians of that era remain trapped, not knowing that their epoch is that of the great scission. It is clearly Plato, who surmounts the Socratic aporia by addressing it at the root, who first performed such a unification in durable fashion. With Plato's strange theorization of the Idea, ontology immediately finds itself hemmed in by axiology, since the world seems to be governed by principles that are both incorruptible and just. Justice is inscribed once more in being, as a harmony of elements in the midst of the Whole. The Cosmos, and its supposedly circular course of celestial bodies, becomes the literal and fascinating image of the Good itself: a supralunary world whose changes display eternity in the very midst of time, its point of departure identical with its point of arrival. The Cosmos depicts the justice that guides the celestial world: circular trajectories allow the planets to follow a course that is uninterrupted and devoid of conflict. They never collide and hence never die, since death and conflict belong to the linear movements of the sublunary world where humans have the misfortune of living and the burden of subsisting. The straight line governs terrestrial time and condemns each thing to asymmetrical becoming (since its commencement and its end are different) and to conflict (since each thing endures the shock of other asymmetrical becomings as well). But this chaotic Earth devoid of beauty – the Greeks never seem to be amazed by landscapes – forms only a minuscule part of the cosmic world. It is the absolute bottom of the cosmos, not its glorified center. Here death and injustice reign, and humans fail to live in harmony with others since they do not take their 'place' in the community. The cosmological Symbol thus consists in *allowing* us *to see* that justice guides the Heavens (the quasi-totality of a finite but immense world) and that the children of the Earth need only lift their eyes to consider the model of beauty and peace that ought to guide their existence.

The collapse of the cosmological Symbol can be linked to the Newtonian decomposition of planetary orbits into linear movements which by nature are identical to terrestrial movements. Far from displaying the eternal harmony of the stars, these movements thus appear as the result, in the strict sense, of relations of force. The difference between the Cosmos and the terrestrial world collapses; the stars and the Earth seem once more to be guided by the absurd and conflictual reign of powers. Justice, disjoined from the real, is unveiled once more as a useful artifice invented by humans, not a veridical principle of the world understood as Cosmos. The voluptuous and libertine skepticism that runs like a thread through the figures of the Enlightenment, powerfully suggested by a physics of forces released from final causes, permits the rebirth of *modern sophists* who demystify a religious tradition that seized the Greek Symbol for its own ends. Yet this splendid liberation of fanaticism is accompanied once more by a cynicism that renews the habitual categories of despair. The death of the first Symbol breathes life back into the first scission, since philosophers no longer possess the celestial escape route for the unification of being and justice.

Faced with the renewed opposition of the priests and the sophists (who have now become clerics and skeptics), the naturalist or romantic Symbol corresponds to Rousseau's attempt to replace the opposition between sublunary and superlunary found in the cosmological Symbol with one between natural and social. The affirmation that 'man was born good' allows us to rediscover an inscription of the Good in the spontaneous being of the *living*, and no longer in cosmic *matter*. The Symbol passes from astral trajectories to compassionate bodies, from the unchangeable ether of celestial entities to the innocence of childlike organisms. In their spontaneous feelings of pity, humans rediscover the ontological reality of the Good. Whatever concerns living nature, animality, or the body becomes the new haven of the goodness that was driven from the supralunary realm. While the Greeks were never amazed by terrestrial realities (Plotinus seems to have been the first Ancient who bothered to tell us that flowers are beautiful), terrestrial nature acquires the privilege of beauty. Rousseau is amazed by the Earth and by Nature in the same way that the Greeks are amazed by the Sky. Rousseau seeks to inscribe the Good in whatever has nothing to do with society; values come to be corporeal, natural, animal, and human, rather than a mere social invention. The essential thing is that society, which is aware only of personal interest, *corrupted* the Good rather than inventing it. Our fervor can thus be reborn from the certitude that goodness is not just an illusion to dupe the naïve, but something that teaches us a truth about being: no longer the being of dead stars, but that of living creatures and their tears.

The romantic Symbol possesses obvious insufficiencies, identical with those that doomed the cosmological Symbol. For pity is no more common in the living than are war, violence, or cruelty. Like everything else, living creatures are the plaything of forces which, for all their impulsiveness, are impersonal none the less. The logic of Romanticism collapses under the weight of illusions borne by a belief in life that is still Greek, and which can survive only in the form of various irrational and amoral vitalisms.

The true successor of the Greek Symbol, the authentic Symbol of modernity, turns out to be the historic Symbol through whose culmination we are living today. Driven from the Cosmos and then from Nature, symbolization now takes History to be that non-human and non-natural entity that finally assures humans of the objectivity of their values. The principle that governs the world is no longer justice, but rather the human community as a whole. The *ruse of history* is a concept that draws its importance from what enacts the most powerful symbolization of values since the Greeks. The anarchic will of individuals seems to produce a result that none of these wills had ever desired individually. In this manner, one rediscovers in History (transformed into a superior and autonomous entity) an objective reality whose own becoming depends on no individual thought or action, but which leads us towards emancipation none the less. The movement of history is not properly human, since it is not the result of any individual will. But like the laws of nature it is not absurd, since it knows a finality whose culmination is Justice. For this principle of process is always posed by the great philosophies of history as the actual accomplishment, quite apart from any good will of empirical subjects, of a Good reinscribed in being in precisely this manner. In its passage from a model inspired by Leibniz's monadology (in which every individual is but an ignorant cogwheel in a harmonious divine plan) to that of Mandeville's fable of the bees (in which the egoism of each individual benefits the wealth of society without anyone having wished it), the historical Symbol culminates in *economism*. The economy finally becomes the ultra-objective principle of a teleology of the Good, whether in its liberal or Marxist version. For the liberal, every economic reverse amounts to a transient retreat amidst a larger movement toward a necessarily positive outcome. For the Marxist, the principle of social becoming occurs through the necessary auto-collapse of whatever alienates humans, and in this way their emancipation is attained. It is an inversion of the liberal scheme (the irrationality of each particular capitalist leads jointly to a general destruction of the existing order that was not desired by the individuals) but now in the manner of a plan of history. Yet what we have lost, with the abolition of communitarian theodicies, *is the ultimate certainty of having the real on our side*. Justice deserts being once more, even once we have arrived in the innermost recess of History. We now live the death of the Symbol of modernity, just as the eighteenth century lived the death of the Greek Symbol. The Symbol is lacking once more, and now as ever we confront the alternative nightmares reborn from their ashes: traditionalism and sophistical immoralism.

Forgetting for the moment all the detailed historical circumstances of their collapse, why has each of the Symbols failed? Because philosophy has always remained prisoner of the metaphysical postulate of real necessity, *and of nothing else*. Once philosophy realized rational necessity by turning it into the property of a being, it was left with nothing but a choice between two illusions:

1. To affirm fallaciously that the necessity of the world is in accord with my own moral ends. In this way, philosophy necessarily falls into the incomprehensible and therefore religious affirmation of such an accord. All the aforementioned Symbols collapse into transcendence. The Platonic Good is inaccessible to dialectic and is found only in ecstasy. The truth of Rousseauist sentiment rests ultimately on Savoyard Faith. Hegelian speculation, where the historicization of the Absolute is accomplished, re-inaugurates a gap between the divine subject capable of *producing* the empirical world starting from a concept alone, and the actual human subject that can only begin from its empirical surroundings in order to attain the concept. All the metaphysical Symbols thus give rise to the irrationality of behaviors stemming from belief. The cosmological easily becomes an article of faith for apostolic Roman Catholicism. The romantic gives way to the Robespierrist cult of the supreme Being. The historical is degraded into the dogma of infallibility, whether of the Party or of the Invisible Hand.
2. To affirm that we can joyously submit our ends to the necessity of the world without falling into cynicism, since virtue procures true happiness by itself. In this way we abandon the idea of universal justice and opt instead for an individual morality that renounces the illusion of a just world in favor of a virtuous submission to the amoral order of the real: a morality that assures us of happiness precisely by renouncing it.

We have not examined this second possibility in detail, because whatever one might say, it is in fact logically dependent on the first thesis. For to claim that the virtuous renunciation of any illusion as to the goodness of the world gives assurance of true happiness is to affirm once more an ontologically mysterious relation between virtue and happiness. To affirm like Epicurus that there is an accord between the most perfect of pleasures and the practices normally considered as virtues is to affirm a coincidence between value and being equal to that of any theodicy one can imagine; once again we live in a world where happiness and virtue come miraculously as a pair. Even the Stoics do not escape this impasse. For if freedom happens not to procure any satisfaction, then in that case nothing legitimates the sacrifices it requires. Let it be called the highest of satisfactions, whatever the nature of this satisfaction may be. In that case this world is definitely the best of possible worlds, which makes the highest of virtues coincide with the most enviable life.

These two positions, both of them ultimately untenable, can be recognized as *reasonable belief* and *virtuous atheism*. Either philosophy attempts symbolization by conceptually establishing that the world is so ontologically saturated by value as to escape the irrational aspect of faith (and its inherent fanaticism) even while renewing the habitual representation of belief in a divine order. Or, philosophy tries to demonstrate an essential relation between virtue and happiness so as to escape the cynicism inherently found in disbelief. These two sorts of attempts can only fail as soon as the necessity of the constancy of the world is admitted. For as soon as *this* world is posed as necessary, only an illusion can make us believe it is a desirable world for a human tormented with the desire of justice. Thus, the illusion of reasonable belief consists in believing that the irrational basis of every theodicy can be avoided. Meanwhile, the illusion of virtuous atheism is to believe that one can renounce every ontological link between being and the Good without ending up in vulgar cynicism, the sole meaningful consequence of such a separation.

These two positions might none the less lead to two extreme solutions which may be irreducible to the basic impasse of such attempts, but which represent its final amplification:

1. To *affirm untruthfully that the world is just, in such manner that this illusion produces the fervor necessary to render the world actually just.* In short, this would amount to utilizing the *power* of this illusion in order to remake the world in its own image. In a previous work ('*Raison et ésotérisme chez Hegel*', unpublished manuscript) I proposed to read the Hegelian system *as if* it corresponded to such an attempt.
2. To affirm that the accord between the world and any particular value is a matter of illusion, but at the same time *to make that*

illusion itself into a value. Namely, we will admit that no value guarantees happiness, and yet we *develop a jubilant happiness over this illusion*. Stated differently, it would be the choice to follow even an illusory value because of the vital intensity generated by such a disciplined belief. It is obviously possible to read the works of Nietzsche in this way.

These two solutions represent the logical consequence of the derealization of all value. If values do not represent anything real, if the ethical requirement rests on no truth and is only an illusion in comparison with being, then the requirement exists none the less *as* an illusion. It is only an illusion, but at least this illusion *is*. It is therefore possible to rediscover a certain being of the 'Good' (in the broad sense of a norm or imperative) by the acceptation, affirmation, or valorization of the illusion that the Good actually is. The obvious result is a contempt for the True, in the name of the conservation of a human aspiration to values. The contemporary ill repute of truth – as something produced by a Stalinized dialectic promoting generalized falsehood in the name of the proletarian Good to come ('not to make Billancourt despair'),[2] or as something resulting from a candid elegy to the myth as a vitally useful illusion – this ill repute can be linked to the domination of these two desperate attempts at symbolization.

The factial, on the contrary, even while maintaining the speculative interest of illusory existence, allows us to avoid breaking with the requirement of truth. For as soon as we accept the ontology of contingency (which teaches the existence *in us* of the idea of justice since nothing corresponds to it in actual reality), *it becomes the very truth of becoming* – the truth of time as advent *ex nihilo*. The more one denounces the requirement of universal justice as a pure illusion belonging to the imaginary realm of the human, the more one emphasizes that with the *advent* of such a chimerical requirement, becoming displays its capacity for producing something that previously did not exist *at all*. Namely, it is an imaginary Good, aimed at by an illusion for which only thinking beings are equipped. It is a Good *at which one aims*, perfectly inexistent in the world that precedes the rise of humanity. And it manifestly exceeds the capacities of matter, in whose midst it has *none the less* emerged in the form of an obstinate hope. Thus, one emphasizes all the more the capacity of time to transgress even its own laws toward the objective advent of justice. For a time capable of making something arise that did not exist before we proclaimed it, since that which is *in* us is nothing *outside* us (the universal *as* illusion), is revealed by producing, *beginning from this same nothing*, the worldly actuality of such a universal. It is not a question in each case of making something exist that previously did not exist at all. The depth of the scission between illusion and reality is thereby reversed in the manifestation of the capacity of time to fill the gap that it itself has forged. Humans can henceforth learn to be astonished, and then even amazed, by the very existence of the illusion in themselves. For the illusion no longer leads them to despair or to faith, but to the lucid hope that the world in the future will be able to reproduce the measureless novelty borne by their thought.

* * *

The factial proposes a new symbolization, the first *non*-metaphysical one. For this time the symbolization is made possible by seizing the radical contingency of worldly laws: a contingency that allows us to found ontologically the hope of justice even while overcoming the former weakening of justice. Value is inserted into a reality no longer identified with a determinate and perennial substance, but rather with the possibility of lawless change. In this way we do not propose that the world is the best or worst of possible worlds, but that it can *actually* be both the one and the other. Thus, we do not abandon our disquietude in the face of the world, but maintain it as a constitutive element of hope (which for Spinoza is necessarily accompanied by fear). But this uncertainty, extended to possibilities exceeding the limits of a nature that can no longer satisfy us, allows us to sketch for the community of humans a project that will be worthy of our desires. It will become worthwhile, on a long-term basis, to remain in a world whose possibilities have once more become extreme, in order that we might *once again* expect something of them. Being is now the realm in which something *can take place*, and if what takes place is the highest novelty of which the real is capable, then this can only be identified with justice for the living and the dead and for those to come. Our aspiration to the Good is based once more on the knowledge of a world that allies with our hope, even while it is shown to be an unparalleled risk, as the power of the advent of contraries more widely separated than ever before.

Excerpt G: The Ethical Scission

Here we encounter the impasse of the ethical scission. The term designates *the contradiction between the present ethics* that awaits the fourth World, *and the ethics to come* that would follow the advent of such a world.

We have seen that symbolization produced a *fervor* resulting from the ontological objectivity acquired by the universal. The hope of justice ceases to be a simple passing fashion and becomes instead the true intuition of the highest innovative power of becoming. What is the immediate practice that is yielded by such a symbolization? Values return to life because they are wagered on the being to come; hope refounds the unity of the human collective, giving it a common project that does not outstrip individuals in the manner of an abstract generality, but is nourished instead on their ownmost experience: that of the boundless refusal of the death of one's neighbor. Humans, through a fidelity initially aimed at those who are closest among the deceased, act to conserve the community in expectation of its ultimate possibility. They do their best to be worthy of the return of those who are beloved, and broaden their concern (through a memory of the other human, ignited by mourning) to encompass all the living and the dead. Humanity can be unified by intensively lived values, because they are founded on the active expectation of an ontologically remarkable event that is accessible to every thinking being.

And yet, the essence of the ethical scission is such that *the realization of this awaiting would abolish its very constituents.* If rebirth were to occur there would no longer be hope, since the object of that hope would already have arisen. There would no longer be a unifying project of the community. There would no longer be anything to expect in the world, since its ultimate advent would have been achieved. (To think otherwise would entail a retreat to the religious postulate of an advent transcending what humans can conceive.) Thus there is no longer a relation between being and value; once again there is a suppression of the Symbol. It seems that the hoped-for rebirth would literally lead us to a new *despair*, in a renewed alternative between a general reign of egoisms and the belief in a transcendent foundation of values, since all the rational elements by which value takes on life would disappear in the very accomplishment of justice.

Here we encounter the problem of what is ultimately desired.

Do we desire the universal? Or do we desire the new egoistic life that seems to promise the accomplishment of this universal? If values rely only on the ontological possibility of rebirth, it seems that the final aim of such an immanent resurrection could consist only in a perfecting of enjoyments that are indifferent to one another. Those who take the recommencement of the body to be an ontological foundation for their unselfish practice of justice will find themselves before a universal that *ultimately* proposes a return to a senseless existence whose benevolence no project can establish. Thus they will have no other choice than to turn toward religion, to rediscover in God the objective support of the goodness that turns out to be lacking in the fourth World.

If the non-religious requirement of the universal is consistent, it ought to be thinkable *even beyond the sudden advent of the fourth World*. In this way we pose the question that had been left in suspense: that of the *philosophical foundation* of the universal, of that which ultimately legitimates the desire for justice. For we now see clearly that if the Symbol is the condition of the universal, if it is that which renders the possibility of justice thinkable by making it possible to surpass the most absurd deaths, it is not the very foundation of this requirement. Thus it is a question of showing how the factial can *ontologically* establish the *value* of the human: the essential human dignity by which every act of justice always draws its legitimacy. Starting from such a foundation, we can determine the exact nature of the contradiction between an ethics ruled by the enthusiasm of the Symbol and an ethics ruled by a truer principle.

Excerpt H: The Absolute and the Ultimate

Founding the requirement of justice seems to lead immediately to a tautology resembling that of the Kantian moral law, which is valid simply because it is valid. For what can be the meaning of the foundation of the universal by something other than itself, if not the subordination of the universal to the non-universal? In this way we end up with the opposite of what we seek: a delegitimation of the universal in favor of a non-universal that would reveal itself as the true source of value. This is what takes place if we found universal values on a transcendent God who corresponds neither to the norms of the true (because of the alogical nature of his existence) nor to the norms of justice (because of the amoral

nature of his reign). In this case one holds that the origin of all
value is Justice and Truth in a superior sense, without any relation
to the accessible meaning of these notions, and thus to any sort of
meaning at all. Even while claiming to provide them with a basis,
truth and justice would be subordinated to the actual irrationality
and immorality of the revealed God, and would thereby subordinate the universal to its exact contrary. This would amount to
a dismissal of the latter rather than a legitimation of it, since the
non-universality of divine transcendence is what would turn out
to have actual value: its conceptual inconsistency as well as its
obvious injustice.

The problem, then, is how to found human dignity in non-
tautological fashion without subordinating the resulting values
to another principle that would contradict that dignity. Here 'to
found' means to relate the ethical requirement to an ontological
eminence of humans, and thus unlike Kant we cannot be satisfied
with founding the value of duty on the sole form of the universal;
the morality celebrated here thus seems to rest on nothing but the
redundancy that I ought to obey the universal because I ought
to obey it. Even if the action can claim only to represent itself (a
decision that no demonstration or fact could ever contradict), it
is still a matter of countering the cynical and religious devaluations of the human by establishing *the essential ultimate status
of the human*. The alternative to be circumvented is the one that
oscillates between a religious foundation of values (which would
relate them to an incomprehensible divine efficacy incommensurable with the universal) and a simple factual acknowledgment
of the pre-eminence of the human species (which would establish
no right other than that of the strongest). Thus it is a question of
demonstrating the *necessary superiority* (*de jure* and not *de facto*)
of the thinking being over all other beings, while refusing the idea
of the necessary existence of such a being, which runs counter to
our ontology.

We have already encountered the principle that enables us to
solve this problem. It consists in maintaining that value rests on
a fact, but a *necessarily uncircumventible fact*: namely, the existence of the thought of the eternal as both actual and contingent.
Stated differently, it consists in maintaining that the human is
the factual but ultimate effect of advent. We recall that the terms
'uncircumventible' and 'final' signify the impossibility that any
emergence could be incommensurable with thought in the way

that thought is with all other beings. The superiority in principle of the human, its eternally unsurpassable unparalleled worth (except for the worth of other thinking beings), is thus accompanied by its essential mortality. The necessity referred to here means that it cannot be circumvented, not that its existence is eternal. To say in this sense that every human qua human has a right to justice ceases to be a tautology, for such an assertion now rests on a remarkable ontological proposition: namely, that *the value of humans cannot proceed from any cause (and in particular not from a divine cause) since every cause is inferior to humans*. In general fashion, the nature of an effect cannot be deduced from the nature of a cause, since by the very definition of advent *ex nihilo* there is *more* in the effect than in the cause. The value of the human is thus drawn from what it is, not from the source from which it arises. That is to say, it is drawn from the *thought* of the eternal of which it is the mortal stakeholder – not from the eternal itself, which only amounts to the neutrality of becoming. The very term 'foundation' refers to the idea of a soil or originary fundament. Against such a procedure, we propose to found the worth of the human in replacing the search for a first cause with the demonstration of a final effect: *the value of the human is not founded by the soil that sustains them, but by the void that outstrips them.*

This proposition is both simple and crucial. The fact that the value of the human is ultimate seems to be such an insupportably banal assertion, yet in fact it turns out to be a rare proposition. For even if such human pre-eminence has been advanced quite often, it never seems to have been founded with the rigor that one might demand for a proposition of this importance. This is true to such an extent that on closer examination, one realizes that *no such thing has ever been seriously maintained*. For if one affirms that humans take their proper value from their knowledge of the Good or of a God that is superior to them, in this case the human has value not by himself but by the object of his knowledge. And if one affirms instead that humans themselves are the most evolved creatures in the Universe, one makes of this thesis nothing more than an acknowledgment of fact on which no right is founded. The affirmation of the impassable value of the human, and the corresponding affirmation that *all* negation of such a proposition tends toward simple barbarism: all of this is in no way established by the most up-to-date version of humanism, which grants the human only a factual and descriptive knowledge of techniques and rules.

It thus provides us with a knowledge that is uncircumventible in principle by any creature, no matter how clever.

Humans acquire value because they know the eternal. But humans do not take their value *from* the object of their knowledge: that is to say, from the eternal itself. It is not the eternal which has value, for the eternal is *only* the blind, stupid, and anonymous contingency of each thing. Value belongs to the act of knowing *itself*; humans have value not because of *what* they know but *because* they know. And this knowledge is plainly the theoretical and absolute knowledge of logical and ontological truths, and the worried and attentive knowledge of our mortality. Certainly, classical humanism can already affirm in banal fashion that humans gain value through their knowledge, and notably through knowledge of their own mortality. But this knowledge by humans of death is thus assimilated to the lucid knowledge of their own limits and insufficiency. If the knowledge of death were nothing but such a negative knowledge, it could not establish the intrinsic value of humans. On the contrary, it could only establish the value of that which is not human and which answers to their essential dissatisfaction: namely, the divine consoler. The factial shows on the contrary that our capacity to think our own death refers to our power of envisaging the real nature of contingency as a possibility of each thing: of all disappearance as of all appearance. The negative knowledge of our mortality thus refers to the positive knowledge of our possible rebirth. It is a knowledge that ceases to designate the sad consciousness of our limit in order to reaffirm the jubilant possibility of its future transgression.

If we can demonstrate the value of the human in its own right, this is of course because we have affirmed the eternal at the same time that we have *de-reified it*. If the eternal *were* (as a thing, or a being), then we would have the Greek knowledge of a determinate and eternal being (a Good, or a God) surpassing the human in worth. If there were no eternity at all, we would have the modern knowledge of a clever animal whose pseudo-value would be consecrated only by the *fact* of a superior and essentially technical *power*. The factial allows us to affirm that there is an uncircumventible knowledge of the eternal, but it removes all value from this object of knowledge by identifying it with the prosaic contingency of each thing. Value thus amounts to the necessarily insuperable fact of the mortal knowledge of eternal contingency.

The unselfish desire of the human toward the human is a desire founded on the knowledge of the effect, not on the power of the cause. It is a knowledge [*connaissance*] of the human as an uncircumventible term of becoming, or rather (which amounts to the same thing) a knowing [*savoir*] of the eternal non-being of the revealed God. With humans, *the ultimate has in fact taken place*: a way of expressing the requirement of justice for every human, whether living or deceased. As the formula emphasizes, the ultimate does not designate the metaphysical absolute, i.e., that which *is* by itself (substance as the first and necessary cause that draws its existence only from itself), but that which *has value* by itself (the final, contingent, and unsurpassable effect of an advent). The ultimate is no longer identified with the non-metaphysical (desubstantialized) absolute of the factial. That is to say, it is not identified with the contingency of the being that gives a reason for itself and for its perennial character. In fact, the ultimate appears only under the form of *the contingent being that knows the absoluteness of contingency*.

What has value is the ultimate effect, not the first cause. By contrast, the ethical mistake *par excellence* consists in founding the end in the origin – in denying that what follows can surpass the beginning, that the contingent thought of the eternal surpasses the eternal, that the human being surpasses the being of beings. The mistake always consists in missing the sole important thing: that which emerges and not the advent itself, the ultimate rather than the absolute, the universal rather than the eternal. And all thought of transcendence, in placing value at the source of advent, in identifying the end with creative power, remains the privileged example of this ethical inversion by which, in Aristotelian terms, one always ends up subordinating final cause (the desirable Good) to efficient cause (the originary power).

Excerpt I: Religion and Prometheanism

We must orient all power towards the universal; we must know how to jettison the ballast of destiny so as not to make of our virtues the sign of being chosen; we are assured in this way of our status as singular humans rather than as monadic individuals. In this way the factial displays its opposition to the *sacralization of power belonging to the religious as such*. For any transcendent position superior to humans and supposedly different from the simple blind power of becoming can only relapse into a subordination of thought to being. Such a third term, neither thought nor being, *does not in fact exist*. To claim that something surpasses the human is to condemn oneself to place the human under the despotism of the eternal, innocent, and amoral power of being qua being. Becoming and its retinue of disasters and cruelties, marked by the stamp of transcendence, would thus acquire a mysterious value ostensibly superior to the morality comprehensible by humans, though identical in its manifestation with the innocent barbarism of pure contingency. This *illusion of the third term* other than thought and being is the habitual manner in which the cult of pure force passes like contraband into respectable thought. All religion, whatever the universality of its *content* might be, is thus condemned *by its very religiosity* to grant a hidden and superior meaning to amoral manifestations of the chaotic power of the world: a pure power to which an equally amoral submission is recommended as our duty.

Thus we can clearly see that Promethean humanism is nothing but a religious vision of the human as self-fabricated. It is an idolization of power by humans: not power in God, but in humans become God. What humans transpose into the religious God is not their own essence, as Feuerbach and the young Marx claimed, but rather the degradation of their own essence. For what humans see in God is the possibility of their own omnipotence: the accomplishment of their inhumanity rather than their humanity. In religion humans are strangers to themselves, because when they submit to God they do not submit to their essence but to the very opposite of their essence. That is to say, they submit to the power of being and not to the possibility of the human. Prometheanism thinks it suppresses the alienation of humans when it reintegrates the transposed God back into humans. But in this way alienation is actually *accomplished*. Humans, instead of revering their own baseness in God, now venerate it in themselves. For in all religion the worst violence (murderous cataclysms, grievous mortal illnesses inflicted upon children, lives absurdly cut down by 'fate') is ordinarily *reserved* for God, who is capable of immense destruction in the name of a Good that no one is authorized to comprehend, let alone judge. But if humans become God, then why should they deprive themselves of the same sorts of actions? All the crimes of God become accessible to humans, and the deified human can always justify them with the same subtlety as that of the theologian deciphering the superior goodness of the Lord in natural catastrophes. Whatever their numerous particular origins, the disasters of the twentieth century stemmed *also* from the fact that humans lowered themselves to the point of only taking themselves to be the equal of God.

The factial is a humanism which, in so far as it is opposed to the religious inversion of values, is equally opposed to the Prometheanism inherent in the classical form of humanism. The mastery of nature ceases to designate only its demiurgic and technical domination, and now refers also and especially to the capacity of humans to extract themselves from their innate powers by an unselfish act that simultaneously achieves the refusal of a supernatural omnipotence. It is from this possibility that we derive the legitimate superiority of humans over anonymous nature, as well as their evident duty of preserving nature. Such is the offering made to the unborn in memory of the expected dead: the perpetuation of a world here below as the hope of its recommencement.

Excerpt J: Fatalism and the Dice-Throw

The preceding considerations allow us to understand that factial ethics cannot be assimilated to a lazy fatalism under the pretext that the advent of the World of justice does not depend on the power of humans, and that it thereby fails to lead to any efficacious action. From this perspective, the 'factial fatalist' would be the one who passively (and vaguely) awaits the happy possibility of justice without undertaking any action toward the universal, since action would not be the source of the advent at which it aims. But in that case the fatalist would avow that he *does not* await such a rebirth, since the desire for the rebirth of the dead has been determined as a consistent desire for justice – that is to say, the desire for justice for all humans, living or dead. Thus, to desire rebirth consists in desiring it as a *condition* of the universal. Such a desire refers in primordial fashion to the attention paid to each individual, and to the stubborn refusal of present or *past* injustice to these individuals. The fervor produced by the Symbol results from the discovery that such a requirement is not absurd, but bears on a truth that is ontological and therefore eternal.

Thus it should not be supposed that the factial would amount to a passive awaiting of the advent. The awaiting that is actually determined by the factial results from a desire that is *preliminary* to justice, which is suddenly revealed as non-absurd to the extreme.

Henceforth I await something from the world (the accomplishment of the universal) even while acting today in accordance with what I await. In turn, the fatalist really just manifests the arbitrary desire of his own vital perpetuation: an individual and capricious desire for rebirth that envisages this rebirth as an end and not as a condition of the end. By strictly subordinating the Symbol to the universal, the factial is awaited as something other than the simple dream of an elixir of life. The ultimate novelty of becoming is merged with the fundamental requirement of thought, which is equally present in every human and thus irreducible to an idiosyncrasy.

But we must go even further in the refutation of fatalism; indeed, not only can rebirth be legitimately aimed at only on the basis of the advent of the World of justice, but *it is also necessary to maintain that the World of justice is itself possible only on the condition that it should be desired in action in the present World*. We contend that passive awaiting of the universal is precisely not an awaiting of it, because this makes the universal into a reality foreign to the thought that requires it. Namely, it is to make of the universal something that it is not, *and in this way to render its advent impossible*. Indeed, the whole point is that if rebirth occurred in such a way that no act of justice had awaited it, it would contain nothing of the universal; we would be dealing only with a blind recommencement imposed anonymously on our humanity. The occurrence of the fourth World requires that it should occur *qua object of hope*, and thus *in response to an awaiting that effectively existed beforehand*. For even if this awaiting cannot bring about the ultimate advent, awaiting alone lends it the status of a *novel* advent: that is to say, an advent of justice hoped for by humans rather than a simple repetitive return of life. In other words, the universal can arise only on the condition that it be awaited as such *in the present*. It must be actively anticipated by acts of justice marked by fervent commitment to the radical requirement of universality, and by the discovery of the non-absurdity of such a requirement. This amounts to affirming that *the final World can commence only on the condition that it be a recommencement*. The World of justice can arise only on condition of *following* the world of thought in conformity with the active hope for it that is deployed beforehand. Stated differently, the fact that the fourth World corresponds *de facto* to a hope that existed anterior to its advent forms part of its *essence*. Each time I act with a view to justice, I renew the awaiting which alone gives meaning to the possible sudden advent of *another* world that would not simply be the repetition of a World of life or thought, but which would actually constitute the final World – the ultimate World of justice.

In this way, one can compare the free act to a throw of the dice. A throw of the dice never guarantees chance, but is that alone which makes chance possible.

This thesis can appear astonishing, even suspicious (i.e., as motivated by a morality of merit) in so far as it claims to condition rebirth by an act that cannot cause it. None the less, it is immediately implied by the status of the ultimate World, which mixes the ontological novelty of the fourth World with the ethical character of the World of justice. Let us try, then, to clarify the status of this *non-causal dependence* of the fourth World on present actions, in recapturing in detail the logic of the preceding argument.

Let us first recall that the recommencement of the human has never been envisaged as an Eternal Return of the Same, a return identical to our present existence, but rather as the sudden advent of a *new* World or *new space of novelties*. We have seen that the advent of life corresponds to the advent of a hidden field of advents that are themselves new (that of species). In like manner, the fourth World ought to be the space of advents of recommenced but not repetitive lives. They are lives charged with the singular *past* of their preceding existences, surmounting the incompleteness and the dehumanizing misery sustained by each of them in the third World, and capable as such of being the field of new inventions of thought, since they recommence without returning to their point of departure. The fact that there should be a new *World* thus implies that rebirth should not be conceived as the phase of a monotonous cycle, but as the hidden resumption of the course of our existence, charged with the memory of its past. It is the condition of desirability of this advent (since justice wants to come about) and it is a condition that does not contravene the immanence of desire (since only *this* life is desired, in its creative dimension). To desire this life again is neither to desire this same life nor to desire something Entirely Other than life.

The World of justice thus constitutes a non-repetitive reconducting of our existence, and we can now maintain that its occurrence depends on our present acts, and even more importantly this World is possible only on the condition of being a *fourth* World, a World charged with the memory of a World of thought that preceded it. For the World of justice, to be charged with a past is not a factual property but an essential one, since a World of justice that occurred without such a passage would not be a World of justice. Let us re-examine the argument that we employed in order to elaborate on this new determination of the universal. The fourth World, we say, is desired in the sense of a World where all existence can in fact be accomplished without being struck down by the injustice of premature death, whether natural or criminal. Nevertheless, if life were thereby *accomplished* (that is to say immortalized, spared since the origin from the lethal injustice of our condition) *without* there having been a *preliminary* desire for this in the struggles of the third World, we would thus be in an improved *third* World, or indeed in a *perfect* one. But it would not be a world that would *surpass* the World of thought. It would only be a question of *our* world, such that all human life would in fact be accomplished in it. Indeed, this World having been given to us without being hoped for beforehand, we would be in a relation of *exteriority* with such an order. It would be equivalent to the one that causes us suffering today, except that it would give us fulfillment to the same anonymous degree that it currently drives us to despair. This would be a World of the demigods: beings who are spontaneously happy, having lived nothing other than this happiness and having never done anything for their condition to be such as it is. These happy people would be in the situation of successful fatalists, individuals indifferent to injustice (having never needed to hope for it, and thus in no need of conceiving it). They would have 'benefitted' from a favorable blow through which they would have passively 'inherited' immortality.

And yet, even if it were identical in appearance to the fourth order, there would actually be nothing universal in such a World. In order for the universal to arise, it should correspond to the realization of a requirement that was *actually* thought and acted. It is necessary that an accomplishment should *respond* to an ethics in such a way that objectivity and subjectivity are not simply in external relation, that this exteriority should be happy or unhappy. In short, the extreme possibility of becoming ought to consist in *accomplishing* the universal aim of the thinker, *which implies that the existence of such an aim, no less than the existence of its object, is a condition for the emergence of the ultimate World.* Even if nothing in my demand is able to provoke the realization of its object, the demand is required in order for the emergence of the ultimate World to be that of an *end* of the rational will.

It will be said that this difference between a perfect third World and the fourth World is purely formal, that it designates no onto-logical reality. After all, by our own admission these Worlds are the same whether or not they correspond to an aim that precedes them. As such, it will be said that nothing can be desired from the World of justice that a World of perfected thought would not already encompass, other than a stubborn conception of happi-ness as only a repayment merited by sorrow. But in truth, there does exist a difference between the two Worlds, for it is only on the preceding double condition (the preliminary existence of hope, and the effectuation in an ulterior World of its object) that time could cause an authentic *novelty* to emerge *concerning thought itself*, rather than just its environment or its vital envelope. If the two previously described orders of immediate perfection and of a justice reactualizing the past lives of men are *objectively* identical, then it is only a difference affecting thought (a difference both *subjective and universal* at the same time) that actually signifies their essential distinction. This difference would not be linked to visible determinations of these two Worlds, but would concern the *representation* of this visibility: it would not be inherent in the Worlds themselves, but in the *relation* of thought to such Worlds. *And this relation, proper to the sole order of justice, is none other than that of beauty.*

This assertion ought to be grasped initially in a sense similar to that which it receives in connection with the transcendental. This is easy to understand: if the fourth order arises, it will correspond *de facto* to our universal aspirations. It will therefore be beautiful, in the sense in which Kant speaks of natural beauty as the non-neces-sary *encounter* of phenomenal mechanisms and our rational ends, even while passing in the midst of the beautiful configuration *as if* the world had been created in conformance with such moral ends: 'as if', because nothing can demonstrate the effective existence of a suprasensible divine will at the origin of such a conformity of fact. According to Kant, it is precisely the *contingency* of such an accord that occasions the feeling of surprise and rapture when the beauty of a landscape or sunset is revealed: manifestations of an order of the world appearing to agree *of their own accord* with our own requirement of meaning. We have daily experience of such an absence of the necessity of beauty, since we often collide with the neutrality of a world directed by laws and forces indifferent to our ends. And thus our sense of wonder when faced with a natural appearance that suddenly, without being implied by any physical necessity, harmonizes with our desire for perfection. But it is precisely this sort of coincidence without necessity that we encounter again in the advent of a fourth World corresponding with our universal requirement: *the beautiful is revealed in this World as the emergence without reason of an accord between reason and the real*, a real that would itself have been established *beforehand* (in the midst of our present World) in its essential absurdity. The beauty of the ultimate World would correspond to the phenomenal emergence of the Symbol: that is to say, with the realization of the harmony between humans and a finally hospitable world that they would be destined to inhabit. A World of the blessed, having had neither the experience of justice, nor the desire for justice, nor the indifference of being towards such a desire, would on the contrary be *deprived of such a possibility of representation*. There would be no rapture in it, because its very perfection would not permit the essential experience of the feeling of beauty: that of a sudden accord *on the basis of a past scission*. Only the re-emergence of the human, only its rebirth as a being of memory, capable of seizing the signification and the contingency of its recommencement, permits the birth of a cosmic beauty of a *re*-conciled world.

None the less, the beauty of the fourth World would not be strictly identifiable with the transcendental beautiful. For in Kant, the 'as if' at which we marvel (everything happens in the beauty of nature *as if* an intelligence had produced it for the sake of our fulfillment), such an 'as if' rests on the *unknowability* of the effective nature of the thing-in-itself. Even if we have no conceptual knowledge to support the assertion, and even if phenomenal appearance seems entirely reducible to the anonymity of mechanism, the unknowability of reality-in-itself permits us to 'think' that it is actually directed by a divine finality. Beauty would be the sensible trace of the providence of this finality. Kantians see in beauty the sign of a possible existence of God, an existence that we cannot know but only suppose, and which we ought to require in such a way as to lend meaning to a universalist morality. The factial reconstructs for the fourth World an 'as if' whose principle is essentially other. For we *know* for our part that no end directs the accord between our aspiration and the world; we cannot make of the accord between subjectivity and objectivity the mark of a providential finality, not even of one that is simply possible. On the contrary, such an emergence would make us reach as far as the nonsense of becoming could go (namely, as far as sense itself) and we would not be able to see, in the contingent accord between nature and our hopes the trace of a possible divinity, but solely the limitless power of a time delivered to itself.

As a result, the beauty of the fourth World does not stem from its being identifiable with the trace of a possible divine will, while happening as if the world resulted from such a will. Rather, beauty will result from the fact that just people in the third World have actually hoped for this World, thereby enabling the possibility that it could arise *as if this hope were the source of it*. Indeed, there is natural beauty only on condition that one should be able to think a worldly reality as if it resulted from a universal intention. In the case of the Kantian transcendental, such a rapport is made into a supposed divine intention. *In the case of the factial, this rapport is turned into a human hope accomplished in the past, and which being now seems to grant*. Thus, only the preliminary existence of just aspirations is able to give rise to the relation of rapture that permits the contingent encounter of hope and being. The factual beauty of the World to come is accomplished as the trace of the *past but actual* hope of just humans, and not as the trace of a *current but hypothetical* divine power. It is the existence of a present hope that offers the order of justice a new but non-objective determination (one that is not presented simply *in* the world, but in *our* connection with the world): a beauty that arises as a gift of the just made across time. It is the gift of a *past* that makes of the fourth World a community inhabited by humans having returned to their condition, rather than a kingdom of demigods indifferent to the heritage of durations.

The fourth World thus corresponds to the surmounting of thought by its non-repetitive but recollective recommencement. Thanks to this, there can suddenly arise (assuming that we have chosen to be free in the third World) a connection between thought and World (that of the Beautiful) which cannot be surpassed. Our current world, as a field of struggle and hope, thus permits us to hope for the emergence of a truly ultimate novelty of becoming (the World of justice, not a perfected world of thought). And in the same way we ourselves, no less than the contingent power of becoming, are the condition of this emergence in which beauty results from our connection with the world, since the final advent can come only from the conjunction between being and act. This does not signify that, by the perversion of a moral rigorism, it would be necessary to *desire* the present order and its procession of miseries. But it is henceforth impossible to hate or regret the present World, which opens up *the very possibility of a history.* This history would be a becoming that belongs to us and would be larger than that of a single World. In this world all humans, with all the gestures they perform, would sketch anew the figure of our re-emergence. What this would offer as its aim would not be the ahistorical and Edenic emergence of a garden of innocents, but the recommencing of an earth weighed down with the memory of humans.

Excerpt K: Incarnation and the Ethical Scission

We are now in a position to understand the exact meaning of the scission between the ethics of the present (an ethics of hope for the advent to come) and the ethics of the future that follows this hope and which thus appears to be, literally, an ethics of despair. In view of such a separation factial ethics seems inconsistent, since it is rendered impossible by the very realization of its object.

Have we resolved this apparent contradiction with the foundation of the universal that we proposed? Only in part. Yes, in so far as we have shown that the Symbol was only the condition of the universal rather than its foundation. Ethics is thereby abolished with the realization of the Symbol, since the universal reposes on the value of the human, and this remains unaffected by the fact of its eventual rebirth. Such an ethics thus no longer takes the form of a desire for justice (of the possible fulfillment of all human existence) but that of a benevolence inherent in a condition emancipated from early death. The universal would cease to designate the requirement of conditions necessary for the blossoming of every life, and would refer instead to the invention of possible links between humans devoted to thought.

Yet such a response remains only partial, for it does not reach the deep meaning of despair inherent in the discovery of the ethical scission. Indeed, what is manifested by such a despair? What it manifests is the *ambiguity* of our awaiting of the Symbol, in so far as this awaiting could be either *philosophical or religious – the despair resulting from a religious awaiting of rebirth*: that is to say, from a desire for justice that sees it not as an ultimate end, but as the trace of something beyond thought. It is the desire of the believer who only wants justice and the universal in so far as these values do not stop with the human, but signal toward a transcendence that both founds and exceeds ethics, a desire that therefore cannot outlast the perspective of a World of justice essentially sufficient in itself. The ethical scission thus poses the immediate question of the *distinction between religious desire and an immanent desire for resurrection*, since only the latter is in a position to escape from the despair of a rebirth that would only open on to the reliving of a life in the world here below.

Let us develop this point. Religion is the position of a transcendence that allows us to avoid making the human into the aim of ethics. What is religious is every incapacity to take the human for the end of action, an incapacity that ends in the submission of humans to the blind power of becoming, identified with a destinal mystery resulting in the incomprehensibility of transcendence. Yet the awaiting of the Symbol can *itself* correspond to a fascination with being. Indeed, *the fervor produced by the awaiting of the Symbol can correspond to the fascination with the productive power of being.* What enthuses me then is my awaiting of *the advent itself* as a mark of the power of novelty of a divinized Real – not the awaiting of *that which* suddenly arises: namely, justice. This form of awaiting is revealed as the last possibility of escaping the universal even while appearing to require it: to desire, by means of a will apparently oriented toward justice alone, something that does not restore the human. Desiring the Symbol by desiring the manifestation of the power of being, and thereby desiring the inhuman, amounts once more to a religious subordination of the end to the origin, or of humans to the power that causes them to be born or reborn. The despair produced by such an advent signifies the kind of awaiting that makes of the Symbol an end of justice (to await the advent while loving the advent; a love of being and not of the human) rather than a condition of it.

In more general fashion, all 'morality' that does not support the perspective of the realization of its object is a religious morality. For what the religious spirit desires is that there should be something *entirely other*: something inconceivable or absolutely inhuman. By contrast, the fourth World opens on to the possibility of an immanent perfection of justice through which the human could live indefinitely in the world that has emerged, with no possible beyond. The one who despairs of the arrival of the advent is thus despairing over the fact that nothing inhuman can arise any longer in the ultimate world: the fact that nothing (no novelty) can still be expected of being and that humans alone, by the possibility of their becoming, should again be the object of hope.

There, in the very midst of the fourth World as we have defined it, there is an indeterminacy such that it is possible to desire that world *either* by accepting the universal or by refusing it. The advent can be awaited either by desiring the subordination of being to humans, or by desiring the subordination of humans to being. Since our method consists in going to the outer limits of what becoming can do once it is 'unharnessed' from empirical constants, we *ought* to integrate into the universal (when possible, meaning *thinkable*) every determination that purifies it, as long as this specifies both the ultimate possibility of time and the highest aim of a thinking being. From then on, the question we must ask ourselves is as follows: where do we locate the indeterminacy that permits such a lack of distinction of two desires that have nothing in common? Stated differently, what is *missing* in the universal as an object of desire that entails our inability to discern the contrary subjective motivations (religious vs. philosophical) for aspiring to it? All evidence is lacking of a link *in the very heart of the object of desire* between the hope placed in being (the advent) and the hope placed in humans (its highest moral possibility). For if this link does not exist in the midst of the awaited World, this desire is split in inconsistent fashion between the hope of rebirth that we place in being, and the hope of the free act that we place in humans. But nowhere in the limit of desire does the fact appear that rebirth should be willed as a condition of the free act. In order to avoid the subjective ambiguity in which we find the religious possibility of despair, it is therefore necessary that the link of subordination or conditionality between advent and the universal should be manifested in the object of our hope. In what should this link consist? The answer is evident: it should be a *gesture* of some sort.

We know that the free act by which we can distinguish the final acceptance of power from its conditional acceptance consists in the possibility that individuals have of abandoning their own power (especially the power into which they were born) in view of an ultimate end. *And yet the sudden advent of rebirth escapes the possibility of such abandonment,* for since it lies outside all possibility of action, we can neither dominate it nor go beyond it.

This implies that there is always some ambiguity (before or after the advent of the fourth World) concerning the nature of the desire for this advent, at least if the universal remains such as it is. The idolatry of being (through which the rebirth would take place), the shared subordination of humans to the becoming on which our fate depends, is an amorality of power inherent in the awaiting of an advent towards which no gesture is possible. The ambiguity of the universal will thus be removed if we think the universal in such a way that there is a possible gesture towards emergence itself, *which amounts to a requirement that the advent of the universal should be incarnated.*

The human mediator between the advent and the specific realities that appear in it ought to be considered as that which not only obtains (by advent ex nihilo) the power of producing the rebirth necessary for justice. It also ought to be considered as that which fulfills the unique gesture of abandoning the power of this advent, once the justice is accomplished for which the advent was (only) the condition.

Five determinations ought to be attributed to this human mediator:

1. The mediator ought to be a person whose action is guided by the universal ('goodness').
2. This person must possess the knowledge or memory of the singular becoming of the living and the dead ('omniscience').
3. This person has the power voluntarily to accomplish the rebirth of the dead ('omnipotence').
4. This person has the power to abolish definitively *their own* former powers (namely, their own omniscience or omnipotence).
5. As a final attribute following from the first four, the mediator *actually and definitively* abolishes their own power once the rebirth occurs.

Only in this way does the mediator accomplish the World of justice. With this unique gesture, the contingency of the mediator's own power is subordinated to a will to become the equal of everyone else. In this way the mediator accedes to the sovereign human possibility of not being the chosen one of its own power, even in this case of omnipotence.

* * *

The 'Christlike' aspect worn by the universal does not make it a 'rational religion', but on the contrary (and herein lies the seeming paradox) an ethics that finally excludes the temptations of transcendence. That which I call *the child* (or *infans*, the Latin term that suggestively designates the unborn child, or a child who does not yet speak) assures the impossibility of any religious vision of the advent. The child is the one who teaches us that its power is not the manifestation of a superior providence, but of contingency alone, of the absurdity burrowed so deeply into itself that it becomes meaningful. The child is the thinking being who teaches its peers that this power has no value in its own right (a value stemming from the transcendent origin of such a power) but solely in the immanent end to which it gives rise: to these peers themselves in so far as they live again. Power is of so little importance that the child abandons it once it has fulfilled its work, manifesting with this gesture a superb humanity. The child is the very incarnation of someone who teaches us the impossibility of despising ourselves with respect to that which makes us human. Thus it cannot be loved as Lord but only as the one who, by a clear consciousness of what is important, knows itself to be equal: the non-elect par excellence. It is that being whose beautiful singularity can be found in having made itself a human among humans.

Thus, the hope placed in being and the hope placed in humans are no longer unrelated; in hoping for the advent of rebirth, we hope by the same token for the extreme possibility of humans. After all, what we hope for is the advent of a becoming that disposes *both* of this power *and* of the possibility of liberating oneself from it. To be worthy of such an occurrence is to be worthy of *infans*: of its possible gesture of liberty in which are conjoined the supreme abandonment of power and the call of all humans to the unequalled value of his own humanity. Since the child is the one who accomplishes the unique gesture (unique because it is linked to the unique passage from the third to the fourth world, not because it is of higher worth than any other abandonment of power) *we can define the hope of the universal as the anticipation of fidelity to the unique gesture.*

Excerpt L: Philosophy and Atheism

The principle of atheism is a *ratification of the religious partition of existence.* The religious consists in the positing of a transcendence which alone is capable of satisfying desire. The immanence *that results from such a partitioning* is thus a limited, finite immanence in which happiness is impossible. This conception of desire permits us to recognize clearly a fundamentally religious ontology: for such ontologies always make the essence of desire rest on failure. As Simone Weil writes, all immanent desire is *contradictory*, and for this very reason it is *impossible* and therefore dedicated to failure. The possibility of happiness in this world is the illusion par excellence of the accursed faculty known as imagination. Devaluation of the imagination, impossibility of the accomplishment of desire: the religious partition of being always ends up with such a figure of immanence, of which Pascal is the obvious forerunner.

In this sense we can say that atheism consists essentially in ratifying the religious partition between immanence and transcendence: for *atheism consists in being satisfied with the unsatisfying territory that religion cedes to it*. Atheism is a strategy of the besieged. One begins by admitting that the territory of immanence is just as religion describes it, then one declares that this territory is the only one that exists, and finally one invents every possible way of rendering it livable *despite* that fact.

Atheism can pursue this aim in one of two ways: renunciation or revolt. In renunciation, the atheist explicitly recognizes the misery of the condition of immanence. Renunciation generally insists on the courage and humility that presuppose the mourning for all transcendence. In revolt, the atheist adopts an attitude of defiance, which in truth amounts to the same thing. This attitude consists in heroically assuming the immanence such as religion describes it, in order to profit from the intense jubilation belonging to all defiance. It is always a question of giving provocative and paradoxical praise to what is habitually present as the manifestation of the misery of our condition: the 'gallant' and 'ironic' joy of our finitude, a superior amusement procured by incessant struggles, a jubilation over our body which is said to be sensitive precisely because it is mortal, etc.

In neither case does the priest have to worry, for the simple reason that *his adversary regrets being right*. In the case of renunciation, the regret is explicit; in the case of revolt, it is masked but still obvious. For revolt is a classically 'demoniacal' attitude, which is to say that it is always religious. What sustains revolt at bottom is nothing other than the joy of defiance: the refusal of a transcendence which is thereby recognized as supremely desirable. This defiance only has value on the condition that those who adopt this attitude recognize the tragic character of immanence, and thus the superior courage supposed by its acceptance. Thus, revolt fully deserves the anathema of its patronymic, 'demoniacal desperation', since it adopts an eminently blasphemous posture: one that would be impossible without the existence of a religion that is renounced but intimately recognized as desirable. This attitude culminates in the pleasure of declaring neither hate nor contempt for religion, but total indifference to it: an indifference that will be developed, repeated, and multiplied by atheists who are always in search of believers in order to flaunt their total lack of interest in matters of the beyond. Only the jubilatory possibility of adopting this intensely reactive attitude renders livable the conditions that it has created. And it is once again the relation with religion, even if one of conflict, that permits those who are in revolt to accept the figure of immanence that religion has always ceded to them. The priest will always be reassured by the heroic opposition of demoniacal rebels, seeing in them nothing more than enemies that he himself has incited.

Unlike the atheist, the philosopher refuses to leave regret in its own camp. Through the concept of immortality, the preceding logic is inverted; the aim of philosophy is not to convince the priest, but to make him *in turn* regret being right (at least in his own eyes). The factial permits us to perform this reversal in the following manner: all that is objectively desirable in the religious can be *repatriated in immanence*, in such a way that philosophy distinguishes itself from religion only by the permanent belief in a *currently* existent God *which can therefore no longer be desired*.

Stated differently, through factial ontology philosophy is in a position to preserve the spiritual awaiting of a divine advent (which is desirable in view of the accomplishment of justice) without faith in a currently existing God. For this belief is precisely the wound of all religion, since it obliges the believer to submit to a being that is essentially amoral, capable in its phenomenal manifestation of allowing or even ordaining the most extreme evil. This submission to a God who is capable of sending the cruellest scourges into the world, which are none the less supposed to be viewed as a manifestation of his love for humans, this pure aberration of religion purely and simply *disappears* in the philosophical divine. Henceforth philosophy turns out to be in a position to bear the hope of religion in immanent fashion, thereby suppressing the endless contortions of the exegetes, following the affirmation of a transcendence that is said to be essentially full of love, even though it is indifferent or even horrifying in its manifestation. The God of the philosophers is thus shown to be without the great and subtle intentions that lend such charm to all the theodicies of the trembling earth.

The notion that the God of the philosophers is no longer on the side of the chaos of nature, but on that of the rebirth of humans in an order worthy of their condition (since this God is no longer accountable for the present atrocities of the world), is a very nice way of making regret change camps. For no one can really want to be saved by a currently existing God against whom such charges are lodged, especially after everything that happened during the past century. But everyone can desire the possible advent of a World of justice for which the child of humans (who is not superior to humans, since the child incarnates their condition of worthiness) should finally be the desired object.

Excerpt M: Conclusion

I. The essential stakes of both Eastern and Western thought consist entirely in a single question: how can we think the unity of Jewish religion and Greek reason? How can we think the unity of the egalitarian messianism of the Jews that breaks with the cyclical time of the pagans (a time that is inegalitarian since it is devoid of promise) and the rational, mathematical, and philosophical eternity of the Greeks? It is a search for the unity of religion and philosophy *without there being a third term to unify them*. All the richness of the problem consists in the fact that East and West have received these two heterogeneous 'truths', *and no others*. The response, in general fashion, thus obeys the following strict (Hegelian) alternative: we will have either a *religious* unity of religion and philosophy, or a *philosophical* unity of religion and philosophy. In both cases the unity obtained is all the more powerful, since it achieves a maximal conservation of the subordinated term: the most rational religion, the most egalitarian and messianic reason. The Middle Ages are entirely consecrated to the elaboration of the religious unity of philosophy and religion. But the factial, for its part, proposes a new means of achieving philosophical unity. Namely, Jewish messianism no longer thwarts the

eternity of mathematical truths, since the latter cease to designate
the real eternity (which is thus without a future) of this world
order and refers instead to the eternal contingency of this world
(which is thus full of promise). The hope of justice supplied by
the promise of Jewish time can be nourished on the mathematical
eternity provided by the immanence of Greek reason.

In this context *the term 'God' does not designate one of the
camps*, that of religion, but *names the battlefield* where the two
camps confront one another. The word presses together the two
truths that are to be combined, since as a Latinized Greek term
that designates the God of the Jews it symbolizes their historical
unity. The Greco-Roman '*Dies*' is translated as 'day' rather than
'sky', the day that fuses light and warmth, meaning knowledge
and hope.

The atheist, in reserving such a name for the object of faith,
shows that he has already confirmed his own defeat. For him the
struggle against religion has to occur through the expulsion of
any divine remainder; nothing that resembles the divine should be
allowed to reside in the homeland of the rational. Philosophy thus
appears to him to be *nourished* by religion, as a form of reason
that preserves in inertial fashion an irrational and archaic remainder of which a consistent atheism ought to be able to rid itself.
But in this way the atheist remains blind to the fact that *the very
borders* of his own territory are religious. For the atheist claims
that all that exists is the world inherited from the priest: a finite
and limited world, submitted to fixed laws, appalling once left to
its own devices. The philosopher speaks of God because he refuses
these borders, because he does not confirm the partition between
immanence and transcendence to which the atheist fully and truly
submits.

'God' is the name given to the stakes of the struggle between
immanence and transcendence: either the revealed God of religion, or the God of the philosophers. This latter God is despised,
and violently rejected by the priests as well as by those who have
renounced the struggle. It is indeed philosophers and they alone
who always confront transcendence, while the atheist merely
barricades himself against it. The atheist stands outside the field
of battle, and confuses the philosopher and the priest just as one
confuses two combatants in a hand-to-hand struggle viewed from
afar. For if philosophy is, as the atheist thinks, a reason nourished
by religion, it is in the same manner that the predator is nourished

by her prey: the philosophical struggle against transcendence that transpires not through a logic of expulsion (removing all religious content from the rational) but a logic of devouring (removing all desirable content from the religious). For the atheist, God is a matter for the priest; for the philosopher, God is too serious a matter for the priests.

The assimilation of philosophy to a *remainder of the religious* ought to be firmly rejected. Quite the contrary: every position that consists in limiting the exercise of reason is religious. Anti-philosophers will always be the *procurers* of the priest; whether or not they are religious in their hearts changes nothing, since the very essence of their enterprise consists in limiting meaning, and for this very reason they inaugurate an *inexpungable* field of nonsense that tacitly legitimates the revelation of a transcendence exceeding all *logos*. And this world inaugurated by the anti-philosopher, a world of unchanging and absurd structures, impassable and incomprehensible, gives us such despair in our need for justice that the religious can only be reinforced by such an enterprise, whose destiny is finally to render this world too unlivable to be fully satisfactory.

All anti-philosophy, all positivism, all scientism, and all logicism thus have a mystical, religious essence, following the brilliant example of the logicism of Wittgenstein. In declaring that rationality is illegitimate outside the scientific framework, these theories condemn reason to being unable to account for the facticity of the laws in the midst of which science always already unfolds, or to respond to the essential questions of existence. This space of nonsense dominates thought today, across diverse enterprises of the ruin of metaphysics with a power perhaps unequalled in history. For no one dares even now to defend philosophy in the full scope of its ambitions: the absolute intelligibility of being qua being and the conceptual apprehension of our immortality.

Contra the views of contemporary atheism, philosophy ever since its metaphysical period can be viewed as the sole historical enterprise that was not religious *in its very project*. Philosophy certainly resembles the religious enterprise in its claim to reach the ultimate principle of being, but it resembles religion in the manner of a rival, not that of a servant. For the very model of immanence is to produce a comprehensible discourse on the world in its ultimate essence. It is the sole model in which *revelation* no longer has any *reason for being*. Thus philosophy is always atheist in act, if not always in speech. This makes it the very opposite of anti-philosophy, which is always religious in act even if frequently atheist in its speech. The authentic tradition of immanence resides in the Platonic divine, and in the gods of Spinoza and Hegel, not in the 'philosophical atheism' of a Heidegger.

The factial is a philosophy, because the factial is a thought of immanence. Yet it is distinguished from all previous metaphysics through the fact that previous systems retain a religious postulate in their enterprise, if not in their project: the postulate that a necessary existence is possible. The factial claims to accomplish the immanent thought of a world through its denial of necessary existence, which is another name for the revealed God. The historical systems of metaphysics all seek a referent that exists in rational discourse, and which is necessary by definition. Thus they maintain by rather diverse routes the notion of necessary existence, which at bottom is perfectly incomprehensible since it is irrational (religious). This failure is the ultimate reason for the configuration of the present world: an illusory and complicitous opposition between sophistry and religion; a disappearance of the opposition between religion and philosophy, thanks to the quasi-total disappearance of the latter.

The project of metaphysics ought to be restored in its legitimacy. As rational beings, humans have access to the essence of the world: an advent without limit, where anything conceivable *can actually arise* in the form of a new constancy. The ultimate aim of the human project thus becomes determinable: an aim that is not reasonable because it is fully rational. That towards which humans aspire, that which they desire, that which has made them suffer for millennia through strange labor pains even as it confers upon them an energy of rare violence, is to give birth to God just as matter gives birth to life and life to thought. We are the possible ancestors of God rather than his creatures, and we suffer because, unlike the animal, which does not know the possible humanity of its becoming, we know the possible divinity of our own. We bear God in our wombs, and our essential disquietude is nothing other than the convulsions of a child yet to come.

There is no necessity for this sudden advent of the divine, since it is only rendered possible by the absolute contingency of all things. Hope exchanges guarantee for possibility, and aims at rupturing the law by a lawless becoming in excess of all mastery. God will be the last-born of humans: the advent whose ultimate novelty will be the recommencement of the human, its rebirth, its renewed struggles and enjoyments. The project of rational beings with reason thus consists in *enduring together*, from generation to generation, by the establishment of a link of fidelity between the living and the dead, in the midst of a world whose knowledge is able to maintain our waiting. It is to endure a totally different historical scale, on a scale of time in which the world assumes a different aspect than the calm indifference of laws. The authentic link of humans with God is thought as a link with the inexistent God of whom humans are the possible ancestor. This link, which makes each of us the possible forerunner of God, I call the divine. The practice of this link in the course of our lives I call the divinization or immortalization of humans; it is the very manner of becoming singular that makes us human. This divinization is not a deification of humans, because it is not a Promethean identification of humans with God. The divine is the affirmation of an uncrossable ontological divide between humans and the omnipotence of the Master, a worthless omnipotence of the revealed God whose happy abandonment inaugurates the philosophical God as justice and as gesture.

Present in each relation, *infans* is the third term by which the unborn intrude into the existence of the living and the dead. It is the focal point where ancestors converge with descendants. It is the promise made to the unborn to refuse the death of those who died too early: the death of those who had nothing to do with death. It is also the promise to refuse its own death. The desire for a child does not break the link between lovers, but transfixes desire to the point of instituting an amorous rupture, by this other being, in a spirit of expectation. *Infans* is such an other through which living and dead humans resonate with the same desire. We wish once more to 'drink with the dead', without a revealed God returning to spoil the party and trouble our intimacy with tombstones. But we also want the living to come drink one day with us ourselves, who are the deferred dead. Together we hope for the birth of *infans*, in view of the rebirth of forerunners, and that is why we seal this promise of desiring again and always living this one sole life.

Nothing guarantees this rebirth. For that reason, hope is not a flight outside the world, since it is born of the knowledge that there is no other. Hope is less a comfort than a difficult requirement. For certainly, only the renunciation of hope is soothing; it is the renunciation of hope which knows how to build me a carcass, soft as a coffin, which assures me till the moment of death of not thinking of death. What is never said is that the harshest mourning is that of the atheist, who knows how to harden himself to the thought of the unavoidable end, to the point of repressing it from his daily preoccupations. It could be that the most intense mourning should in truth be immortal mourning which confronts possible rebirth, which forbids itself the temptation of faith, in order to conserve and transform day after day the original violence of separation. For, hope being also our torment with respect to a possibility that nothing necessitates, to maintain this hope imposes the acceptance of a possible failure to accomplish what is hoped for. And to envisage that perhaps nothing will happen anyway leads to sadness, to a nostalgia for which it is hard to lose our fondness. But the memory of the dead remains a gift to the living. It is a memory at which we grasp so as to delight ourselves with the contingency of all things, with the eternal nonsense that necessarily makes it possible to hold reunions beyond the grave. Social and political activity, amorous and parental life: all these practices have a possible immortalization in which the process of an encounter can be modified.

The memory of the dead is manifested in giving assistance to the living. In the memory of the dead, there is fidelity to the divine. In the fidelity to the divine, there is the amorous knowledge of the promise of the world.

II. The philosophical divine is not a religion: has anyone ever seen a believer deny the existence of God? Nor is it an atheism: has anyone ever seen an atheist believe in God? The divine carries both atheism and religion to their ultimate consequences so as to unveil their truth: God does not exist, *and* it is necessary to believe in God. More deeply, the divine links these two assertions, which attain their truth only through this link.

To the atheist who rightly affirms the inexistence of God, the divine responds that *it is necessary to believe in God because he does not exist*. Only the inexistence of God guarantees his possible advent, since only immanence thought in absolute form permits an advent without limit. The divine pushes the immanentism of the atheist to the limit, by getting rid *of what remains to him of the religious*: namely, it gets rid of his *belief* in laws that are necessary and none the less inexplicable in their necessity, and thus properly irrational. This belief of the atheist institutes the field of an unyielding transcendence that the divine, for its part, simply discards.

Henceforth, to believe no longer means to have faith, and no longer to believe in the law. It is to hope for a justice *worthy of the name*. The divine ceases to alienate the human from what it can do, unlike atheism which always separates the human from what remains its living work. Atheism diminishes humans and humiliates their projects, by deposing what it believes to be a simple myth. But this 'myth', the belief in God, is nothing other than the trace in humans of the madness of the world without God: capable of everything and thus capable of God. The divine, on the other hand, is opposed to the great temptation of the atheist, this Prometheanism that appeals to the debased deification of humans. Separated forever from all omnipotence, humans can learn to love life to a sufficient degree as to assume its possible victory.

Unlike the divine and its anti-Promethean glorification of humans, all the contemporary enterprises of 'demystification' are religious projects that debase humans and their claims to exceed finitude. It is a mocking enterprise of demystification that only allows our species a few mediocre projects compared with what we are capable of envisaging. It is a sarcasm of humans toward humans, and thus a hatred of oneself. But the project of humans has to be worthy of humans, and if the philosopher conceives God as this project, it is because he knows that one cannot limit what humans want, *because one cannot limit what a world can do*. The divine thus shares neither the superstition of the atheists toward the laws of the world, nor their devaluation of the human, which is always imprinted with pious humility.

The divine desires infinitely, but he does not desire the Infinite in the manner of the believer: the Infinite as an omnipotent extrapolated God, alienated from the strength of the human. The divine infinitely desires this incarnated *finite* being, the child of humans through which there comes to pass the sole deed worthy of humans: justice. Philosophy knows very well that, whatever might be the strength of the mockery from unbelievers and even from the religious, one can never extinguish the splendid desire that makes of humans something other than a clever beast or a lukewarm, mediocre individual. And he also knows that even in those who refuse God to humans, despairing of their world in the weakness of the ends they propose, one can be very sure of discovering those who are too often heard praying at the altar, fleeing this world that is so overwhelming because it is so false, which the atheist thus means to impose on them. Religion is the undercurrent of a world that is not infinitely desired: a world not seized in its infinite power of advent and loved for the eternal promise of which its madness is the guarantor.

To the believer who rightly affirms that it is necessary to believe in God, the divine responds that *to believe in the existence of God is not to believe in God but to believe in existence*. It is because he believes in the existence of God that the priest does not believe in God. For to believe that God exists is to make of him a God who is not only love, but also and especially omnipotence. It is the God who created this world with all its injustices, the God-master that one must fear as much as love. To believe in the existence of God is inevitably to venerate his existence as master and as incomprehensible power. If love for the existing God is effectively always 'sinful', it is because it always remains burdened with the love that is *also* accorded to the impenetrable designs of the one who governs. To believe in the existence of God is not just an error, but a mistake that forbids all authentic belief in God. To this mistake, which the virtuous atheist has always intuitively guessed without grasping its essence, and which ruins all religion to the core, we will give the double name of blasphemy and idolatry. In this way we send such condemnations back to the place from which they came, so as to annul their oppressive power.

It is *blasphemy*. To say that God exists is the worst of blasphemies, for this amounts to saying that God reigns over the world in a sort of *grand politics*, without ever having been weak enough to modify his designs to prevent the atrocities that have taken place on earth. It is to say that this world is as God has willed it, in projects impenetrable to just humans, through a cruelty that cannot be understood. It is to turn the divine hope of humans into an object of fear, and to insult the very essence of the goodness by means of the most worrisome sophisms. It is an attempt, in the terrible style of the theologian, to prove to Dostoevsky's unbeliever that there is in fact a certain divine goodness in allowing a child to be devoured by dogs.

To say that God exists is to make him the worst of masters. All these analyses of alienation, of the inexpungable reactivity of all religion, are perfectly fitting on this point. Religion invents a master worthy of the name in order to confound it with the Good itself. It is religion, and religion alone, which reverses values; illness, murder, and extermination become mysterious and destinal manifestations of a Good that is disfigured by such theogonies.

Blasphemy towards God consists in identifying him with the creator of this world, fusing the veridical God which is only love with the religious God who is only power. It is for this reason that the best of believers have always attempted, through reasoning of the most tragic subtlety (and subtlety is always the management of an impasse), to remove God from existence and make him a being of such transcendence that he is outside being, beyond being, indifferent to being. In short, they have tried to avoid the blasphemous expression that *God exists*, even while attempting to avoid the immanent expression that *God does not exist*. But the divine has no need of such virtuosity, knowing that the belief in God is the responsibility taken by humans towards the child not yet born, and that the words '*the divine inexistence*', clear and pure as moonlight, guarantee hope for as long as a just person remains in existence. The God worthy of hoping for is the one who has the excuse of not existing.

It is *idolatry*. From the blasphemy of belief in the existence of God we can immediately infer the essential idolatry of *all* religion. For we know that if God is indeed the horrifying and incomprehensible being, he ought to be loved as such by the believer. Whatever the sincerity of the love carried to God, this love is always crossbred with deference for the mighty and cunning master who by holding back his strength is all the more threatening in his strange supposed affection for us. If God is amoral omnipotence, inaccessible to all moral comprehension, he is also the one *through whom* such a strength can arise: the strength of the illuminated, of the prophet, of the fanatic, of he who manifests the amoral force of the creator God in his own behavior by his condemnations, his anathemas, his bestowals of fate, his threatening cries of rage: in short, by a behavior adequate to the manifest violence of the hidden God.

All religion is thus parcelled out between two basic attitudes. There is the sanctity of those who follow Elder Zossima and see in God only love because they believe in him. And there is the superstitious mysticism of the ascetic Father Ferapont, who sees in God only power because they believe in his existence. And where the first God is only a violent good, the second God is nothing but maledictions, threats, and obscurantist magic. We should not be astonished that even a religion founded on benevolence and forgiveness continually turns into hateful fanaticism. For if religion is both love and hate, this is because it believes simultaneously in God as the amorous promise of the rebirth of the dead, and in the existence of God through the servile and malicious desire for an omnipotent master.

If the cynic is a bigot who does not know it, the fanatic is a blasphemer who has forgotten it. At bottom both are united. For the cynic, if God does not exist then everything is permitted; for the fanatic, if God exists then everything is permitted *to him*. But the rational believers who believe due to their love of the Good, and the virtuous atheists who do not believe due to their love of the True, are themselves neither believers nor atheists. Lost in the false oppositions of our time, they are and remain the stateless people of philosophy.

If the divine is not an atheism, this is because atheism remains burdened with superstitious belief in the perennial character of laws. If the divine is not a religion, this is because religion remains burdened with cynical submission to the power of a master. If the divine is not atheism, it is because atheism devalues the desire for justice that makes humans into beings of such singular worth. If the divine is not a religion, it is because religion dismisses what is most noble in humans, by making earthly horror the sign of a divine goodness that is thereby travestied. The philosophical divine thus faces two catastrophic and constitutive illusions of contemporary history: *the first being that God exists, the second being that one can do without Him.*

III. Humans can establish four different links with God, of which only three have been explored so far:

1. *Not believing in God because he does not exist.* This is the atheist link, which occurs in countless variations that all lead to the same impasse: sadness, tepidity, cynicism, and the disparagement of what makes us human.

   It is the immanent form of despair.
2. *Believing in God because he exists.* This is the religious link, in countless variations, all leading to the same impasse: fanaticism, flight from the world, the confusion of sanctity and mysticism and of God as love and God as power.

   It is the religious form of hope.

3. *Not believing in God because he exists.* This link, which is not confined to a specific doctrine, expresses all the various forms of revolt toward the existent God. It is the Luciferian position of rebellion against the Creator which expresses a reactive need to hold someone responsible for the evils of this world. This demoniacal revolt in the face of all the disasters of existence would rather hate God than declare him inexistent. This vision of the world encompasses the position of subtlest indifference toward God: 'even if God exists, he does not interest me; he is of no interest as regards the pleasures and struggles that occupy all finite existence.' It is a superb indifference that mixes apathy towards God (and all displays of indifference are nothing but hatred trying to be as hurtful as possible) with classical atheism, whose impasse it aggravates to the limit: cynicism, sarcasm toward every aspiration, hatred of self.

4. Only the fourth link, the philosophical link and immanent form of hope – *believing in God because he does not exist* – has never been systematically defended.

   It has now been done.

   The four possible links of humans with God are henceforth known.

   One must choose.

Notes

1. Here I follow Brassier in translating Meillassoux's French coinage *factual* with the English neologism *factial*. For an explanation of this decision (which is fully supported by Meillassoux himself), see Brassier's note 6 to Chapter 3 of *After Finitude*.

2. The phrase 'not to make Billancourt despair' is often attributed to Jean-Paul Sartre (apparently inaccurately) as his reason for refusing to criticize the Soviet Union. Billancourt is a western suburb of Paris, site of the global headquarters of Renault, and a longtime stronghold of communist workers.

Works Cited

Works by Quentin Meillassoux

After Finitude: Essay on the Necessity of Contingency, trans. Ray Brassier, London: Continuum, 2008.

'Badiou and Mallarmé: The Event and the Perhaps', trans. Alyosha Edlebi, *parrhesia* (2013), 16, pp. 35–47.

'Le Cogito contre le sujet – ou comment sortir de l'anthropologie par le doute', unpublished lecture delivered in Toulouse, France, on 18 November 2008, at conference entitled 'Pour une approche non-anthropologique de la subjectivité', Université de Toulouse le Mirail.

'The Contingency of the Laws of Nature', trans. Robin Mackay, *Environment and Planning D: Society and Space* (2012), 30, pp. 322–34.

'Decision and Undecidability of the Event in *Being and Event I* and *II*', trans. Alyosha Edlebi, *parrhesia* (2014), 19, pp. 22–35.

The Divine Inexistence, excerpts translated by Graham Harman from the unpublished French manuscript of *L'Inexistence divine*, pp. 224–87 of the present volume.

'History and Event in Alain Badiou', trans. Thomas Nail, *parrhesia* (2010), 12, pp. 1–11.

'The Immanence of the World Beyond,' trans. Peter Candler, Adrian Pabst, and Aaron Riches, in Conor Cunningham and Peter Candler (eds), *The Grandeur of Reason: Religion, Tradition, and Universalism*, London: SCM Press, 2010, pp. 444–78.

'Interview with Quentin Meillassoux (August 2010)', conducted and translated from the French by Graham Harman, pp. 159–74 of the present volume.

'Iteration, Reiteration, Repetition: A Speculative Analysis of the Meaningless Sign' (aka 'The Berlin Lecture'), trans. Robin Mackay, unpublished manuscript. The leaked pirate version online is cited here

288

with Meillassoux's permission, and is available at http://oursecretblog. com/txt/QMpaperApr12.pdf (audio recording of the 20 April 2012 lecture available at http://www.spekulative-poetik.de/speculative-philosophy.html).

'Metaphysics, Speculation, Correlation,' trans. Taylor Adkins, *Pli: The Warwick Journal of Philosophy* (2011), 22, pp. 3–25.

The Number and the Siren: A Decipherment of Mallarmé's Coup de Dés, trans. Robin Mackay, Falmouth: Urbanomic, 2012 and New York: Sequence Press, 2012.

Personal communication, electronic mail to Graham Harman, 3 September 2010.

Personal communication, electronic mail to Graham Harman, 4 September 2013.

Personal communication, electronic mail to Graham Harman, 26 March 2014.

'Potentiality and Virtuality', *Collapse* (March 2007), II, pp. 55–81.

'Raison et ésotérisme chez Hegel', unpublished manuscript.

'Spectral Dilemma', *Collapse* (May 2008), IV, pp. 261–75.

'Speculative Realism', with Ray Brassier, Iain Hamilton Grant, and Graham Harman, *Collapse* (November 2007), III, pp. 306–449.

'Subtraction and Contraction', *Collapse* (November 2007), III, pp. 63–107.

Works by Others

Badiou, Alain, *Conditions*, trans. Steven Corcoran, London: Continuum, 2009.

—, *Logics of Worlds: Being and Event 2*, trans. Alberto Toscano, London: Continuum, 2009.

—, 'Preface', in Quentin Meillassoux, *After Finitude: Essay on the Necessity of Contingency*, trans. Ray Brassier, London: Continuum, 2008.

—, *Being and Event*, trans. Oliver Feltham, London: Continuum, 2007

—, *The Century*, trans. Alberto Toscano, Cambridge: Polity, 2007.

Bennett, Jane, *Vibrant Matter: A Political Ecology of Things*, Durham, NC: Duke University Press, 2010.

Bergson, Henri, *Time and Free Will: An Essay on the Immediate Data of Consciousness*, trans. F. L. Pogson, New York: Dover, 2001.

Brassier, Ray, *Nihil Unbound: Enlightenment and Extinction*, London: Palgrave, 2007.

Bryant, Levi, Nick Srnicek, and Graham Harman (eds), *The Speculative*

Turn: Continental Materialism and Realism, Melbourne: re.press, 2011.

DeLanda, Manuel, *A New Philosophy of Society: Assemblage Theory and Social Complexity*, London: Continuum, 2006.

Deleuze, Gilles, *The Logic of Sense*, trans. Constantin Boundas, New York: Columbia University Press, 1990.

—, *Nietzsche and Philosophy*, trans. Janis Tomlinson, New York: Columbia University Press, 1983.

Fakhry, Majid, *Islamic Occasionalism: and its Critique by Averroës and Aquinas*, London: Allen & Unwin, 1958.

Hallward, Peter, unpublished manuscript quoted with Hallward's permission.

Harman, Graham, 'Johnston's Materialist Critique of Meillassoux', *Umbr(a)* (2013), 1, pp. 29–50.

—, *Bells and Whistles: More Speculative Realism*, Winchester: Zero Books, 2013.

—, 'A New Look at Identity and Sufficient Reason', in Harman, *Bells and Whistles*, pp. 227–56.

—, 'The Current State of Speculative Realism', *Speculations* (2013), IV, pp. 22–8.

—, 'Meillassoux's Virtual Future', *continent*, (2011), 1.2, pp. 78–91.

—, 'Dwelling With the Fourfold', *Space and Culture* (2009), 12:3, pp. 292–302.

—, *Prince of Networks: Bruno Latour and Metaphysics*, Melbourne: re.press, 2009.

—, 'DeLanda's Ontology: Assemblage and Realism', *Continental Philosophy Review* (2008), 41:3, pp. 367–83.

—, 'Quentin Meillassoux: A New French Philosopher', *Philosophy Today* (Spring 2007), 51:1, pp. 104–17.

—, *Tool-Being: Heidegger and the Metaphysics of Objects*, Chicago: Open Court, 2002.

Heidegger, Martin, 'On the Essence of Ground', in *Pathmarks*, ed. William McNeill, Cambridge: Cambridge University Press, 1998.

—, *What Is Called Thinking?*, trans. J. Glenn Gray, New York: Harper & Row, 1968.

Johnston, Adrian, 'Hume's Revenge: À Dieu, Meillassoux?', pp. 92–113 in Levi Bryant et al. (eds), *The Speculative Turn: Continental Materialism and Realism*, Melbourne: re.press, 2011.

Latour, Bruno, personal communication, 21 February 2007.

—, *Science in Action: How to Follow Scientists and Engineers Through Society*, Cambridge, MA: Harvard University Press, 1987.

Mabille, Bernard (ed.), *Ce peu d'espace autour. Six essays sur la méta-physique et ses limites*, Chatou: Les Éditions de la Transparence, 2010.

Marx, Karl and Friedrich Engels, *Communist Manifesto*, Hollywood, FL: Simon & Brown, 2010.

Melville, Herman, *Moby-Dick*, in *Redburn, White-Jacket, Moby-Dick*, New York: Library of America, 1983.

Nietzsche, Friedrich, *Thus Spoke Zarathustra*, trans. Adrian Del Caro, Cambridge: Cambridge University Press, 2006.

Ortega y Gasset, José, *Phenomenology and Art*, trans. Philip Silver, New York: Norton, 1975.

Perler, Dominik and Ulrich Rudolph, *Occasionalismus: Theorien der Kausalität im arabisch-islamischen und im europäischen Denken*, Göttingen: Vandenhoeck & Ruprecht, 1999.

Philonenko, Alexis, *La Liberté humaine dans la philosophie de Fichte*, Paris: Vrin, 1966.

Plato, *Collected Dialogues*, ed. Edith Hamilton and Huntington Cairns, Princeton, NJ: Princeton University Press, 1961.

—, *Meno*, trans. W. K. C. Guthrie, in Plato, *Collected Dialogues*, ed. Edith Hamilton and Huntington Cairns, Princeton, NJ: Princeton University Press, 1961.

Polieri, Jacques, 'Le livre de Mallarmé: A Mise en Scène', trans. Gabrielle Goff and Martin Goff, *The Drama Review: TDR* (Spring 1968), 12:3, Architecture/Environment.

Rancière, Jacques, *Mallarmé: The Politics of the Siren*, trans. Steven Corcoran, London: Continuum, 2011.

Rees, Martin, *Just Six Numbers: The Deep Forces That Shape the Universe*, New York: Basic, 2001.

Şaul, Mahir, 'Claude Meillassoux (1925–2005)', *American Anthropologist* (December 2005), 107:4, pp. 753–7.

Susskind, Leonard, *The Cosmic Landscape: String Theory and the Illusion of Intelligent Design*, Boston: Back Bay, 2002.

Thomas-Fogiel, Isabelle, *Critique de la représentation: Étude sur Fichte*, Paris: Vrin, 2000.

Turgenev, Ivan, *Fathers and Sons*, trans. Richard Freeborn, Oxford: Oxford University Press, 2008.

Vernes, Jean-René, *Critique de la raison aléatoire, ou Descartes contre Kant*, Paris: Aubier, 1982.

Whitehead, Alfred North, *Religion in the Making: Lowell Lectures, 1926*, Bronx, NY: Fordham University Press, 1996.

—, *Process and Reality*, New York: Free Press, 1978.

Žižek, Slavoj, 'An Answer to Two Questions', in Adrian Johnston,

Badiou, Žižek, and Political Transformations: The Subject of Change, Evanston, IL: Northwestern University Press, 2009.

—, *Tarrying with the Negative*, Durham, NC: Duke University Press, 1993.

Žižek, Slavoj and Glyn Daly, *Conversations with Žižek*, Cambridge: Polity, 2003.

Index

293